The Complete Idiot's Reference Guide to Upgrading Your PC

A Windows 95 Dream Machine and How to Get It

If you want Windows 95 to run like a dream (or you just want Windows 3.1 to run better), upgrade your PC to match these standards:

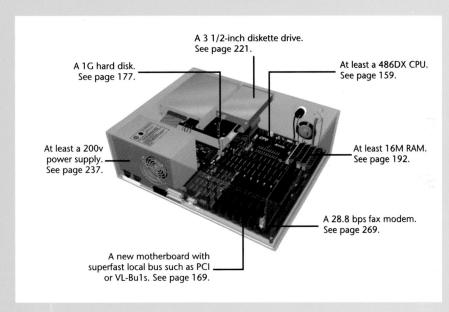

A 3 1/2-inch diskette drive. See page 221.

A 1G hard disk. See page 177.

At least a 486DX CPU. See page 159.

At least a 200v power supply. See page 237.

At least 16M RAM. See page 192.

A 28.8 bps fax modem. See page 269.

A new motherboard with superfast local bus such as PCI or VL-Bu1s. See page 169.

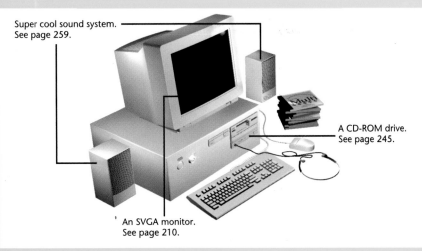

Super cool sound system. See page 259.

A CD-ROM drive. See page 245.

An SVGA monitor. See page 210.

que®

What My PC's Got

Before you start adding stuff to your computer, you should make a record of what you currently have (see Chapter 4 for details on how to find this information). Then take this card with you when you shop for new parts so that you can make sure that what you buy is compatible with what you already have.

Upgrading Your PC, in a Nutshell

1. Get the right part for your system.

2. Prepare for disaster by creating an emergency diskette before you do anything else.

3. Discharge your body's static by touching something metal.

4. Unplug the computer and open up the system unit.

5. Plug in your new gadget.

6. Plug the PC back in, turn it on, and check for signs of life.

7. Close up the system unit.

8. Introduce your PC and Windows to its new friend by running a setup program and changing some settings in DOS and/or Windows.

Equipment	My PC
PC brand/model	_____
CPU	_____
BIOS	_____
O/S	_____
Total RAM	_____
Type of RAM	_____
Max. amount of RAM	_____
Hard disk type	_____
Hard disk brand	_____
Hard disk size	_____
2nd hard disk type	_____
2nd hard disk size	_____
Diskette drive A:	_____
Diskette drive B:	_____
Total # drive bays	_____
No. unused drive bays	_____
CD-ROM type	_____
CD-ROM settings	_____
Monitor type	_____
Video card	_____
Modem type	_____
Modem settings	_____
Expansion bus type	_____
No. slots available	_____
Network type	_____
Network card setting	_____
Mouse type	_____
Mouse settings	_____
Tape backup type	_____
Tape backup setting	_____
Sound card type	_____
Sound card settings	_____
Other	_____

The COMPLETE IDIOT'S GUIDE TO

Upgrading Your PC

by Jennifer Fulton

A Division of Macmillan Publishing
201 W. 103rd Street, Indianapolis, IN 46290 USA

For Scott, who taught me that I could fix just about anything on a computer with a screwdriver, a paper clip, or a hair pin (OK, I learned that one on my own).

©1996 Que® Corporation

International Standard Book Number: 0-7897-0681-4
Library of Congress Catalog Card Number: 95-72565

98 97   8 7 6 5 4 3

Interpretation of the printing code: the rightmost number of the first series of numbers is the year of the book's printing; the rightmost number of the second series of numbers is the number of the book's printing. For example, a printing code of 96-1 shows that the first printing of the book occurred in 1996.

Screen reproductions in this book were created by means of the program Collage Complete from Inner Media, Inc., Hollis, NH.

Printed in the United States of America

Publisher
Roland Elgey

Vice-President and Publisher
Marie Butler-Knight

Editorial Services Director
Elizabeth Keaffaber

Publishing Manager
Barry Pruett

Managing Editor
Michael Cunningham

Development Editor
Lori Cates

Technical Editor
Martin C. Wyatt

Production Editor
Mark Enochs

Copy Editor
Rebecca Mayfield

Cover Designers
Dan Armstrong, Barbara Kordesh

Book Designer
Kim Scott

Illustrator
Dan Swenson

Cartoon Illustrations
Judd Winick

Technical Specialist
Nadeem Muhammed

Indexer
Gina Brown

Production Team
*Steve Adams, Claudia Bell, Jason Carr, Bryan Flores, Sonja Hart, John Hulse,
Clint Lahnen, Bob LaRoche, Glenn Larsen, Stephanie Layton, Julie Quinn,
Kaylene Riemen, Laura Robbins, Craig Small, Kelly Warner, Todd Wente*

Contents at a Glance

Contents

Introduction

You are an intelligent, mature adult. You can balance the department budget, plan the annual weeklong sales meeting, and get the copier to collate (and staple!). Yet there's something about a computer that makes you feel foolish.

But, hey, at least you learned how to use the thing for something other than a desk ornament. Somehow that should be enough, but now you're feeling silly again because you just tried to install a new program using the CD-ROM drive—and your PC doesn't have one.

Looks like it might be time to upgrade.

Why Do You Need This Book?

With so many "upgrade it yourself" computer books on the market, why do you need this one? Well, first off, this book doesn't assume that you want to become a computer technician in your spare time. Instead of overloading you with technical mumbo jumbo, it shows you how to do about any repair or upgrade you'd want to try, while guiding you along with simple-to-follow steps and illustrations.

With this book's help, you can perform many common upgrades, including:

➤ Adding more RAM.

➤ Upgrading the CPU.

➤ Adding a second hard drive.

➤ Installing a new sound card or a CD-ROM drive.

➤ Getting your new modem to work.

➤ Preparing your computer to run Windows 95.

Also, if you think something's broken and you're not sure whether to replace it or not, this book will help you in that department, too.

How Do I Use This Book?

First, start with the problem. If a computer nerd tells you that your PC needs more RAM and you're not sure if he's talking about a football team or your computer, turn to Chapter 3, "Taking a Look Inside." That, and Chapter 2, "Taking a Look Around the Back," are the places where you'll find all the computer stuff that nerds assume you already know.

Once you find out that RAM is the same thing as memory, you could jump over to Chapter 15, "Make Mine More Memory!," to learn how to go about adding memory to your PC. Want some alternatives before you try an upgrade? Then check out Chapter 7, "Examining Your Alternatives."

The best part about this book is that you don't have to read anything unless you need to. Just find the chapter that talks about your problem and go to it. If you do choose to read this book all the way through, you don't necessarily need to read every chapter in order. If there's something you should have read that came before, I'll tell you about it so you can review that chapter if you need to.

The Complete Idiot's Guide to Skipping Chapters

Here's what's in store so you can skip things you don't have time to deal with right now:

Part 1: First Steps Down the Upgrade Path

This part's full of background fodder, which you'll need to know if you're not sure what kind of computer you have, or what kind of stuff it already has in it. Here you'll also find help on whether or not to upgrade as well as some nifty alternatives to try.

If you're thinking about upgrading to Windows 95, there's a whole chapter full of hints that will make the whole process easier. And, if you're sticking with Windows 3.1 for a while longer, there are some tips in this chapter as well on how to make the going easier.

Not sure what the problem is, and whether or not it's time to replace a part? Check out the last chapter in this section for help deciding what to do.

Part 2: Easy Upgrades

Want to get your feet wet without drowning in a sea of upgrades? Try the replacements in this section first. You won't even break a sweat—I promise.

Part 3: Really Revving Up Your PC

Here you'll find step-by-step instructions for the most common kind of upgrades, including CPU, hard disk, memory, video, floppy diskette drives, and power supply upgrades.

Now, when you buy your upgrade component, specific installation instructions are shipped with the product. Chances are, though, that those instructions are meaningless to humans; so this section decodes everything for you.

Before you even think about opening your PC for the first time, read the first chapter in this section. It'll help you avoid many common mistakes (and even some uncommon ones).

Part 4: Upgrades That Will Make Your Neighbor Jealous

Was your neighbor the first one on the block with a video cam, a satellite dish, or a cell phone? Well, this part provides sweet revenge. Learn how to upgrade your PC with the latest and greatest (some of which you may actually use to get work done). For example, you'll learn how to install a CD-ROM drive, a sound card, a fax modem, and a tape backup.

Part 5: Getting Your PC to Figure Out What You've Done

If you ever thought you were dumb, wait until you finally get your new part installed. You see, your computer's so stupid that it won't know what you've done until you actually *tell it*. So once you've made your upgrade, you can jump to this section to learn how to get your computer's internal BIOS, DOS, or Windows to recognize all your hard work. You'll even learn how to edit your configuration files when necessary (oh joy).

Sometimes adding a new modem or a sound card causes a conflict with an existing device. When that happens, you may have to change some settings to get everything to live together peacefully. The last chapter in this section, "Fiddling with Ports, IRQs, Addresses, and Such," will show you how.

Special Reminders

As you use this book, watch out for these special reminders that will help you find just what you need:

Skip this background fodder (technical twaddle) unless you're truly interested in nerdy details.

In these boxes, you'll find a hodgepodge of information, including easy-to-understand definitions, time-saving tips, hints for staying out of trouble, and amusing anecdotes from yours truly.

Acknowledgments

Thanks to the great people at Que for allowing me to write a computer book for regular people. Special thanks to Martha O'Sullivan and Lori Cates for their help and support during the writing of this book.

My very special extra thanks goes out to Chris Krane at Elektek, for his help with the printing chapter, and to David Sokolowski at Evergreen Technologies for the information on CPU upgrades. Thanks again, guys!

Trademarks

Part 1
First Steps Down the Upgrade Path

My brother-in-law always buys the latest and greatest gadgets. He bought a VCR, microwave, Ginzu knives, cellular telephone, Thigh Master, video cam, and a satellite dish before anyone else I know. It's ironic when he boasts that his dish or his beeper is only six months old, while, in the next breath, he complains his computer equipment is six months old already. If you're one of those people who always has to have the best, you'll find owning a PC pretty frustrating. After all, whatever's new in the computing world today is already history tomorrow.

If you think owning a PC is frustrating, upgrading one can be even more so. In this section, you'll learn how to avoid some upgrades and how to ease into the ones you absolutely have to have.

Chapter 1

The Top Ten Things You Need to Know

Maybe you're standing there in the book store right now, wondering whether you should attempt this upgrade thing or not. Well, first of all, if you can heat up a can of soup, you can probably master all the "skills" necessary to upgrade your computer. Of course, having this book to guide you along doesn't hurt.

No, I don't expect that first paragraph alone to convince you to lay out a few dollars to buy this book and try your hand at upgrading. Before you decide *not to try*, read my top ten truths about upgrading:

1. A Computer Is Really a Hard Thing to Break

This one I know you won't believe, but I'm going to try anyway. Although I don't recommend it, you can probably *drop* your PC without causing any damage. I mean it—these babies are tough. And no, they don't explode if you do something wrong. They may not work right until you fix the problem, but they don't explode. So you can ditch the safety glasses.

Also, if you've ever changed the windshield wipers on your car, you can easily manage simple upgrades to your PC. That's because unlike the wipers, the parts on a PC are designed to fit only one way, so they're almost mistake-proof.

2. For Most Upgrades, All You Need Is a Good Screwdriver

The truth is, you don't have to be a master mechanic to upgrade your PC. Any part you have to add or remove is held in place by simple screws. So if you've ever used a screwdriver before, you've got all the mechanical skills you need.

I know—taking a screwdriver to a couple of thousand dollars worth of computer equipment sounds a bit scary, but hey, you've done crazier things.

3. Your Chances of Electrocuting Yourself Are About the Same As Winning the Lottery

The first time I ever looked inside a PC, I was more than a bit scared that I would touch something accidentally and electrocute myself. Even with the computer unplugged, I was convinced that spare voltage was just waiting for me somewhere. Of course, my fears turned out to be unnecessary.

Now, sure, you can accidently touch something in your PC and short it out—that is, if you've been shuffling your feet back and forth over a nice wooly carpet. (Don't worry; you'll learn exactly what to do to avoid shocking your PC and other problems in Chapter 12, "Before You Open That Box.")

4. You Don't Actually Repair Anything

You replace it. That's right. Unlike your car, which has components you repair by carefully taking them apart piece by piece so that even the guys who write Chilton's manuals are hard-pressed to get them back together again, you fix the parts on your PC by replacing them. So if your diskette drive starts messing up, you don't open it and try to replace the what's-it. Instead, you just chuck the thing and replace it with a new one. And believe it or not, it's cheaper than trying to get some computer store to attempt to repair it. (Most computer stores just replace the thing anyway and charge you for the full repair.)

5. It'll Cost You Less Money If You Do It Yourself

Well, if this doesn't get you to try an upgrade yourself, probably not much else can. My thinking is, you've already invested quite a few dollars in your computer, so why part with any more than you have to? I mean, I'm sure you can find someone to add that new hard disk, sound card, or whatever for you, but it won't come cheap. In fact, having somebody else do it may just cost you more in labor than the part is worth!

6. Or It Could Cost You More...

If you have a really old PC, you could end up replacing a lot of things just to upgrade the one thing you wanted to upgrade first. For example, if you add a 3 1/2-inch diskette drive to an older PC, you may have to upgrade its BIOS (some chips on the motherboard) and even DOS.

Other times, you upgrade one thing, only to decide that something else no longer looks as good, so you have to upgrade it too. For example, you might add a CD-ROM drive so you can play some new game, only to decide that your monitor or your sound card is lousy.

You don't have to hide your wallet—before you start any upgrade, I'll tell you exactly what you're up against and give you a rough estimate of what it will cost.

7. Upgrading Is a Real Learning Experience

After you upgrade something on your computer, no matter how hard or how easy it turns out to be, you learn something. After you've seen your PC's innards, your word processing program isn't so scary anymore. I'm not saying you'll suddenly start a career as a computer technician, but when something starts acting funny, you'll find that you're no longer afraid to try a few things before you call Joe down in MIS.

8. Learning to Upgrade Gives You Power

After months of sweat, you finally learned how to use a mouse and then Windows. After that, you figured out how to wrangle a report out of your word processor and print it.

So after months of making you feel like a fool, now you stand there, ready to take a screwdriver to the darn thing. Talk about sweet revenge.

9. You'll Probably Have to Upgrade If You Want to Run Windows 95

You've been bitten by the marketing hype, and now you've decided that you just have to have Windows 95. Trouble is, chances are really good that unless you bought your PC *yesterday*, you're going to need to upgrade something just to run it. Yes, you can put it off, but eventually you'll buy some new program that requires Windows 95. You may as well bite the bullet now—but don't worry—I've included a special chapter dedicated to Windows 95 upgraders just like you.

10. Some Upgrades You Can't Really Put Off

If you can start your PC, get a cup of coffee, schmooze in the break room for 20 minutes, come back, and your PC's still loading Windows, you can get mad or you can get used to it.

Some upgrades are necessary whether you want them to be or not. A PC, like any other mechanical device, will wear out sometime—but when it does, you can use this book to help you replace the worn out part.

Chapter 2

Taking a Look Around the Back

In This Chapter

➤ What's hanging around behind your computer

➤ How to decide where to plug everything in

➤ Serial and parallel ports revealed

➤ Other things you can learn about your PC by just nosing around

After months of sweating over the decision, you finally made an investment of your hard-earned money (or at least money you hope to hardly earn) and bought a computer. Now the decision is over, the computer's installed, and you've seen your software actually running for a minute or two. So why not relax, because after all, the hard part's over, right?

Wrong.

I know. I know. You're thinking, why should I worry about what makes the thing work when the sales guy promised that all I had to do was switch the computer on, "point and click" on some corny little picture, and everything would happen automatically?

The problem is that one day you'll get the urge to run some new software, and in order to do that, you'll probably have to install Windows 95. So you'll march down to the local computer store, and, as you're standing in the check-out line, you'll glance at the back of the box at the list marked "System Requirements," only to discover that your one-year-old computer is now an antique. In other words, your PC is going to need an *upgrade* just so you can install Windows 95.

Or maybe you've decided to bypass the Windows 95 madness for a while, but suddenly your mouse starts going on the fritz. Or maybe your boss just told you that you're being transferred to Outer Nowhere, and you're going to have to "telecommute" by modem with your coworkers in the office.

In any case, like it or not, one day you'll realize that the computer store guy lied, and you really do need to know how the dumb PC works because now you have to upgrade it. No, as much as you may want to, you can't just take it in to some computer store and say, "Upgrade this thing," because at the very least, you'll have to tell the guy *what* to upgrade. Plus, the more you know, the less likely you are to pay $500 for a $50 part. Luckily, learning more about your PC is what this and the next chapter are all about.

So What Kind of PC Do I Have?

Before you can answer that question, you need to know more about the various types of PCs. Basically, PCs are named after the CPU (or "brain," if you prefer) they contain. You'll learn more about CPUs later in this chapter, but for now, all you need to know is that they don't have names like Jack or Bob. Instead, they have mostly numbers for names.

Maybe you have some vague memory that your PC has a 386/33 CPU, but you may not have paid any more attention to that seemingly meaningless string of numbers than you pay attention to an ordinary license plate. Well, the first part you need to look at is the "386" part.

A 386 CPU is a newer CPU than a 286. A 486 is newer still, and the 586 (otherwise known as the Pentium) is the latest and greatest. As you might expect, newer generally means faster. Sometimes I say the CPU is the "brain" of your computer, which is all well and good, but it's really more correct to say it's the "engine" of your computer. If you think of the Pentium (or 586) as the computer equivalent of a V8 engine, then that makes your 486 like a V6, your 386 like a four-cylinder, and a 286 like...well, a gas-powered weed-whacker.

Tell Me Doctor, Can the Patient Be Saved?

By now you're probably wondering what kind of "engine" your PC has, and whether it's worth trying to "save" with an upgrade. I'll get to that in due time, but for now, here's a description of some general characteristics of each class of PCs, along with some tips as to whether or not you should try to upgrade them.

The IBM PC, released in 1981, is one of the granddaddies of all PCs. It contained a CPU with the name 8088, and it's as old as dirt. If you have one of these PCs, consider donating it to a museum. The IBM PC was only capable of running 64K of memory—which is only a droplet of the amount you need to run Windows 95. Remember that 286 weed-whacker? Well, compared to it, the original IBM PC is like a hole-punch. Upgradable? No way, Ray.

Soon after IBM released the original PC, it released something called the XT (short for eXtended Technology). The XT has a somewhat faster CPU than the older PC model, but it's still museum fare. Although XTs contain expansion ports, XTs aren't really "upgradable" by today's standards because the expansion ports are designed for attaching silly things like electronic equipment such as seismographic equipment and home security systems. So don't bother upgrading an old XT, either.

Almost immediately after IBM released the XT, other companies started offering PCs similar to it. The first to do so was Columbia Data Products (may it rest in peace). A company called Leading Edge soon followed, and then came Compaq. These copycats created what became known as the IBM-compatibles, or simply, *clone* PCs. A clone XT has similar components, so you shouldn't try to upgrade it either.

Clone PC
A PC based on the original IBM model, which means it was meant to run DOS and DOS programs. Newer clones can run Windows or OS/2 Warp instead.

Check This Out...

In 1984, IBM introduced the AT (short for Advanced Technology). It soon became the standard for all other PC-type computers. The AT has a 286 CPU, which as I already said, is the weed-whacker of CPUs. Although you can upgrade an old AT, you have to replace everything in order for it to run any modern programs, such as Windows programs. You're better off in most cases simply chucking an AT or similar PC and buying a new computer.

At some point, IBM introduced a joke called the PCjr. You knew it was a PC because it had the IBM logo on it; but that's where the resemblance ended. This was the computer that introduced the world to the "chiclet keyboard" (you can imagine what it looked like) and another innovation that faded into history: cartridge DOS. Yes, MS-DOS on a little cartridge that looked like one of today's Sega games. IBM marketed the PCjr exclusively to the home user, who at that time was busy buying real computers such as Apple, Radio Shack, Atari, Commodore, and so on. All of these brands shredded the PCjr in the quality department. None of them, however, was IBM-compatible, but strangely enough, neither was the PCjr, if you can believe that marketing decision. If you bought a PCjr, I'm sorry to tell you that you better plan on buying a new computer (that is, if the PCjr didn't make you want to give up on computing altogether) because it isn't upgradable.

In the late '80s, Compaq introduced a new class of PC called the 386—again after the name of the CPU it contained. This time, it was Compaq that made the first 386s, beating IBM to market by several months. When Compaq took the lead, it redefined the definition of "upgradability," allowing PC owners to upgrade memory, hard drives, and, even CPUs. If you own a 386 PC, you'll find that it's not really all that good for running today's software, but it's definitely upgradable. In fact, a lot of today's upgrade chips are designed specifically for the old 386s.

PCs manufactured today are either 486s or 586s (Pentiums). They don't require a lot in terms of upgrades, but as my husband says, "Every PC can use *something*."

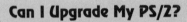

Can I Upgrade My PS/2?

IBM makes a line of computers it calls the PS/2s. Older PS/2s use a design called MCA, which is short for Micro Channel Architecture. The problem with MCA is that it never really caught on, so you'll have trouble finding MCA cards to upgrade them. IBM eventually gave up the fight, so newer PS/2s (now called PCs, as in PC60 and PC80) use a design called ISA (short for Industry Standard Architecture), which is pretty standard. In fact, most computers sold today are the ISA type. You'll learn more about MCA, ISA, and their friends in the next chapter.

Now let's just take a look at the outside of a typical PC and see what we can discover.

The Case

A big case called the *system unit* stores your computer's guts. (Some people think that the big box is called the CPU, but the CPU is actually a chip inside the system unit itself. More in a minute.) There are different sizes of system units, and for the most part, you don't really need to care, as long as you get upgrade parts that will fit into your computer's system unit. The big problem with some system units is their small height or *width*, which you'll see in a minute. (By the way, the size of a system unit is described as its *footprint*.)

Older desktop cases, such as the XT and AT cases, are big, about seven or eight inches tall. The floppy diskette drives inside are large too, which explains the need for such a big case. PCs of this type fall into the XT and AT classes, so you may not want to attempt to upgrade them. In some cases, the newer parts sold today don't work in them anyway. Expansion cards designed for the AT, for instance, probably don't fit in an XT because an AT card needs two slots, and the XT expansion bus provides just one.

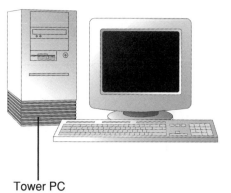

System units come in all shapes and sizes.

Slimline or small-footprint PC   Tower PC

The newer desktop cases are called *slimline* or *small-footprint* cases. About half as tall as the older cases, these don't take up as much room on a desktop. You won't have any problem finding parts to work with these PCs, however, today's desktop cases don't contain as much room to expand (such as empty drive bays and open expansion slots) as a tower system.

A *tower case* is named so because it stands on end. This type of case is usually placed under or next to a desk, on a special stand which keeps it from falling over. The attraction of a tower case is that it looks cool while also leaving your desktop uncluttered. The big benefits of a tower case, however, are more room for expansion devices and more space for ventilation.

The Power Sockets

At the back of the system unit are a couple of power sockets. These connect inside to a *power supply*, which you'll learn about later. You connect the PC to a wall outlet through one of these power sockets. The second socket isn't used a lot, because it's for supplying power to the monitor. Not such a hot idea as it turns out because the monitor uses more power than anything else in your PC. Plugging it into the system unit causes a big power drain and may prevent you from installing other devices safely. You plug today's monitors directly into their own wall socket.

Check This Out...

Suppress Your Surges!

Actually, you don't really want to plug your computer directly into a wall socket. That's because, even if the power is off, the PC can get spiked (hit with a sudden surge of electricity) during a storm, wrecking its delicate innards. So connect your PC and the monitor to a *surge suppressor*, which blows itself up in order to stop an electrical surge from getting to your computer.

Plug it in, plug it in.

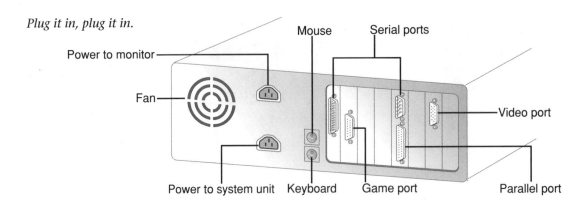

The Video Port

Once you plug your monitor into a power source, you still need to connect it to the system unit itself so it can get a picture from the computer. You do that through a special *port* (uh, connector) called the video port.

You find video ports on your video card. Although the video card is contained inside your PC, the video port is located on the outside, for your plugging convenience. Unless you have a really, really old computer, you have a video card. The video card controls the content and quality of what appears on the monitor. The video card and the monitor work hand in hand, so you have to be sure that the type of monitor you use works with whatever video card you choose. There are lots of different kinds of video cards, of varying quality:

Missing a Video Card?

Some older PCs with local bus technology have the video controller on the motherboard instead of on a card. This makes them an exceptional pain to upgrade, because you have to disable the video controller in order to add a newer one on a video card. But it can be done, and I'll tell you how in Chapter 16.

Color Graphics Array (CGA), Enhanced Graphics Array (EGA), and Hercules Graphics (monochrome)   These types of video cards are older, and they don't produce the crisp graphic images or the wide array of colors that modern video cards do. Also, they don't work with Windows.

Video Graphics Array (VGA)   Not exactly an antique, but still not as good as SVGA. VGA provides a fairly good image that's perfect for working with Windows.

Super VGA (SVGA)   The most popular type of video card and monitor sold today. The SVGA is like VGA only better, with crisper images and more color variety. The crispness of an SVGA monitor enables you to decrease the size of objects in Windows (to fit more stuff on the screen), and yet still distinguish each object clearly.

Video reality.

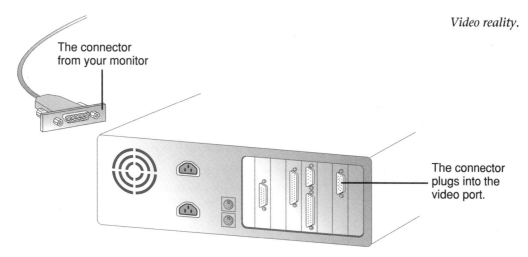

The connector from your monitor

The connector plugs into the video port.

A Rule of Thumb

All CGA and EGA video connectors have 9-pin male connectors (pins) at the end of the cable, while VGA connectors have 15-pin male connectors (pins) at the end of the cable. All video cards have female connectors (holes).

Your video card has a 9-hole connector. If your PC uses VGA or SVGA, you have a 15-hole connector instead.

Graphics Accelerator Card

Displaying the pretty pictures that are popular today in Windows, OS/2 Warp, and so on, slows down your computer because it takes time to plot where each dot of color goes. A graphics accelerator card is a special card with a unique chip which helps the CPU make these precise calculations more quickly. People used to have to buy the video card and graphics accelerator cards separately, but now the acceleration function is part of the video card, as you'll learn in Chapter 16.

The Keyboard and Mouse Ports

Not on the Back? OK, sometimes you find the keyboard connector on the front or side of the PC, instead of in the back. Some computer manufacturers just have to be different, even if it doesn't make sense.

There are usually two special ports (connectors) on the back of the system unit, for the keyboard and the mouse. I say *usually,* because sometimes the mouse is connected to a generic port called a *serial port,* which you'll learn about in a minute.

On most computers today, the keyboard and mouse ports are small, round connectors called DIN connectors. (Don't ask me why—okay, it's short for Deutsche Industrie Norm. See, I told you you wouldn't want to know.) Since they look pretty much the same, little icons such as a small mouse help you identify which is which.

The type of mouse that plugs into these round connectors is called a PS/2-style or bus mouse, because IBM introduced this style connector on its PS/2 computers.

Any Other Port in a Storm

Your computer comes with at least two generic connectors—the *serial port* and a *parallel port.* These two connectors differ not only in how they look, but also in how they work and in what types of devices you can connect to them.

Be Sure to Line 'Em Up The plug for your keyboard (and probably your mouse also) is round, so you'll want to make certain the pins on the plug make contact with the right holes. Make sure you align the notch on the plug with the notch on the connector. This ensures that you insert the plug correctly.

First of all, think of a port in a shipping area: it's a place to drop off and pick up supplies. In the case of your PC, a port is a place where a device such as a printer or a modem can drop off or pick up data.

A serial port handles data one bit at a time. (Remember that eight bits make up a *byte,* which is equal to one character, such as the letter S.) A serial port is not the fastest port on the block, but it is the most precise. Serial ports are popular because they connect lots of devices people want to use, such as a mouse, modem, scanner, and so on. So in a lot of cases, computers have two serial ports for people to connect things to.

Serial ports come in two sizes, 9-pin and 25-pin. Functionally, they are the same; you just need to connect your device to the proper size port. If you need to connect a 9-pin device such as a modem to a 25-pin connector, pop on down to your local Radio Shack for a converter. They're cheap and easy to use.

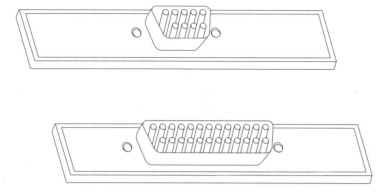

Serial ports come in two varieties.

A serial port has a nickname, COM port, because these ports are used to communicate with other devices such as a modem or a mouse. Your computer can distinguish up to four COM ports, but a lot of programs, including the first releases of Windows 3.1, recognize only the devices you attach to the first two. This makes serial ports pretty precious, indeed. To add to the confusion, an internal device such as a modem uses up one of these ports without being connected to the outside part of the port. If you then connect two other devices to the serial ports on the outside, you end up with trouble. If you suspect such trickery, turn to Chapter 24 for help.

A parallel port is faster than a serial port because it handles data one whole *byte* at a time, instead of one bit. A parallel port transmits an entire byte each time, so sometimes one bit gets scrambled, causing a "J" to turn into a "P". Extra pins in the parallel port transmit extra information to help the device at the receiving end verify that it gets the right data. If needed, the data is simply re-sent. Parallel devices include printers, tape backup units, and even portable hard drives.

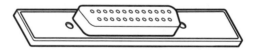

Parallel ports have 25 holes.

Parallel ports look like inverted serial ports, because they have holes, not pins. Like serial ports, parallel ports also have a nickname, LPT (Logical Printer) ports. Although MS-DOS is capable of recognizing up to four LPT ports, some computers can use only two. Few people own more than two printers anyway, so this is generally no big deal.

15

Fun and Games

Your PC may have one other port, called a game port. A game port is typically located on a sound card. There currently are three types of game ports, the most common having 15 holes. You plug in a joystick or other game device into this kind of port for hours of fun (that is, until you realize that your big presentation is due tomorrow and that, although you still have three aliens to kill, it's not even close to being done).

You may be able to plug a MIDI device into the game port also, so you can pretend you're Springsteen with a synthesizer.

The Least You Need to Know

Before you attempt to upgrade a PC, you should know a little about how it works. In this chapter, you found out some mighty interesting facts, such as:

➤ The CPU is the PC's brain (or engine, if you prefer). This is where the processing takes place. Upgrade this, and your PC can think faster.

➤ You shouldn't bother to upgrade anything older than a 386 PC.

➤ A clone PC is one which was based on the original IBM PC. Basically this means it's not a Mac.

➤ A tower case is one which is vertically oriented, whereas a desktop case is horizontally oriented.

➤ Video ports and your monitor work together. Most likely, when you upgrade one, you upgrade the other.

➤ Your PC has only a few serial and parallel ports, so you should be picky about what you decide to connect them to.

Chapter 3

Taking a Look Inside

In This Chapter

➤ What lurks inside your computer

➤ The truth about your PC's guts: RAM, the hard disk, and so on

➤ The beauty of expansion slots

A person has many parts—a heart that pumps blood, a stomach that changes food into energy, and a brain that processes information (but, in my case, not before 10:00 a.m.). A computer also has many parts, each serving its own function. The *system unit* (the big box that everything plugs into) contains most of these parts.

As you learned in the last chapter, your PC's system unit may be a regular desktop model (which lies horizontally under the monitor), or it may be a tower model (which sits vertically on the floor, under the desk). Here's a quick lowdown on what you normally find inside a system unit:

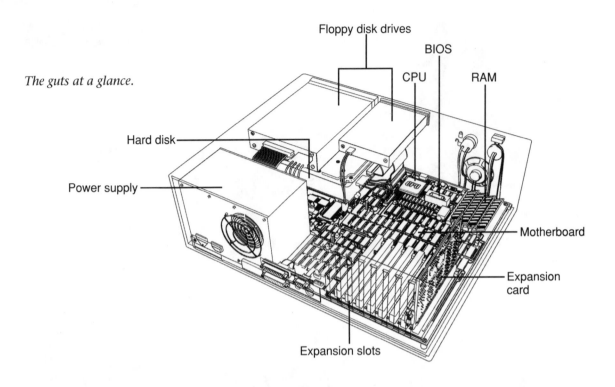

The guts at a glance.

Item	Description
Motherboard	Basically the "floor" of the system unit, the motherboard electronically connects all the other parts of the computer.
CPU	Nicknamed the "brain," this part performs all those fancy calculations. Upgrade this, and you can make your computer faster.
BIOS	If the CPU is the brain, then the Basic Input/Output System is the computer's "instinct." It's your computer's main program; it tells your computer how to run a program or read input from the keyboard or a disk drive.
Memory	Nicknamed "RAM," memory is the "work area" of the computer. Upgrade this, and the computer has a bigger area in which to work.
Hard disk	This is where the computer stores programs and permanent data (stuff that you create and then save). Upgrade this, and you can install more of those mega-do-it-all programs you love.

Item	Description
Floppy disk drive	A floppy drive enables you to transfer stuff from one PC to another, or to store data that you don't need on the hard disk all the time. All PCs come with at least one of these, so you probably don't have to upgrade this unless yours breaks down.
Power supply	This is the thing that powers it all. After upgrading, you may find that you need more juice to run all your new toys. In that case, you can upgrade the power supply.
Expansion slots	These gizmos enable you to add new junk to your PC such as an internal fax modem, a tape backup, or a CD-ROM drive.

The Motherboard Has All the Right Connections

The motherboard is a circuit board usually located on the floor of your PC. Every computer part has access to it, either directly or through a cable.

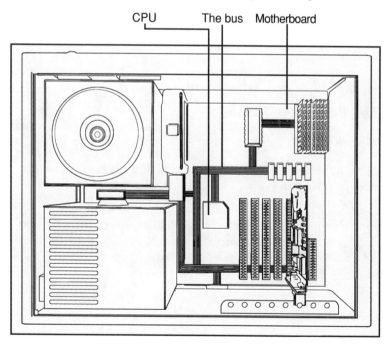

CPU The bus Motherboard

Get on the bus.

The motherboard is like a small city. Etched onto its surface are computer leads running from the CPU (a computer chip which acts like the brain of your computer) to all the other parts. These computer leads form an electronic highway called the *bus*. Like commuters at rush hour, computer instructions ride the bus from memory, the hard disk, or wherever to the CPU and back again. (An instruction must go through the CPU—it can't go from memory directly to the hard disk, for example.)

What? Replace Your Mother(board)!?

The motherboard is not something you'll generally want to replace. Everything connects to the motherboard. If you replace it, you have to unplug everything and then figure out where each piece fits into the new motherboard. On the other hand, if you can't upgrade your CPU any other way, or you want a faster bus, then replace the motherboard. However, you may want to find someone who can replace it for you instead of doing it yourself.

The only part of the bus you really need to worry about is the I/O (input/output or data in/data out) bus. Problem is, the I/O bus can take only so much data (or passengers) each time around. Most computers use a 16-bit I/O bus, which in English means that it can carry two *characters* of eight bits each.

The Local Bus Gets There Faster

Most computers built today include a *local bus*, which is a super expressway for VIP data heading from the CPU to some special peripheral such as your video card. For example, with a VESA local bus, you don't have to worry that your computerized sales pitch will stop for a five minute snoozer to gather more video data, giving your victims (uh, clients) time to sneak off.

Another type of local bus is a high-speed transfer bus called PCI (Peripheral Component Interconnect). PCI local bus is faster than VESA local bus (VL-bus), and it's built into most 486DX4 and Pentium PCs. More on PCI later in the chapter.

The Power of One Little Chip: The CPU

The CPU is the brain of the PC gang. Like a big brother, the CPU orders around all of its younger siblings: the hard disk, the floppy disk drives, the monitor, and so on, telling them what to do and when to do it.

If the CPU is a slow thinker, then things in PCland don't get done very fast. For example, if you can start your PC, get a cup of coffee, locate the last jelly donut, waste twenty minutes talking to Dan about his car problems, and return to your desk only to find that Windows is still starting up, then you've got a slow CPU.

CPUs have two numbers that help you identify them. The first number is the CPU type, such as 386, 486, and Pentium (or 586). A 486 is faster than a 386, and so on. Just in case you were thinking this is too easy, some chips have letters such as DX and SX. An SX chip is slower than the same type DX chip. For example, a 486SX CPU is slower than a 486DX CPU.

Don't Throw Out That Old PC!

Intel makes most of the CPUs used in PC-compatibles. In 1989, Intel began making CPUs upgradable. Rather than throwing out the whole computer when a faster CPU comes along, people can now take out the old CPU and plug in a new one (or in some cases, leave the old CPU in, and put the new CPU right on top of it).

For example, if you own an AT-style computer with the 80286 CPU, then you can replace the old CPU with an 80386SX CPU. You can't just plug in a standard 386 CPU (also called a 386DX) in place of an old 286 (it's too fast), but in most cases you can replace it with a 386SX, and even a 486.

Here's the Lowdown on the SX/DX Business

A 286 is just a 286, no SX or DX, thank you very much. A 386SX is like a 386DX (known to his friends as just 386), except that the 386SX doesn't "talk" as fast to the other PC components. A 486SX is like its cousin the 486DX (or just 486 if you prefer), except that it doesn't do math quite as fast. The DX chip (such as the 486DX) is always released first, then later on, the SX chip (such as the 486SX) is released at a lower price.

If you hear about a chip with the letters "DX2," it's a clock-doubled chip. This type of chip has an internal clock that runs at twice the speed of the motherboard clock. For example, a DX2 chip on a 20 MHz PC runs at 40 MHz. Megahertz, as you'll discover in a moment, is a way of measuring the speed of a CPU chip. Adding a DX2 chip speeds up the PC's processing, but not the speed of the bus (which shuttles the data around). This lets you put a faster CPU on a slower motherboard if you want.

A "DX4" overdrive chip's internal clock can run at up to three times the speed of the motherboard. These clock-doubled (or -tripled) chips either plug next to your existing CPU, or they replace it. Some even clamp onto the socket of your existing CPU without actually requiring you to pull the old CPU out first. You'll learn more about overdrive chips in Chapter 13, "Getting Your PC to Go Fast."

You may also hear of a 486SL CPU, which is exactly like the 486SX, but it includes a feature that allows it to turn parts of itself off when necessary to conserve power. This makes it more expensive, but ideal for a laptop that just loves to run out of power at 20,000 feet when you're flying to a big presentation.

A CPU's second number, measured in megahertz (MHz), tells you how fast the CPU "thinks"—the higher the number, the better. For example, a 100 MHz 486 CPU is faster than a 66 MHz 486 CPU.

If you want to know what kind of CPU you have, look at the front of your PC, which probably has a number on it like 4DX2-66, which means that you've got a 486DX2 CPU that runs at 66 MHz.

Check This Out...

Math Coprocessor

The purpose of a math coprocessor is to process numbers on behalf of the CPU. By dividing the workload in this way, the CPU can concentrate on other things, such as updating the display. The math coprocessor chip is normally included with a PC, but if your PC is missing its math coprocessor, you can buy one to plug into a special slot on the motherboard. If your computer doesn't have a math coprocessor and you don't buy one, then the CPU handles math itself along with all of its other chores. Fortunately for new computer buyers, CPUs sold today come with a math coprocessor built-in.

Basic Instinct: BIOS

BIOS is short for Basic Input/Output System, and it's a set of instructions that tells the computer how to "talk" to its friends: the keyboard, the hard disk, the floppy disk drives, the monitor, the printer, and so on. Just like your instinct tells you to duck when someone throws a brick at you, the BIOS handles the automatic functions of the PC, such as updating the display or reading data from a diskette. It also tells the CPU to pay attention when you start pressing keys on the keyboard. Handling these simple chores gives the CPU time to breathe between calculating the square root of 234,567,483,094 and spellchecking a 200-page document.

The BIOS also handles repetitive tasks, such as the rigmarole the PC goes through to start up each morning. You see, when you start your PC, the BIOS checks everything out to make sure they're functioning properly. For example, it checks out the keyboard to make sure that it's plugged in, and it checks out memory to make sure a RAM chip hasn't committed suicide in the middle of the night. This part of the BIOS, by the way, is called the POST, or *Power-On Self-Test*.

Another important function of the BIOS is to kick-start the operating system (DOS, Windows 95, or OS/2 Warp to name a few). After the POST, the BIOS loads the operating system into memory and then tells it, "OK, George, I brought 'er in. Now, this baby's yours." From here, the operating system handles the big jobs, sending requests to the CPU. The lowly BIOS continues to run—fetching data, watching for key presses, and scanning for mouse movement.

Check This Out...

Name That BIOS Want to know what brand of BIOS you have? Just start your PC, and watch for a message on-screen, like **AMI BIOS (c)1992 American Megatrends**.

The BIOS is stored on one or more ROM (read-only memory) chips, located on the motherboard (in newer systems, there is just one ROM chip). *Read-only* means that the stuff on the chips is meant to be permanent; non-nerds like you and me can't change it, accidently or otherwise.

Techno Talk

blah blah blah blah blah bl b

Upgrading the BIOS

Why would you ever want to upgrade your BIOS, and can you even do it? Yes, you can, and as to why, well, because the BIOS handles all the computer's basic input and output and computer technology is outdated weekly, there's a chance that if you own a PC that's older than a few years, your BIOS may not be able to handle all the new toys you might want to add, like a 3 1/2-inch floppy diskette drive and a fancy VGA monitor.

The PC's Think Tank: RAM

RAM is short for random-access memory, and it's basically the computer's work area. The computer stores data and instructions here temporarily while it waits for the CPU to do something with them. For example, when you start a program, your computer places it into RAM. The CPU then carries out the program's instructions as needed. When you create something, such as a letter to my editor telling her what a great book you think this is, your computer stores that letter in RAM so that the CPU can make your changes to it.

RAM is not a permanent thing, however. When you restart the computer, it erases everything in RAM. That means I'll never get to hear your wonderful words of praise unless you save your letter to the hard disk (or at least print it out) before you turn the computer off.

Check This Out...

Megabyte
Memory today is measured in megabytes. A *byte* is the amount of memory it takes to store a single character, such as the letter "J." A kilobyte is roughly one thousand bytes, and a megabyte is roughly one million bytes. (OK, if you've just gotta know, it's really 1,048,576 bytes.)

Now, because RAM is the computer's working area (or desktop, if you will), it places a limit on the amount of things you can ask your computer to do at one time—because there's only so much room on that desktop. You see, if you want to work on something, the computer must move that something into RAM. Now, if you try to run Windows without a lot of memory, your computer shuffles work out either to a temporary place on the hard disk, the TEMP directory, or to a huge unseen monster of a file called the swap file. By doing this, your computer reserves RAM for the stuff on which you currently need to work. This back and forth business really slows things down, believe me. That's why adding more RAM is probably the best thing you can do for a computer. (More on Windows in Chapter 6.)

The Different Types of RAM Chips

There are two different types of RAM chips: DRAM chips and SRAM chips. A dose of electricity must constantly refresh DRAM chips (dynamic RAM chips), or they lose their data. DRAM is the most common type of RAM chip. SRAM chips (static RAM chips) don't need to be refreshed as often, so they are faster. So why doesn't your computer have SRAM chips instead of DRAM chips? Probably because they cost big bucks.

DRAM chips aren't down and out though. Newer PCs use an improved DRAM chip called EDO DRAM, short for *extended data out*. But who cares when all you need to know is that these new DRAM chips are still cheaper than SRAM chips, yet they really zoom!

What's the Cache?

Actually, your PC may have a few of these SRAM chips in its *cache*. A cache is a special area where the PC keeps data that it has been using a lot. The idea is that if the PC requests the data several times, chances are it will do it again, so why not keep the data someplace where the CPU can get to it fast? The data in the cache is constantly evaluated so that it contains only the most popular data.

RAM chips are located on the motherboard in rows. If you're lucky, your PC comes with each row of chips prefabricated in one strip, called a SIMM, or *single in-line memory module*. If you upgrade your RAM, you can just snap in some SIMMs, and you're done. If your PC doesn't use SIMMs, then you're stuck inserting each chip in a row individually. (Ugh.) These chips are called DIP chips, short for *dual in-line package*.

SIMMS Are Simpler to Insert

DIP chips are bug-like, with tiny legs that have to fit exactly into the corresponding holes on your PC's motherboard. Ironic...this makes them little buggers to insert. The development of the SIMM was in direct protest to this nonsense; the chips are already "installed" on the SIMM, all you have to do is slip the SIMM into its slot. No chance for broken legs here.

There are other chip types as well, although they aren't necessarily popular. One, called a SIP (short for *single in-line package*) looks like a DIP chip on its side, but with only one row of legs. A ZIP (short for *zigzag in-line package*) is like a SIP but with two rows of pins. A SIPP (short for *single in-line pin package*) is kind of like a SIMM—but looks are deceiving. You can *easily* insert a SIMM into a slot, but a SIPP is much more difficult to insert. A SIPP has legs just like a DIP chip, which (yes, you guessed it) you can easily bend by accident.

Various RAM chips.

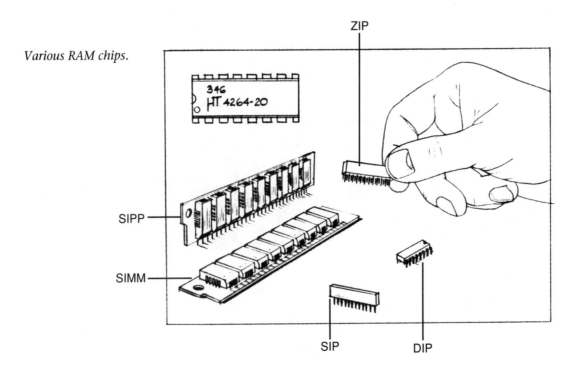

ZIP

346
HT 4264-20

SIPP

SIMM

SIP   DIP

More Chips Don't Necessarily Mean More Memory

A series of RAM chips (or a single SIMM with several RAM chips on it) works together to form a single segment of memory. For example, if your PC uses DIP chips, you might insert several 1 M RAM chips into an empty row on your motherboard; you may think that you're updating your PC by several megabytes because you're using so many chips, but instead, you're updating it by *only one* megabyte.

It's more likely that your PC uses SIMMs, rather than DIPs. Dealing with SIMMs makes it easier to understand this "it takes several 1 M chips to make up 1 M of memory" nonsense. A SIMM looks like a single unit of memory, although if you look at one closely, you can see that a 1 M SIMM really contains an entire row of these 1 M DIP-like chips. The simplicity of using SIMMs is that when you insert a 1 M SIMM, for example, you add one megabyte in a single step, instead of having to insert each of the separate DIP-like chips.

The bottom line is that you can only update memory in units called *banks*. Your PC's BIOS determines the size of a bank; but a lot of PCs have SIMM slots in banks of two, which means you have to add at least two SIMMs each time you add memory. And sometimes your PC's BIOS restricts you to adding memory in certain increments, such as 2 or even 4 M at a time, placing extra restrictions on what you can or can't do when adding memory. See Chapter 15 for help.

Save It for the Hard Disk

The hard disk is where you store your permanent data, like programs, and the stuff you create with them, such as letters and things. When you look inside your PC at the hard disk, all you see is a boring metal case about the size of a sandwich. You can't see or touch the hard disk itself; it's protected against the smog, smoke, pollen, and other crud that you and I breathe everyday without even thinking about it.

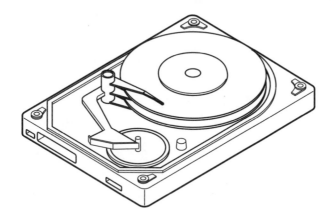

The guts of a hard disk.

If you could open up the hard disk, you'd see that it's actually a series of disks that look like CDs suspended on a central hub. The platters are coated with magnetic particles to form a pattern that, when translated from the ancient Sanskrit (OK, the bits and bytes), forms your data. Read/write heads float between these platters, eagerly waiting to grab this data when you request it.

The hard disk is connected to the motherboard through a controller card that plugs into one of the expansion slots. You find the expansion slots along one side of the motherboard; you plug a card (a controller card, a modem, a network adapter card, or whatever) into one of these slots to connect it to your computer. (More on expansion slots in a minute.) There are lots of different types of hard disk controllers; you'll find out about them in Chapter 14, "Solving a Hard Disk Problem."

Read and Write
Reading is the process of retrieving data off a disk. Writing is the process of saving data onto a disk.

Some computers come with removable hard disks—mostly for security reasons. Press a release button, pop out the hard drive, and then hide it with your diamond tiara so no one can snoop through your stuff. By the way, the computer should be off when you're performing all these shenanigans. Also, if your computer has a removable hard drive, it's a simple task to replace it with a larger capacity disk.

Partitioning and Formatting Your Hard Disk

How exactly does a computer save data onto a magnetic disk? Glad you asked. First, you have to understand that your computer usually treats the hard disk as one unit, although you can divide the hard disk into smaller units called *partitions*. You give each of these partitions a letter, such as C. In order for your computer to start using a new hard disk, you have to partition it using a command called FDISK. Basically all you're doing with FDISK is telling the computer the size of each partition, which, like I said earlier, is usually the same as the actual hard disk itself. For example, if you decide to add an 800 M hard disk to your PC, you can treat the whole thing as one drive or partition, or divide it into two partitions (such as C and D).

After you partition a hard drive, you format it. Formatting is a process that divides each platter into tracks and sectors. A track is a circle on which the hard disk actually places the data. Each track is divided into parts called sectors. When you save a file to the hard disk, it divides that file into segments that fit into the individual sectors. The location of a file is kept in something called the FAT, or file allocation table, which is located on the first sector of the hard disk.

With a Floppy Disk, You Can Take It with You

Floppy disks (also known as floppy diskettes, or simply *diskettes*) are wonderful little marvels that enable you to copy data onto your PC's hard disk and to copy data back off. You use diskettes to copy new programs onto your computer's hard disk. You can also use them to copy your own data from the hard disk onto a diskette, in case something ugly happens to the originals. When you fix the something ugly, you can then copy your original data back onto the hard disk.

Don't Forget to Back Up!

Data loss is the number one totally rotten thing that can happen to a computer user. To protect yourself, create a *backup*, which is essentially the process of copying the hard disk's data onto something else, such as a series of floppies. If you have a lot of important data (and with today's large hard drives, it's easy to have a lot), you can install a tape backup drive to back it up (see Chapter 14 for information about doing this). It's a lot easier than using a bunch of diskettes, believe me.

Basically, diskettes are small, portable, plastic storage squares. *Diskette drives* are slots located on the front of your PC; insert a diskette into the proper size slot, and the diskette drive reads the data on the diskette. You can also write data to a diskette; this is how you get data from your PC to somebody else's PC, such as a coworker.

3 1/2-inch diskette drive   5 1/4-inch diskette drive

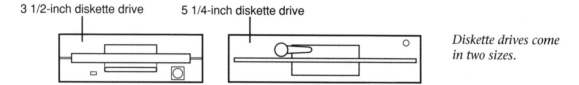

Diskette drives come in two sizes.

Diskettes come in two sizes. The larger size, 5 1/4-inch, is not used very much anymore because the smaller size, 3 1/2-inch, actually holds more data (go figure). If your PC has only a 5 1/4-inch drive, you can add a second diskette drive in the more popular 3 1/2-inch size. A 5 1/4-inch diskette is floppy, which means that you can bend it (but of course, don't actually do this, because it ruins your data). This is where the *floppy* in floppy diskette comes from. The term "floppy" isn't used much anymore, because the newer and more popular 3 1/2-inch diskettes are hard. (At least on the outside.)

Diskettes also come in several *densities*. The denser the disk is, the more data it can hold. That's because the data is more densely (or more closely) packed together on the diskette. A *high-density diskette* holds more data than a *double-density diskette* of the same size. For example, a double-density 3 1/2-inch diskette holds 720 K. A high-density 3 1/2-inch diskette holds twice that amount, 1.44 M.

Write-protect tab   Protector ring

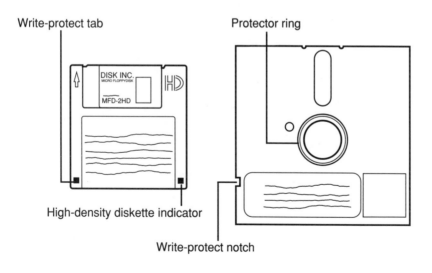

Diskettes come in two sizes, 3 1/2-inch and 5 1/4-inch.

High-density diskette indicator

Write-protect notch

I'm Your Density

How can you tell a double-density diskette from its high-density counter-part? Well, hopefully, they're marked. If not, on a 3 1/2-inch diskette, you can look for the *high-density diskette indicator*—a little hole on the opposite side of the write-protect notch. On a 5 1/4-inch diskette, it's a little harder to tell. I usually just look at the big hole in the center of the diskette. If I see a protector ring (kind of a white edge along the inner part of the hole), then the diskette is double-density. If the protector ring is not there, then the diskette is high-density.

Expanding Your PC's Horizons: Expansion Slots

Located at the back of the system unit is a row of slots called *expansion slots*. Expansion slots enable you to expand the capabilities of your computer. Plug something into one of these slots, such as a modem or a sound card, and the computer can use it.

Expand your PC's capabilities with expansion cards.

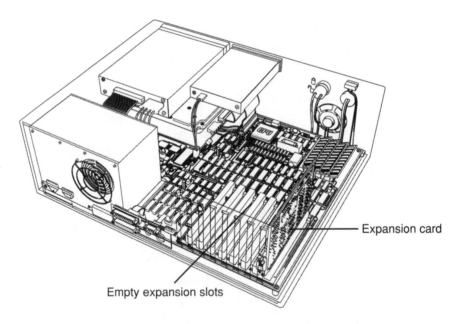

Expansion card

Empty expansion slots

Of course, nothing in life is that easy. Expansion slots come in several types, and you've got to get a card that fits into the type of slots your computer has. (More on that in a minute.) Also, your computer has only so many of these expansion slots, so when you use them all up, that's it.

What can you find already occupying some of your computer's expansion slots? Well, a video card that controls your monitor, for one. You'll also find one or two disk drive controller cards that control your hard disk and the floppy disk drives. You may also find an I/O (input and output) card that provides a serial and a parallel port on the back of your PC.

The list of cards you may have is huge: you may have a card that runs your mouse (or the connector may run directly off the motherboard). You may have a modem, a network adapter, or a joystick controller. If you add a CD-ROM drive, you may need something called a SCSI (pronounced "scuzzy") or an ATAPI IDE controller to run it, or it may run off of a sound card. If you add a scanner, there's a controller card for that. Want to edit your own videos or watch TV on-screen? That's another couple of cards. If you work at home, you can add a telephony card to manage those irritating sales calls. If you're a musician, you may want to add MIDI interface for your digital musical instruments. And believe it or not, you can add an extra fan to cool your system with an extension fan card. Sometimes you can save a few expansion slots by buying a multifunction card that combines several functions in one.

> **Check This Out...**
>
> **Expansion Cards** The things that you plug into expansion slots are called *expansion cards*. Sometimes you'll hear someone call them expansion *boards* instead of cards.

> **Check This Out...**
>
> **Any-Port-in-a-Storm** Ports are connectors at the back of your PC. Think of the various ports a ship visits to pick up or deliver cargo—in this case, the "cargo" is data. Through the ports, data enters and leaves the system unit. For example, you connect a printer to a port so you can print data.

Now, earlier I told you that there are several types of expansion slots in your PC. Again, you have to remember to match up the right size card to fit in the size expansion slot you want to use.

An 8-bit card has a single tab on the bottom which fits into an 8-bit expansion slot. "Eight bits" describes the amount of data that can travel from the card to the CPU in a single clock *cycle*. Eight bits is equal to one *byte*, or the length of a single character. Most PCs today don't use 8-bit slots because they are too slow, but you'll find them on old 286s and 386s.

Make Sure You Have Enough Slots

Before you go off the deep end and start buying things to expand your PC, you need to count the number of open slots and then fill them with the to-die-for items first. That way, you don't run out of slots before you add something you consider critical.

An 8-bit expansion card and slot.

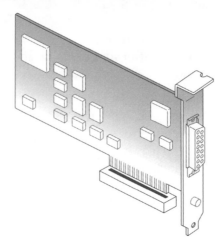

16-bit expansion slots are the most popular today. A 16-bit expansion card has two tabs on the bottom which fit into a 16-bit slot. A 16-bit card is twice as fast as an 8-bit card, because it passes twice as much data to the CPU with each cycle. A 16-bit slot is also known as an ISA (Industry Standard Architecture) slot. You'll find ISA slots on 386s, 486s, and Pentiums.

Cycle

Everything happens in a computer within a cycle. For example, if you read a file from the hard disk so that you can make changes to it, then the hard disk reads a small amount of the file per cycle, until it reads the entire file. The speed of the computer's CPU determines the number of cycles per second in the computer.

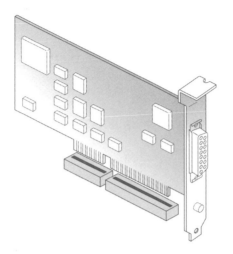

A 16-bit expansion card and slot.

EISA is short for Extended Industry Standard Architecture, and it's not terribly popular. An EISA slot is 32-bit, so it's fast, but not a lot of companies make EISA cards. An EISA card has two tabs on the bottom. You won't find an EISA slot in your typical run of the mill PC—but if you bought a PC from your employer, and it was an expensive one (at least at the time your office bought it), then it may have EISA slots.

VESA is short for Video Electronics Standards Association, and this type of slot is a direct link to the CPU. VESA local bus (known to his friends as VL-bus) is usually used for video. Updating today's cool graphics on-screen is a boring, time-consuming task, so video is one of the most important things to benefit from this direct link to the CPU. For example, if you're into the new video-in-a-window stuff, this kind of card actually makes the video seem not-too-boringly-slow. Like EISA, it's also a 32-bit expansion slot. VESA cards have four tabs on the bottom. You used to find VL-bus slots in just about every PC sold in the last few years, but nowadays you're more likely to find PCI slots (wait, I'll talk about them in a minute) instead.

An EISA expansion card and slot.

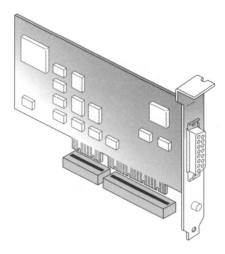

A VESA expansion card and slot.

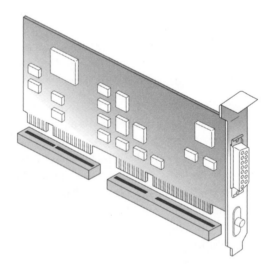

You can find MCA, short for Micro Channel Architecture, slots on older IBM PS/2 computers. Like EISA, MCA slots are also 32-bit. Trouble is, like EISA, MCA never really caught on, so not a lot of companies make MCA expansion cards. Also like EISA, MCA cards have two tabs on the bottom; but they're different sizes, so they don't fit into anything but an MCA expansion slot.

PCI is short for Peripheral Component Interconnect. You find PCI slots on 486DX4 and most Pentium computers. PCI cards are 32-bit, and they have two tabs on the bottom.

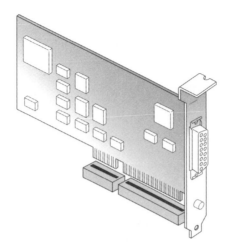

An MCA expansion card and slot.

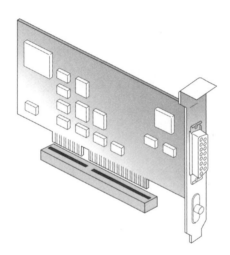

A PCI expansion card and slot.

Just in case you don't think all this slot business can get any more confusing, you should know that some cards work with slots other than their own. Confusing? This table helps:

Slot	Kind of PC in Which You Find It	Types of Cards It Takes
ISA	286, 386, and 486 PCs	8-bit or 16-bit cards
EISA	Mostly Power PCs	EISA and 16-bit cards
VESA	Mostly 486 PCs	VESA (VL-bus) and 16-bit cards

continues

35

continued

Slot	Kind of PC in Which You Find It	Types of Cards It Takes
MCA	Older PS/2s	MCA cards only
PCI	Pentiums	PCI cards only
PCMCIA	Laptops	PCMCIA cards of the right type

But I Have a Laptop!

Well, laptops don't come with expansion slots per se, but with PCMCIA (Personal Computer Memory Card International Association) slots. These slots make it easy to insert one thing (such as a CD-ROM drive) and later replace it with something else (such as a modem) as your needs change. You insert what is essentially a credit-card sized expansion board into one of these slots in order to "install" the device that's attached to it.

There are several PCMCIA standards; laptops usually come with several Type II and Type III slots. Type III are mostly for removable hard disks, while Type II handles everything else. You need to make sure that the upgrade item on your list comes in a compatible PCMCIA type to fit the slots your laptop has. The easiest way to do this is to contact the manufacturer of your laptop.

The Power Supply and Battery

Inside the system unit is a big gray box with lots of wires running out of it, connecting it to, well, basically everything. This gray box is the power supply. Unless you bought your PC off a truck from some guy who talked in a whisper (and who offered to throw in a Rolex for an extra $50), your PC already comes with one of these.

A Shocking Fact Don't ever, ever open the power supply box to try to "fix" it. Doing so (even with it unplugged) may fix you dead.

Now, why does the computer have an internal power supply, when you plug it into the wall? Well, the power supply takes your ordinary household current (AC) and "gentlizes" it to the lower voltage current (DC) that your computer's delicate parts prefer.

The power supply also contains a fan, which cools down your PC's components. This is very important, especially if your PC has one of those fast CPUs, such as a Pentium.

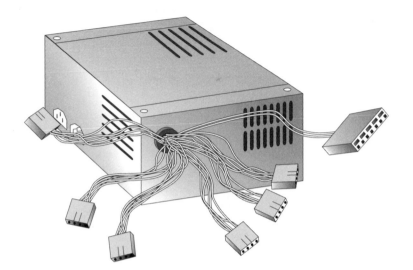

A typical power supply.

So why should you concern yourself with the power supply? Simple. If you start adding tons of stuff to your computer, you may need to upgrade the power supply as well. Standard wattage is 180, but if you have a big system, you may need 220 watts or higher.

Besides the power supply, there's also a battery in your PC. What for? Well, it powers a tiny chip that helps the PC remember important stuff even after you turn it off, such as the current date and time. Most batteries last about three years before you have to replace them. You'll learn how to do this in Chapter 18, "Powering Up the Power Supply."

The Least You Need to Know

Before you attempt to upgrade a PC, you should know at least a little about how it works, such as:

➤ The motherboard is the "floor" of the system unit, and everything connects to it.

➤ The motherboard uses an electronic transportation system, called a bus, to transfer data back and forth between devices.

➤ The BIOS handles routine tasks such as reading and writing data, updating the monitor display, and monitoring keyboard and mouse activity.

➤ RAM is the working area of the computer. Add more RAM, and the PC can handle larger workloads.

➤ You use the hard disk to store permanent data. To take data with you, copy it to a floppy diskette.

➤ Your PC's expansion slots enable you to connect new devices easily.

➤ The power supply converts an ordinary household current into a lower voltage current that the delicate parts of your PC can handle.

Finding Out What Kind of Computer You Have

In This Chapter

➤ Simple ways to get DOS to tell you what it knows

➤ The real truth behind the CONFIG.SYS and AUTOEXEC.BAT hoopla

➤ The secrets Windows keeps

➤ Pulling CMOS (vital system info) from your PC's innards

Before you start thinking about upgrading your PC, you need to know some things about your computer. For example, you need to know what kind of CPU it has, how much memory it has, and how things are currently set up. This kind of information will help you tell whether or not you can actually do the kind of upgrade you have in mind on your particular PC. Vital stuff to know *before* you start actually tearing things apart, don't ya think?

Once you've done some serious snooping using the tips you find in this chapter, be sure to complete the following list as best you can:

Relax...This Is Not an SAT

At this stage in the game, don't feel bad if you can't complete this entire list, or even understand what you're supposed to put in most of the blanks. You'll learn more about your computer as you go along. If you want a head start on this list, try locating your PC's original invoice—it'll help you fill in a lot of the blanks. Also look at the front of your PC and other devices for model names and numbers. For example, a model number 486SX/33 tells you that you have a 486-33MHz CPU. Copy down as much as you can and then use the tips in this chapter to learn more.

Equipment	My PC
PC brand/model (e.g., Compaq)	_____
CPU (e.g., 486SX/33MHz)	_____
BIOS (e.g., AMI, 11/11/92)	_____
Operating system (e.g., DOS 3.3)	_____
Total RAM (e.g., 4 M)	_____
Type of RAM chips (e.g., 120ns DIPs)	_____
Maximum amount of RAM my PC can handle (e.g., 16 M)	_____
Hard disk type (e.g., Conner IDE)	_____
Hard disk size (e.g., 340 M)	_____
Second hard disk type	_____
Second hard disk size	_____
Diskette drive A: (e.g., 5 1/4-inch)	_____
Diskette drive B: (e.g., 3 1/2-inch)	_____
Total number of drive bays (e.g., 4)	_____
Number of unused drive bays (e.g., 2)	_____
CD-ROM type (e.g., NEC Multispin 6x SCSI)	_____
CD-ROM controller settings (e.g., IRQ12)	_____
Monitor type (e.g., VGA)	_____

Equipment	My PC
Video card (e.g., Hercules Graphics)	_____
Modem type (e.g., USRobotics 14.4FAX ext.)	_____
Modem settings (e.g., COM2 IRQ3)	_____
Expansion bus type (e.g., ISA)	_____
Number of expansion slots available	_____
Network type (e.g., Novell Netware 4.01)	_____
Network card settings (e.g., DMA 4)	_____
Mouse type (e.g., Logitech serial)	_____
Mouse settings (e.g., COM1 IRQ4)	_____
Tape backup type (e.g., Mountain 350 M)	_____
Tape backup setting (e.g., DMA 5)	_____
Sound card type (e.g., SoundBlaster 16)	_____
Sound card settings (e.g., IRQ7 DMA 3)	_____
Other (e.g., game adapter)	_____

In this list, you probably ran into a lot of terms you don't understand, including COM, DMA, and IRQ. You'll learn about a lot of terms as you go along, but these three I thought I better clear up right here.

COM refers to a COM or serial port. Each COM port is assigned a particular I/O address that enables the PC to communicate with the device assigned to that port. Serial devices, such as a modem, mouse, or a serial printer, are assigned to these ports. Internal serial devices such as a modem also use a COM port. Your PC can have devices assigned to up to four COM ports, although only two can be in use at any one time. So knowing which COM port your various serial devices have been assigned to helps a lot when troubleshooting a problem with a new device.

DMA is short for Direct Memory Access channels, and they're the high speed communications channels your hard disk, floppy disk drives, tape backups, network cards, and sound cards use.

IRQ is short for interrupt request. Various devices use IRQs as a kind of tap on the shoulder to the CPU to gain its attention. The system timer, keyboard controller, COM ports, LPT ports, hard disk controller, floppy drive controller, and so on use IRQs. So fighting to get your new device a free IRQ is the number one cause of hair loss. In addition, many devices stake out particular I/O address (a particular area in memory). When you install a new device, you might run into a conflict if that device tries to use an address which some other device calls "home."

For help setting ports, DMAs, IRQs, or I/O addresses, see Chapter 24.

What DOS Can Tell You

After checking your original invoice for information (that is, if you still have it), you may still end up with some blanks on your equipment list. That's okay, because DOS has some commands that you can use to find out more.

Techno Talk

DOS Is Still with You

Even if you use Windows, you can still get DOS to tell you some stuff about your PC. To get to the DOS prompt, double-click on the **MS-DOS Prompt** icon in the Main program group. Type the command you want and then press **Enter**.

To get back to Windows, type **EXIT** and press **Enter**.

If you use Windows 95, you can get to the DOS prompt by selecting **MS-DOS Prompt** from the **Programs** menu. Again, just type the command you want and press **Enter**. To get back, either type **EXIT** and press **Enter**, or just click the **Close** button to close the window.

Check This Out...

Communicating with DOS With DOS, you type commands at the prompt (that C:\> thing) and you press **Enter** to get results.

First of all, to find out what DOS version you're using, type **VER** and press **Enter**.

You see something like this on-screen:

    MS-DOS Version 5.0

Now, if you happen to have DOS version 5.0 or higher, you can use the following command to figure out how much memory (RAM) you have. Just type **MEM** and press **Enter**:

You see something like this:

Microsoft(R) Windows 95
  (C)Copyright Microsoft Corp 1981-1995.

C:\WIN95>mem

Memory Type	Total	Used	Free
Conventional	640K	83K	557K
Upper	155K	155K	0K
Reserved	128K	128K	0K
Extended (XMS)	15,461K	109K	15,352K
Total memory	16,384K	475K	15,909K
Total under 1 MB	795K	238K	557K

Largest executable program size   557K (570,256 bytes)
Largest free upper memory block   0K   (0 bytes)
The high memory area is available.

Look at the *total memory* number to see how much you have. For example, it looks like I have 16,384K. Memory is shown in *kilobytes*, which are roughly equal to 1,000 bytes. To convert to megabytes (which are roughly equal to 1,000,000 bytes), divide by 1,000. So if I take 16,384 and divide it by 1,000, I learn that I have about 16 M of RAM.

To see what size hard disk you have, type **CHKDSK** and press **Enter**.

You see something like this:

Volume Serial Number is 1303-2525

511,344,640 bytes total disk space
8,798,208 bytes in 142 hidden files
2,310,144 bytes in 266 directories
415,039,488 bytes in 6,197 user files
85,196,800 bytes available on disk

8,192 bytes in each allocation unit
65,509 total allocation units on disk
13,489 available allocation units on disk

655,360 total bytes memory
570,576 bytes free

To figure out how big your hard drive is, look at the first number, which is listed as "total disk space." You see that it's listed in bytes; this is about as useful as ice in Alaska. To convert the number to megabytes, divide by a million. So I'd take 511,344,640 and divide by a million, which gives me 511 M. If you have a thing for decimal points (and accuracy), you can divide by 1,048,576 instead. (1,048,476 is the actual number of bytes in a megabyte.)

Cheating with Microsoft Diagnostics

Very few computers (even if they look exactly alike on the outside) contain the same equipment on the inside. Even the most well-known brand names may contain internal parts made by who knows what other manufacturers; every week or so, somewhere on the assembly line, a part made by one of these so-called "other" (or "third-party") manufacturers replaces a part from some other "other" manufacturer. Even the mighty BIOS chip (which tells your computer that it's a computer when you turn it on), is sometimes replaced on the assembly line with another version. So even if you can find the owner's manual that came with your PC, you may not be able to rely on it to tell you what type of stuff your PC actually has.

To get some serious snooping done, you need Microsoft Diagnostics, which you can call MSD after you get to know it better. One problem: you'll only find MSD on your PC if you have Windows or DOS version 5.0 or higher.

Check This Out...

I Don't Have It

If you don't have MSD, you can still find out some more information about your PC. Just restart it and watch the screen. You'll see a message telling you what kind of video card you're using, along with what BIOS you have, and its creation date.

For example, when I boot my system, I see this:

AMI BIOS (c)1992 American Megatrends

This tells me that I have the 1992 version of American Megatrends BIOS.

MSD digs down into your system and then displays what it finds. Unfortunately, this list includes only the things that the good folks at Microsoft decided you might want to know—so it's not complete. At least it gives you a good start at completing your equipment list. One warning though—the Surgeon General has rated most of this junk hazardous to your sanity, so avoid prolonged exposure whenever possible.

To start Microsoft Diagnostics, type **CD\DOS** and press **Enter**. Then type **MSD** and press **Enter**. (If you're doing this from Windows, you'll get an error message telling you that the results will be skewed. Back out of it, exit Windows, and try again at the real DOS prompt. You'll get better results. If you're using Windows 95, restart the PC in DOS mode—which you can do by shutting down Windows and choosing the DOS mode option in the dialog box that appears.)

You see something like this on-screen:

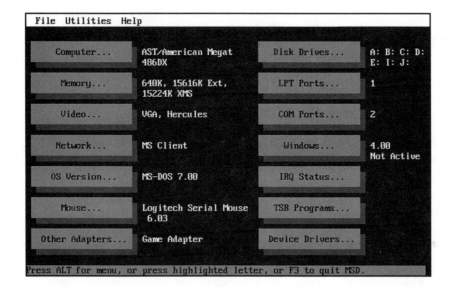

MSD can tell you a lot about your computer.

To find out more about a particular component, just click on its button. For example, if you want to learn what kind of video you've been using all these years, click on the **Video** button. To return to the main screen, click **OK**. When you've learned all you can, open the **File** menu and select **Exit** to return to the DOS prompt.

By the way, if you're curious, the reason the screen tells me I have Windows 4.0 is because I'm using Windows 95. (Jealous? Don't be.) Windows 95 is basically Windows 4.0, if you think about it, because the last version of Windows was 3.x. Anyway, I restarted the PC with DOS, so it's showing as "Not Active." You may see some similar nonsense. Don't worry, because when you restart the PC again, Windows 95 will activate itself automatically.

Just Print It

Why bother writing this all down, when you can take a snooze while MSD prints this all out for you. Turn your printer on, open the **File** menu, and select **Print Report**. Click the box next to any of the items you don't want to print to deselect them and then click on **OK**. (Um, if you print everything, plan on a looong coffee break.)

Snooping Through the Configuration Files

After you find out all that DOS can tell you, it's time to move on to bigger fish: the configuration files. You see, when you start your computer, it yawns and stretches, performs a couple of quick sit-ups, and then reaches for the computer equivalent of a cup of coffee, otherwise known as the configuration files, AUTOEXEC.BAT and CONFIG.SYS.

So why are these files so important, and what have they got to do with finding out what's in your PC? Well, after you add something to your PC such as a new video card, you need to make changes to the configuration files in order to get the card to work. (You'll learn why in just a minute.) Usually you find a setup diskette with your new card; this setup diskette makes the necessary changes to your configuration files for you. In any case, if you look at the configuration files later on, these same changes provide you with another important clue in "The Case of the Unidentified Computer Equipment."

Always Keep Copies

The installation of some new device may change a configuration file, so you should keep updated copies of all your configuration files on diskette. That way, if the change inadvertently causes you some "minor" inconvenience (such as preventing you from starting your PC), you have some way to undo it. Don't worry, I'll show you how to create this and other forms of insurance in Chapter 12, "Before You Open That Box."

CONFIG.SYS

The CONFIG.SYS file enables you to add information to customize your PC so that it will work with all those extras you may add one day, such as a CD-ROM drive, a sound card, or a tape backup. CONFIG.SYS contains other information as well, but mostly it contains the names of *device drivers*, which act as interpreters between "foreign objects" (such as a mouse) and your PC. Through the right device driver, your computer can "talk" to just about anything, including things that didn't even exist when you bought your computer.

You see, each time you turn on your computer, it starts up the device drivers. Each device driver acts as a sort of translator between whatever applications you're running and the device that it controls, such as a printer. Your application issues some command to "da printa," and the device driver translates the command into something that your specific HP LaserJet 5P printer can understand.

To see what device drivers and other settings your CONFIG.SYS contains, type **TYPE C:\CONFIG.SYS** at the DOS prompt and press **Enter**.

Your computer shows the CONFIG.SYS file on your screen. Here's what my CONFIG.SYS looks like:

```
DEVICE=C:\DOS\HIMEM.SYS
DEVICE=C:\DOS\EMM386.EXE
BUFFERS=10,0
FILES=40
DOS=UMB
DOS=HIGH

DEVICEHIGH /L:1,38064 =C:\DOS\DRVSPACE.SYS /MOVE
DEVICEHIGH /L:1,11648 =C:\MVCD6  /D:MSCD000 /N:1
DEVICEHIGH /L:1,35514 =C:\COMM\FAX\SATISFAX.SYS
DEVICEHIGH /L:1,33696 =C:\PROAUDIO\TSLCDR.SYS /D:MSCD0001 /R /P:3
DEVICEHIGH /L:1,11712 =C:\PROAUDIO\MVSOUND.SYS D:3 Q:7
```

What does all this mean? Basically, who cares, except for the lines that begin with DEVICE or DEVICEHIGH. These are the lines that load device drivers during startup. However, you can ignore the HIMEM.SYS and the EMMM386.EXE lines; these load device drivers that help your computer deal with memory. Ignore the next one as well, because it loads DRVSPACE.SYS, a driver that helps your PC talk to a compressed hard disk.

With the next four DEVICE lines you've struck gold, because these lines load device drivers for stuff attached to your PC. Look at my CONFIG.SYS file. The first line loads a device driver for a Media Vision CD-ROM drive. The next one loads a driver for an Intel SatisFAXtion

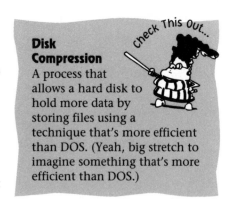

Disk Compression
A process that allows a hard disk to hold more data by storing files using a technique that's more efficient than DOS. (Yeah, big stretch to imagine something that's more efficient than DOS.)

modem, and the next two lines load drivers for a ProAudio Spectrum sound card. By looking at your DEVICE and DEVICEHIGH lines, you can tell at least the brand names of the devices attached to your PC.

AUTOEXEC.BAT

The AUTOEXEC.BAT file contains commands that your PC automatically "executes" (carries out) for you at startup. It's as if you actually type each of the commands yourself, except you don't have to move a finger. One of the things the AUTOEXEC.BAT may contain is a command to load a device driver for a new computer part. True, most device drivers live in the CONFIG.SYS, but sometimes they get a hankering for something new, and they turn up in the AUTOEXEC.BAT. Another common use for the AUTOEXEC.BAT file is to automatically start Windows 3.1 and your favorite programs when you start the computer. (If you have Windows 95 on your computer, you know that it automatically starts without you having to type anything.)

To see what your commands are in your AUTOEXEC.BAT, type **TYPE C:\AUTOEXEC.BAT** at the DOS prompt and press **Enter**.

Here's what my AUTOEXEC.BAT's got in it:

```
@ECHO OFF
LH /L:0;1,45456 /S C:\DOS\SMARTDRV.EXE
LH /L:1,13984 C:\DOS\SHARE.EXE /1:500 /F:5100

SET TEMP=C:\WINDOWS\TEMP
PROMPT=$P$G
PATH=C:\DOS;C:\WINDOWS;D:\UTILITYS;C:\LOGMOUSE

C:\LOGMOUSE\MOUSE
```

Unfortunately, unlike the CONFIG.SYS, you can't look for the word DEVICE to point out where the device drivers are hiding. Some device drivers are loaded into "high" memory here through the LOADHIGH command ("LH" to its friends). Most LH-loaded drivers, however, don't drive physical devices (things you can hold and touch); instead, they drive virtual devices (things that only exist in the mind of your computer). For example, the line, LH /L:0;1,45456 /S C:\DOS\SMARTDRV.EXE is loading a virtual device driver called SMARTDrive, which creates a disk cache. Why would anyone want to do that? Well, the secret's in the sidebar coming up. In any case, you can't always look at the LH lines for clues to your PC's equipment list.

But some of the LH lines actually do load device drivers for physical devices, such as a CD-ROM drive. So how can you tell whether an LH line is pointing to a real or an imaginary device? Good question, but when I'm not sure about what a particular device does, I go to the DOS prompt and type **HELP** followed by the name of the device driver. So in my case, I type **HELP SMARTDRV** and press **Enter.** Then I wait to see what happens. If Help turns up something, then I know the device driver is a figment of DOS' imagination—in other words, it's a DOS virtual device driver, and totally useless for helping me complete my equipment list. But if Help turns up nothing, I know the device driver is not something DOS made up, and that it must be pointing to a real device such as a CD-ROM drive or a mouse.

More about Virtual Devices

If you're just dying to know more about virtual devices, here are a few examples. One popular virtual device driver is SMARTDRV, which creates a disk cache (pronounced "cash") in memory. A cache is like a bank, except this one stores the most popular data at any given moment. Because getting data out of memory is quicker than trying to get it off the hard disk, a cache can make your PC faster by allowing it quick access to the data it uses the most.

Another popular virtual device driver is SHARE, which fools DOS into letting more than one program use the same file. Windows uses SHARE so that it can keep more than one program running at the same time.

You may find device drivers in the AUTOEXEC.BAT that aren't loaded high. One example in my AUTOEXEC.BAT is the very last line, which loads a device driver for a Logitech mouse. So to sum it all up, I didn't really learn a lot from my particular AUTOEXEC.BAT. All I learned is that I have a bunch of virtual device drivers attached to nothing and a device driver for a real device—a Logitech mouse. You may or may not learn more about your PC from your own AUTOEXEC.BAT, but of course, you'll never know until you try.

WIN.INI and SYSTEM.INI

Windows insulates you from the drudgery of DOS with its fancy graphics and cute icons. Windows insulates itself from DOS too, through its own configuration files, WIN.INI and SYSTEM.INI. Under Windows, the CONFIG.SYS and AUTOEXEC.BAT load the device drivers that DOS uses. SYSTEM.INI loads the Windows version of the drivers for the same devices.

You see, when you tell Windows that you've just installed a new device (something you'll learn how to do in Chapter 23), Windows makes a note in SYSTEM.INI so that it can remember which drivers to use. You remember *drivers*—they're the files that help a PC communicate with the specific devices you add on, such as a printer or CD-ROM drive. WIN.INI is less geeky than the SYSTEM.INI; it contains boring but important stuff, such as the colors you like and the amount of spacing you prefer between icons.

Both WIN.INI and SYSTEM.INI contain text; this means that you can use Windows' Notepad program to read the stuff that's in them. Just start Notepad and open the files as usual—they're in the \WINDOWS directory. But don't expect great enlightenment; they aren't meant to contain anything *you* can make sense of—they're for Windows to use. But if you look closely for the word "device" you might learn the name of a device or two, such as your printer or your mouse.

Windows keeps track of what your PC has with its own configuration files.

And when it comes to upgrading, you won't be dealing with either of these files directly, but I thought you might want to know what they're for, because they might come up in conversation—especially if that conversation is with some technical support guru. One last word here—if you open either of these two files using Notepad, just make sure that you look and don't touch—in other words, don't make any changes to the files, or some part of Windows may not work properly.

Surely There's an Easier Way

If you have Windows 95, there's an easier way to discover what kind of equipment you have. Just open the Control Panel and double-click on **System**. Click on the **Device Manager** tab. You'll see everything listed. Just click on the tiny **plus sign** in front of any device you want to know more about. If you want to get real nosy, you can also select a device from the list and click on **Properties**.

Don't Forget the "Sea Moss" (CMOS)

Ever wonder what day it is? Ever wonder how your PC knows, even though you don't? Well, the answer's in the CMOS (pronounced "sea moss").

CMOS is short for Complementary Metal-Oxide Semiconductor, and it's a chip inside your PC that stores important information such as the current date and time. Once information is typed into the CMOS, it stays there, thanks to a tiny battery which helps it remember, even when you cut off the computer's power supply.

Life Before CMOS

Some older PCs (museum trash mostly, such as old XT types and the original PCs) don't have a CMOS; instead, these PCs use several DIP switches or jumpers to tell them what kind of hard disk they have, and how much memory. A DIP switch by the way, is like a light switch; it only has two settings: on or off. A jumper is a couple of tiny metal poles set close together, like goal posts. To turn on a particular jumper, you cover the two posts with a rubber clip, which I'll show you how to do in Chapter 24.

By setting a series of these DIP switches or jumpers in a certain pattern of off/on/off/ off, or whatever, you actually provide your PC with what today passes for CMOS information in any modern computer.

Think of CMOS as a kind of big day planner for your PC, chock full of important information such as how many disk drives it has, and what type they are. CMOS keeps track of other stuff too, such as the amount of RAM your PC has. But, just like what happens if you lose your own day planner, if your PC loses the information in CMOS (such as when the battery finally dies), it is dead in the water—*literally*.

BIOS and CMOS, Why Do They Sound So Similar?

Well, yes, you have a BIOS chip inside your PC. And yes, you also have a CMOS chip. However, they are not the same thing, nor do their purposes overlap.

The BIOS is like a butler, performing all the menial input and output tasks which are beneath the lordly CPU. If a disk needs to be read, for instance, then the CPU dispatches the BIOS to read it, and so on.

The CMOS, on the other hand, is like a reminder pad to which the CPU can refer whenever it forgets basic information, such as how large the hard disk is, or how much memory there is.

So, while your CMOS is still in good health, copy down the information it contains. That way, when the battery supporting the CMOS dies, and your PC ends up with amnesia, you can re-create the CMOS data by typing it back in. Just turn to Chapter 13, "Getting Your PC to Go Fast," for information about replacing the battery. Then jump to Chapter 24 to learn how you can restore your PC's "memory" (CMOS).

How you get to the stuff CMOS contains depends on your PC, but it's probably one of these three ways:

➤ Reboot your computer and press **Ctrl+Alt+Escape** or **Ctrl+Alt+S**. You can also try **Ctrl+Alt+Enter** or **Ctrl+Alt+Insert**.

➤ Reboot your computer and watch the screen for a message telling you what key to press for **Setup**. Then press it. (It may tell you to press **F1** or **F2** or even **Delete**.)

➤ Restart your computer with a Setup diskette in drive A. (This is usually what you need to do for an AT-type 286 PC.)

➤ Uh, remember that an XT or earlier type PC doesn't have a CMOS program. Instead, CMOS is set up by moving a bunch of jumpers on the motherboard.

Still No CMOS
If you try all these things and still no CMOS, look in your owner's manual for help.

Once you get the CMOS open, copy down the information it contains. Don't worry if you don't understand what it all means, because your PC does. Just make sure you copy down the information *correctly*. Or, if you've got a printer, turn it on and press **PrintScrn** to print it.

Device	CMOS Setting
Hard disk C type	_____
Hard disk C settings	Cyls ___ Hds __ WPcom __ LZ __ Sec __
Hard disk D type	
Hard disk D settings	Cyls ___ Hds __ WPcom __ LZ __ Sec __
Diskette drive A type	_____
Diskette drive B type	_____
Base memory	_____
Board memory	_____
Extended memory	_____
Display type	_____
Other stuff:	*Setting:*
_____	_____
_____	_____
_____	_____
_____	_____
_____	_____

Follow the on-screen instructions for getting out of CMOS. You're probably safe with just pressing **Esc**, as long as you don't actually change anything.

While we're on the subject, if you add a new disk drive to your PC, add more RAM, replace the motherboard, or change any other basic component, you're going to have to run your PC's Setup program to tell CMOS about it. Don't worry—you'll learn how to do that in "Part 5: Getting Your PC to Figure Out What You've Done."

The Least You Need to Know

Finding out what kind of computer you have is an important step down the road to Upgrade City. Here are some clues to help you find your way:

➤ Start by looking at your original invoice for information.

➤ To find out what DOS version you're using, type **VER** at the DOS prompt.

➤ To find out how much memory you've got, type **MEM**.

➤ To discover the size of the hard disk, type **CHKDSK** at the DOS prompt.

➤ A great way to find out lots of information is to use Microsoft Diagnostics. Just type **MSD** at the prompt.

➤ The system configuration files, CONFIG.SYS and AUTOEXEC.BAT, also provide clues. Check out their device driver lists.

➤ A *device driver* is a file which helps your PC communicate with its devices, such as a sound card, fax modem, a CD-ROM, or a tape backup.

➤ CMOS is a special chip which keeps track of some of your PC's basic "ingredients," such as the number of disk drives it has, the size of the hard disk, and the amount of memory.

➤ If your PC's battery goes dead, your CMOS info is lost forever, so you need to make a copy of your CMOS information before disaster strikes.

What You Should Know Before You Upgrade

I know. The only thing you've ever upgraded was your airline seat. Maybe the mere thought of upgrading your computer brings a vision of possible *electrocution* (or *execution* by your boss if you accidentally destroy your computer). Or maybe the thought of an upgrade brings visions of another kind—of money flowing out of your pocket and into a gray box with a TV on top.

In this chapter, you'll learn what type of upgrades fit both your risk tolerance and your wallet.

First, What CAN You Upgrade?

There aren't many limits to how you can upgrade your computer. For instance, you can upgrade your PC by adding something new to it, such as a CD-ROM drive. Or, as the need arises, you can replace an old part with something that's better or faster.

But what, exactly, *can* you upgrade? Well, this list tells you about some of the more popular upgrades, and whether or not they're possible for your PC:

Replace the Mouse or the Keyboard

Your keyboard is sticky, and you can't locate the "E" anymore. Or your mouse is simply erratic. There's no need to put up with either inconvenience, because replacing the mouse or keyboard is an easy task.

Not a lot of worries here about whether or not you can replace your keyboard or your mouse—as long as the cable fits, use it. See Chapters 9 and 10 for the details.

Add a Printer

If you emptied your pockets when you bought your PC a year ago, now may be the best time to add that printer you've been eyeing. Prices are down, so a laser printer is now affordable, and so is a color printer, for that matter. Besides, it's a simple upgrade for any computer. Jump on over to Chapter 11 and give it a try.

Add Memory

If your PC is slow and you use Windows, adding memory is your best upgrade. You won't believe the difference another 8 M of RAM makes, even on an old dinosaur.

A warning, however: you can only add memory to your PC if the motherboard can support the total amount. For example, if your motherboard can only handle a total of 16 M, then that's all you can have, period.

It helps if the motherboard has open memory sockets in which you can put the RAM chips you want to add. There are other things to look out for as well. For instance, be sure you buy memory chips that are compatible with your system. Before you run off to the old memory store, don't forget to check out the advice in Chapter 15.

Add Another Hard Disk and a Tape Backup

If you use Windows like me, you probably ran out of room on your hard disk about six months ago. It's amazing how quickly a couple of programs and their data can eat up

100 M. (If you want to see how much room your hard disk has left, go to a system prompt and type **CHKDSK** and press **Enter**.)

So if your hard disk's crowded, instead of copying files onto diskette and then copying them back again when you need them, just bite the bullet and add another hard drive. Hard drives are relatively inexpensive and LARGE! (I'm talking a gigabyte here—that's one thousand megabytes, or three times the size of most hard drives sold about a year ago.) While you're at it, add a tape backup to make the job of protecting all that data a simple one.

Of course, in order to add a hard disk or a tape backup, you need to have *room*. For your PC, this means empty *drive bays* (these "shelves" into which you can place new hard disk drives, floppy disk drives, tape backups, or CD-ROM drives are visible from the front of your PC). If you run out of "shelves," you severely limit your upgrade possibilities.

Can't wait for the step-by-steps? See Chapter 14.

Add a CD-ROM Drive or Sound Card

To get current with today's programs, you're going to need a CD-ROM drive to install most of them, and probably a sound card to hear them. (Okay, you can install some programs using diskettes, but that is really getting more and more rare, since it's cheaper to produce a program on CD-ROM.)

To install a CD-ROM drive, you need an empty drive bay. Otherwise, you have to settle for an external CD-ROM drive, which hangs off the side of your machine like an extra foot and costs at least $100. Check out Chapter 19 if you want to know more.

To install a sound card, you need to be sure that your PC has an empty *expansion slot*. An expansion slot is an all-purpose connector that enables you to add just about anything to a computer—even things that weren't invented when you bought your PC. Trouble is, your PC has only so many of them, and you will use them up quite quickly. You may have to open up the PC to see if you have any open slots available, so see Chapter 20 before you invest in sound equipment.

Replace the CPU

If you have a need for speed, replace the CPU. (Caution: You may or may not be able to do this, depending on your PC's motherboard—see Chapter 13 for specifics.) But if you can replace an old 386 with a newer 486, you won't believe the difference in speed. It's like going from a Taurus to a Ferrari.

Add a Modem

Yes, Virginia, there's a world out there, and it's waiting for you. With a modem and some kind of online service like CompuServe, America Online, Prodigy, or Microsoft Network, you can blab with friends, grab free software, and get more advice than a couple on their wedding day.

The good news is that you can add a modem to any PC. The bad news is that sometimes it's a pain to get a modem to work with all the other stuff in your PC. See Chapter 21 for details.

Upgrade the Video

If you can't hardly see anything on the screen anymore because your monitor is so fuzzy and Windows' icons are so small, do your eyes a favor and add a better graphics (video) card.

Of course, if you have to do this, it may mean that you need to add a new monitor, depending on what type of monitor you have. See Chapter 16 for how-tos.

There's lots more you can upgrade or replace, as you'll see in upcoming chapters.

The Laptop Liability

A laptop is like a PC that's been left in the dryer too long. If you have a laptop, I'm jealous. It's a mini-miracle that you can take literally anywhere.

Also, if you have a laptop, I'm sorry. It's a major headache to upgrade.

Why? Because you can only upgrade most laptops with special (a computer word which means "expensive") parts designed specifically for your laptop's make and model. So once you finally locate the correct part, it'll cost you plenty. Then you're stuck with the problem of actually getting the part into the laptop.

Don't fret over it too much, though, especially if you just bought your laptop. That's because newer laptops come with fancy slots called PCMCIA slots. PCMCIA is short for Personal Computer Memory Card International Association. Lots of manufacturers make stuff that fit into these slots, such as CD-ROM drive adapters, external hard disk controllers, memory cards, modems, and so on. Just buy one of these gizmos, shove it into the slot, and bammo, it's installed (well, more or less.)

Your laptop may not be the easiest thing to upgrade.

Nothing Is That Simple

PCMCIA is not the beauty that it appears to be. Although there are many cards that say they are PCMCIA-compatible, there are at least four different flavors, or types, of the PCMCIA standard, so there's no guarantee that a particular card will work with your laptop. The best solution is to check with the manufacturer and see if anyone has ever used the card in your particular brand of laptop.

Second, Is It Worth Upgrading?

Actually, that's pretty much up to you to decide. Some things you should consider include:

➤ Your tolerance for annoying parts that don't want to cooperate

➤ The size of your wallet

Check This Out...

Whoa. What Is That?
No, BIOS is not some foreign language. If you don't recognize some of these upgrades, take two quick steps back to chapters 2 and 3 for a translation.

➤ Your bravery level

➤ The amount of aspirin still left in your Excedrin bottle

To help you, here's a list of possible upgrades, with my ratings for both difficulty level and cost:

Difficulty Level: EZ
                        Not so bad
                        Harder, but worth it

Cost: Geo
            Cadillac
            Porsche

Type of Upgrade	Difficulty Level	Cost
Battery		
BIOS		
CD-ROM drive		
CPU		
Floppy drive		
Graphics card		
Hard disk		
Joy stick		
Keyboard		
Math coprocessor		
Memory		

Type of Upgrade	Difficulty Level	Cost
Modem		
Monitor		
Motherboard		
Mouse		
Power supply		
Printer		
Scanner		
Sound card		
Tape backup		
Video capture board		

There's No Tellin' Where the Money Went

Beware of what a lot of people call the "upgrade cascade." Sometimes upgrading one thing causes you to upgrade something else because the old thing is no longer compatible, or it's stinky slow. For example, if you go multimedia and add a CD-ROM drive and a sound card, you better have at least 8 M of RAM to get the thing to work right. If you have only 4 M, you'll find yourself adding more. See how the upgrade cascade works? On an old PC, you can quickly end up spending almost as much in upgrades as you would on a new PC. The bottom line is, it's cheaper to get all the goodies you want in a new PC than to add them later.

Before you open your wallet, be sure to check out Chapter 7, which contains several easy things you can do with DOS to speed up a slow PC. Best of all, they're free! Also, if you've just bought Windows 95 or are contemplating it, check out Chapter 6 to find out how to make it run at its best.

PCs That Just Aren't Worth the Trouble to Upgrade

Deciding to scrap a PC rather than upgrade it is often a personal decision, like deciding to buy a new car instead of keeping the old one a few more years. So I can't really tell you what to junk, but I'll give you some leading indicators of old age.

If your PC is a 286, donate it to a museum.

If your PC is a 386, consider scrapping it if the upgrades you're considering will cost over $1,000. Also, don't expect miracles in the speed department, because you're stuck with a slow motherboard, even if you replace the CPU.

If you own a PCjr, send it back to IBM.

If your PC uses only brand-name parts, and you can't seem to find them anywhere, hey, then, somebody's telling you something.

Even if you have to chuck the PC, you may be able to salvage its parts by replacing only the motherboard in your existing PC. By the way, you'll have to scrap any motherboard with a surface-mounted CPU (the CPU is "glued" to the motherboard) if you want to upgrade the CPU.

If your laptop is a 286, junk it. If your laptop is a 386, you may be able to upgrade it, but it will be a lot of work.

What's Involved in a Typical Upgrade?

Do you have your heart set on a new sound card, or CD-ROM drive, or other gizmo, but you're not at all sure if you're ready for what lies ahead? So you can get a better idea of what you're getting yourself into, here's a list of steps you follow during a typical upgrade:

1. **Get to know your PC** Before you introduce your new "friend" to the PC gang, you need to know where it's going to go and whether or not it'll get along with every one else. To do that, you'll probably need to know a lot more about your PC than you do now. So be sure to check out Chapters 2, 3, and 4 before you do anything else.

2. **Get the right part**   This one's hard, but if you arm yourself with a thorough knowledge of your PC's guts plus the specific tips you'll find in every chapter, you should do fine.

3. **Prepare for disaster**   Most upgrades involve opening up the PC. Sounds pretty scary, doesn't it? That's OK—most dangers can be easily eliminated (or easily repaired) by taking a few simple precautions, such as backing up your data and creating an emergency diskette, which you'll learn how to do in Chapter 12.

4. **Figure out what to do next**   Just kidding. Before you do anything else, you should read (yes, I said read) the instructions that came with the new part. They may tell you to check out a text file on an enclosed diskette. That's easy to do. For example, if the file is called README.TXT (as they invariably are), insert the diskette and type **TYPE A:README.TEXT| MORE** at the DOS prompt. Write down anything you find that's interesting or relevant.

Survival Kit An emergency diskette is a diskette that you can use to start your PC when the darn thing doesn't start in the normal way. An emergency diskette has a copy of the operating system (usually DOS), and the configuration files, CONFIG.SYS and AUTOEXEC.BAT, in addition to some useful get-me-out-of-here utility programs.

5. **Unplug the computer and open up that box**   Most parts require *surgery,* meaning you have to open up the PC to install them. Of course, make sure you unplug the computer before you do that. Also, some PCs are a booger to get open, so see Chapter 12 for help. Once the box is open, there are some simple procedures you can follow to make sure you don't damage anything. Again, see Chapter 12. Some parts connect externally, through ports on the back of the PC. With these, you just smile and skip this step.

6. **Connect the new toy**   This involves plugging some part of the new device into the computer, either through a cable, or through some kind of funky connector. This step isn't so hard once you figure out exactly where you're supposed to plug in your new toy—not too hard if you follow the step-by-steps you'll find in each chapter.

Get Your Tools Together   To open your PC, you'll probably need a special set of screwdrivers and other tools. Chapter 12 contains a complete list of supplies you need to walk the upgrade trail.

7. **With the cover still off, plug the PC back in, fire it up, and check for signs of life**   Yes, I said with the cover off. All you want to do here is test to see if the new part is connected, so you can quickly correct it if it's not, *before you put the cover back on.* Say you're installing a new hard drive, but your PC doesn't recognize it right away. However, if the drive turns on (you hear its usual bleating as it comes to life), you know that you've cleared one of the biggest hurdles. If something's really, really wrong, generally the motherboard tells you by beeping a whole lot. In such instances, turn the PC off, unplug it, try reconnecting things, and then fire it back up to test your adjustments. I know, this is scary stuff, but as long as you don't touch anything inside the PC while the power's on, you'll be fine.

8. **Close up the box**   This one's a snap—just repeat step 4, only backwards. Once you put the box back together, plug everything back in and start up the PC.

9. **Introduce the computer to its new friend**   Most parts come with some kind of program called Setup, which makes changes to the configuration files so that your computer can talk to the new part. This process usually consists of sticking the Setup diskette into the drive, typing a command such as **SETUP**, **INSTALL**, or some such thing, and then sitting back while the Setup program does its thing. After you install the part, see Chapter 22 for help. If you run Windows, there may be some additional setup thingies you have to do as well, but have no fear—they're explained in graphic detail in Chapter 23.

The Least You Need to Know

Deciding whether or not to upgrade a particular PC is sometimes a hard decision, because many factors come into play. Consider these:

➤ Some PCs are so old you can't upgrade them. Others aren't worth the trouble or the expense.

➤ Some laptops are just as hard to upgrade as old PCs, either because replacement parts are expensive, too difficult to install, or unavailable.

➤ When deciding whether it's worth upgrading a particular part, be sure to consider the expense, the difficulty factor, and your tolerance level.

➤ Beware of the upgrade cascade, a phenomenon which causes you to buy additional parts just to get the first part to work. For example, adding a new hard disk may force you to upgrade the power supply or add an additional fan.

➤ To complete a typical upgrade, you need to get to know your computer. This helps you make sure you buy parts that work in your PC.

➤ Once you buy a part, read all the instructions that come with it so you install it properly. Look for README files which include cautions for specific PCs.

Chapter 6

Upgrades That Make Windows 95 Happier

In This Chapter

➤ What makes Windows 95 such a big deal

➤ Which upgrades make Windows 95 the happiest

➤ Oh, yeah, there's stuff about Windows 3.1 too

➤ And some ways to make Windows run faster without upgrading your hardware

Windows 95 is a pumped up version of Windows 3.1, which means that it's faster, easier to use, and contains less than half the fat. Unfortunately, (or fortunately, depending on your point of view) Windows 95 doesn't look very much like Windows 3.1. And it can't always run on a computer that can run Windows 3.1.

Whoa. Take two steps back.

Yep, that's right; even though your old PC is currently running Windows 3.1, that doesn't guarantee that it can run Windows 95.

Before you get all bummed out, take a look at Windows 95 and see if it's even something you need right now. If you decide to upgrade to Windows 95, you'll find a listing in this chapter that tells you exactly what your PC will need. If you decide to stick with Windows 3.1 for a while, there's no need to suffer; there are several things you can do to help it run faster, and I'll discuss them at the end of this chapter.

Let Me Introduce You to Windows 95

The first thing you probably notice about the new Windows 95 is that its windows, including Program Manager, seem to be missing.

So where are the windows?

Well, after you start a program, the window frame that normally surrounds it is still there, but the group windows—those little boxes such as "Main" and "Applications" that grouped various icons together—are gone. Instead of starting a program by opening several group windows to find its icon and then double-clicking on it, you open several menus and then select the program's name from a list. Easier? I dunno. It took me a while to figure out where everything was. However, if you like clicking on icons, you still can. Just click on the program file and drag it onto the desktop to create a shortcut icon.

The next thing you notice about Windows 95 is that it's sporting a whole new look:

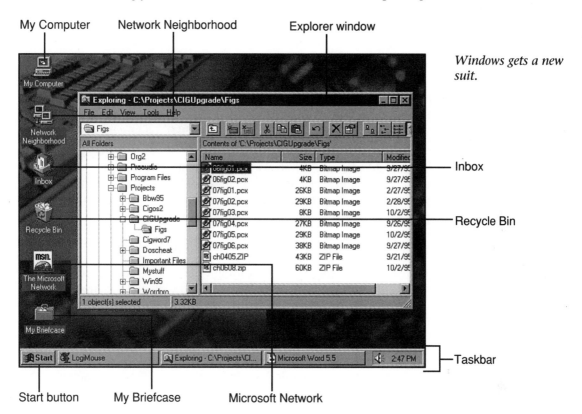

Windows gets a new suit.

Here's what's behind the new duds:

➤ **Taskbar**   It's the gray strip at the bottom of the screen, and you use it like you used to use the Task List—to jump from one program to another. Because the taskbar stays visible, you don't have to fumble for the Ctrl and Esc keys like you do to view the Task List.

➤ **Start button**   This one's easy to spot because it has the number one seat on the taskbar. Click here to view endless menus.

➤ **Explorer**   Bye-bye File Manager. In its place is a retooled version called Explorer. Easier to use? Maybe—but it takes some getting used to, since it works a bit differently than its papa. But at least you can give a file a decent name, such as "Sales figures for 1st Quarter" instead of some dumb DOS name like SALES95.WK4.

➤ **My Computer**   Think of this as your PC's attic—you won't come up here very often. But if you do, you can learn lots of things about your computer—that is, if you can find anything at all, what with the silly way My Computer works, compared to Explorer.

➤ **Network Neighborhood** You won't find Mr. Rogers here. Instead, you find a listing of all the computers, printers, and whatnots connected to your office network. (If you're working at home and aren't connected to a network, you won't see this icon.)

➤ **Inbox** The Inbox is your local "post office," only instead of *receiving snail mail* (uh, letters delivered by your friendly neighborhood postman), you use the Inbox to send and receive mail through your network's e-mail system and whatever online service you use (such as CompuServe or Prodigy). You can also connect to Microsoft Fax, if you want to send a fax instead. (Of course, to send or receive a fax or to use an online service, you'll need a modem.)

➤ **Recycle Bin** In the old Windows, if you deleted a file, it was pretty much gone. Oh, you might have been able to get it back if you had the Undelete tool installed on your computer, and you used it quickly enough. The Recycle Bin definitely makes getting back files you accidently delete a lot easier. The only problem is that the Recycle Bin doesn't empty its own trash: you've got to do that job on its behalf when you're ready to say a permanent good-bye to your recently deleted files.

➤ **Microsoft Network** "Hey, here's an idea," thought Microsoft, "Just in case our customers don't already have an online service, why don't we make it super-easy for them to sign up for ours?" Which you can do, by the way, just by double-clicking on the **MSN** icon. Presently, MSN is similar to other online services such as CompuServe, Prodigy, and America Online.

➤ **My Briefcase** Who said you can't take it with you? Well, if you have a laptop and you transfer files between it and your desktop PC all the time, this little gadget makes it easy to keep the files in synch.

What You Need to Move to Windows 95

There is a pretty good chance that if your PC can run Windows 3.1 now, it can probably run Windows 95. Trouble is, it may not be able to do anything else. In other words, you may be able to get Windows 95 installed on your old PC, but you probably won't be able to get much done, because your PC will probably be a lot slower.

So what do you really need to run Windows 95? Well, use this table to tell:

What Microsoft Says You Need	What Works Even Better
386DX CPU	Windows 95 is basically a snail on slow compuers. So get yourself a 486SX, 486DX, or a Pentium CPU.

What Microsoft Says You Need	What Works Even Better
4 M of memory (RAM)	No way do you want to run Windows 95 with anything less than 8 M—it'll just be tooooo slooooow. If you want nirvana, try at least 16 M.
40 M of free hard disk space	I really have no idea where Microsoft got this number. My Windows 95 directory takes up 116 M, but of course, I installed *everything*. If you're picky about what Windows 95 features you install (yes, you can pick and choose what features to include during the installation), you may be able to get away with 85 M.
VGA monitor	Yes, you can still make a long-distance call from a rotary phone, but why would you want to do this? So instead of viewing all those cute icons and great graphics with a simple VGA monitor, get a Super VGA. For speed, add an accelerator card.
That's it	Other things you may want to think about getting include a CD-ROM drive, a tape backup (to protect all that data), a modem (the better to dial up some online service with, my dear), and a sound card (for listening to all the new Windows sound effects).

So how much will all this stuff cost you? Well, let's look at our shopping list:

Item	What It'll Cost Ya
Faster CPU	$200
Extra hard disk	$500 for about 1 G
More memory	$200 to $280 for 4 M
SVGA monitor	$400 to $450
Video card	$175 to $200
CD-ROM drive	$200
Tape backup	$200 for 800 M
Fax modem	$100 for 14.4 bps
Sound card	$100
Total bill	$2,075 to $2,230

Of course, if your PC actually needs this much work, pitch it and get a new one; it will cost about the same. A better strategy is to add what you need now, such as more memory, a larger hard disk, and a faster CPU. In any case, once you decide what you can afford to add, check out the individual chapters for step-by-steps.

Upgrading Your Software

If you upgrade to Windows 95, do you have to upgrade all your programs to their new Windows 95 versions? Well, no. Most Windows 3.1 applications run just fine—in fact, better—under Windows 95. But there are some 3.1 applications that, like some cats, just don't take well to new surroundings. If you need to make sure that your program will run okay under Windows 95, contact the program's manufacturer.

Also, keep in mind that you can't save documents with longer filenames in Windows 95 with a 3.1 application unless you upgrade your program—because the 3.1 application simply won't let you. If you try to use a 3.1 application to open a file that was given a long name in Windows 95, you will see that the file's name has been given a different, abbreviated name that fits the old naming conventions. The file will still work OK, but you may have to do some guessing to figure out which file is which.

Check This Out...

Plug and Play with Windows 3.1 If you buy a Plug and Play device and you don't upgrade to Windows 95, that's okay. The device will work perfectly well under Windows 3.1. Just don't expect the system to automatically install the device for you. Don't worry—I cover all the details in Chapter 23.

So what do you get for your upgrade dollar? Well, Windows 95 applications are obviously designed to run specifically with Windows 95. So, unlike Windows 3.1 programs, they can take advantage of all the speed Windows 95 has to offer. Unfortunately, there aren't too many Windows 95 applications that you can buy—the Microsoft suite of products of course: Word, Excel, PowerPoint, etc., and a handful of utilities. But more (including the Lotus suite: Ami Pro, 1-2-3, Approach, and so on) will arrive soon.

Of course, you can still run DOS programs under Windows 95, although I'm not at all sure why you'd want to, because it's like using a Ferrari to navigate rush hour traffic. But if you must, you'll be glad to know that DOS programs run better under Windows 95. In fact, incredibly better—if you can give such praise to a DOS program.

Plug and Play

One thing you probably hear about every time Windows 95 is mentioned is something called *Plug and Play*. So what does it mean? Well, it's basically a newer technology that allows devices (such as your printer) to identify themselves to your computer, so your computer knows exactly how to talk to them. Does this mean that you have to run out and get specially marked Plug and Play devices to work with Windows 95? Nope. Although there are such things as specially marked Plug and Play devices, Windows 95 is perfectly capable of identifying most of the common devices anyway. But if you decide to add a new device, you may want to make sure that it's Plug and Play or Windows 95 compatible.

Plug and Pray

The truth behind the Plug and Play hoopla is rather dismaying: in order to get PnP to work, you have to have three elements working together: a PnP operating system (that's Windows 95), a PnP device (such as a CD-ROM drive, hard disk, or whatever else you want to add to your PC), and a PnP-compliant BIOS. The BIOS is a chip (or a bunch of chips) on the motherboard that control the basic input and output of your PC. Unless you bought your PC yesterday, you don't have a PnP-compliant BIOS. To get one, you gotta upgrade the BIOS (that is, if an upgrade is available). See Chapter 13 for help in that department.

So what do you get with Windows 95 on a non-PnP PC? Well, a pretty nice operating system that's still better at identifying new devices than Windows 3.1 ever was. A little wonder called the New Hardware Wizard tries hard to identify whatever device you throw at it. You might still run into trouble, but if you need help prodding Windows 95 to install your new device, see Chapter 23.

Something Else to Consider Before You Upgrade

Before you upgrade to Windows 95, make sure that you can upgrade your utilities as well, such as your backup program, anti-virus program, and rescue utilities. Do not use a Windows 3.1 utility under Windows 95, unless you like to play Russian Roulette with your data.

So far, Norton Utilities is the only well known utility package available for use under Windows 95, and it does not contain a backup program. This shouldn't be a problem because Windows 95 includes one of its own, but that program doesn't recognize most tape drives, including Mountain and Colorado. So if you use a tape backup, be sure to contact the manufacturer and obtain an upgrade diskette for Windows 95, or you'll be out of luck.

Before You Switch to Windows 95: Upgrades That Make Windows 3.1 Happy

If the last section gave you sticker shock, don't worry—there's no hurry to switch to Windows 95. If all you're looking for is a faster PC, there's a lot you can do to make Windows 3.1 run better:

Put your affairs in order   With a little utility called DEFRAG, you can reorganize the files on your hard disk so that it doesn't take Windows so long to open the files when you need them. See Chapter 7, "Examining Your Alternatives," for more information.

Give your existing memory a boost   Using another utility called SMARTDrive, you can help Windows make the best use of the RAM your PC has. See Chapter 7 for the how-tos.

Stretch your limits   Both Windows 3.1 and Windows 95 are happier when you give them more memory—which makes this the single best upgrade for your computer. Adding just 4 M of RAM costs you only $250, but it makes a huge difference! See Chapter 15, "Make Mine More Memory!" for help.

Double the hard disk, double your fun   If the only problem you have right now is that you're running out of space for new programs, then why not double the hard disk? It's easy with DoubleSpace or DriveSpace. See Chapter 7.

Make a permanent commitment   When Windows runs out of memory, it pushes the stuff it's not currently using out of RAM and into something called a *swap file*. This swap file is a temporary thing, which is great if you're short on hard disk space. But, if you've got the room, you may want to switch to a permanent swap file on your hard disk, which speeds up Windows 3.1 considerably. See the next section for the complete lowdown.

How to Speed Up Windows Without Upgrading

If you use Windows 3.1, one of the simplest ways to speed the darn thing up is to switch to a permanent swap file. (If you use Windows 95, the swap file is already as fast as it's gonna get. See the box for more details.)

The Windows 95 Swap File

Windows 95 combines the "best" of the temporary swap file and permanent swap file business in Windows 3.1. The swap file in Windows 95 is *dynamic,* which is a fancy way of saying that it changes its size as needed. Also, the Windows 95 swap file works in a non-contiguous space (just like the old temporary swap file in Windows 3.1), but unlike Windows 3.1, there's no penalty in performance.

So you get the benefit of a temporary swap file (you don't have to permanently allocate hard disk space when the swap file may never use it) and the benefit of a permanent swap file (speed, baby, speed). Also, Windows 95 can place its swap file on a compressed drive, such as drive C, so chances are, it can be larger than the one you used under Windows 3.1.

And if this is almost too good to be true, there's more: Windows 95 sets up its permatemp swap file without any help from you. The only thing you may ever want to do is change the hard drive it uses (which is drive C), but even that is rare.

You see, when you run Windows and you start up all your programs, you can quickly run out of memory (RAM). Even though Windows can juggle multiple programs at once, you are only one person, and for the most part, you can only work on one thing at a time. So when you start a program, open a few files, and then switch away from the program for a while, Windows takes the stuff you're not currently working on and "swaps it out" of memory by copying it to the hard disk temporarily, to a place called the *swap file*.

When you installed Windows 3.1, it created a temporary swap file, which means that it staked out some space on the hard disk each time you started Windows and then removed itself when you exited. If you don't have a lot of space on the hard disk, then the temporary swap file ends up being pretty tiny and pretty worthless. In addition, it takes Windows longer to access a temporary swap file because the file itself is broken into tiny bits and scattered all over the hard disk.

If you do have some room on the hard disk, it's worth the trouble to create a permanent swap file. Windows then stakes out a permanent area on the hard disk for swapping things out of memory. A permanent swap file provides faster access because the file is *contiguous*, which for a big word, simply means that all of its parts are together on the hard disk, making it easier for Windows to get data out of it.

Memory Is Even Faster

Even though a permanent swap file is faster than a temporary one, it's a turtle compared to the real speed demon—your computer's memory. Memory is a lot faster to access than anything on the hard disk. So if you can afford to upgrade anything, memory is the best way to spend your bucks, especially if you plan on using Windows. See Chapter 15 for help.

The only negative here is that you need to have room on a *non-compressed drive* to create your permanent swap file. This non-compressed drive is usually drive H. If you find that you have some room on drive H, then here's what you do to create a permanent swap file under Windows 3.1: In Windows, exit all your programs; open up the **Control Panel** and double-click on the **386 Enhanced** icon; click on the **Virtual Memory** button to see the Virtual Memory dialog box; click on the **Change** button; and the dialog box expands faster than your stomach after a Thanksgiving dinner.

Reorganize Your Disk, First

Before you switch to a permanent swap file, you should reorganize your hard disk first. See the section, "Reorganize the Hard Disk," located in the next chapter.

The Virtual Memory dialog box expands so you can create a permanent swap file.

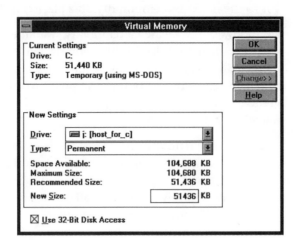

Now, open the **Type** list and select **Permanent**. If you see an option to **Use 32-bit Disk Access**, select it (well, read the box first, then decide if you want to try this option). That's it—click **OK**. Windows asks if you really, really want to create a permanent swap file. Click on **Yes**. You need to restart Windows, so click **Restart Windows**.

Big Drive? Read This

Some of the really huge hard disk drives (a gigabyte or more) don't work with the 32-bit Disk Access feature of Windows 3.1. If you have one of these gargantuan drives, and you chose the 32-bit option, restarted Windows, and saw nothing but the dead of night, then go find the manual that came with your hard drive (hopefully your dealer gave it to you).

You may have to install a special driver to make your hard disk work with 32-bit disk access; the most common one is called Disk Manager (Western Digital and some other brands provide it with their drives). The manual tells you for sure. Next, find the diskette that contains this driver and use the automatic setup procedure that runs from DOS to install it.

If you can't find a driver and you need to use Windows now, then you can undo the 32-bit access thing, with a little work. Type **CD\WINDOWS** and press **Enter**. Then type **EDIT WIN.INI** and press **Enter**. Use the down arrow to go through the file until you find the line: 32BitDiskAccess=Off. Change the Off to **On**, save the file, and exit EDIT. You can now use Windows again.

RAM Doubler

You can almost double your RAM with a software program called RAM Doubler for Windows. Of course, it doesn't actually increase the physical amount of RAM that you have, but it does manage it better than Windows can.

Like Windows, RAM Doubler shuffles things in and out of memory as needed, saving them temporarily on the hard disk until they're called for again. The reason that RAM Doubler can squeeze more memory space out of RAM is that it also compresses (shrinks) the information in RAM, kinda like DriveSpace does for the hard disk.

Other Ways to Speed Things Up

Here are some other ways to get Windows into gear:

Use Your Startup Group Wisely

In other words, make sure that Windows automatically starts up only those programs that you truly use every day. If you're in doubt about the usefulness of something, take it out of the Startup group. And this goes for Windows 95, too. I used to have my Inbox in my Startup group, but I didn't always use the thing every day. So instead of waiting for Windows to load it on days when I might not use it, I just removed it from the Startup group.

If you use the same documents every day, put the documents in the Startup group, instead of the program you used to create them. For example, if you have a sales spreadsheet that you use every day, put it into the Startup group, and not Excel or Lotus 1-2-3. Windows then opens Excel or Lotus 1-2-3 for you during startup and loads your spreadsheet automatically.

Get Rid of Unused Fonts

Get rid of fonts you don't use. Practically every program comes with loads and loads of fonts, most of which you probably don't use. A list of the names of all these fonts is in the WIN.INI (a Windows configuration file). Windows reads this list every time you start it. In addition, the font files themselves sit on the hard disk, taking up room. Getting the extra fonts out of there saves time in starting Windows, in addition to making room on the hard disk.

Now, if you're at all nervous about removing a particular font, copy it to a diskette first. You can reinstall it later if you decide that this was all some cruel mistake. To get rid of a font in Windows 3.1, open up the **Control Panel** and double-click on the **Fonts** icon. Highlight the fonts you want to murder and click on **Remove**. You see a warning; to remove the font from the WIN.INI and from the hard disk, click the **Delete Font File From Disk** option. Click **Yes**, or if you're committing mass-murder, click on **Yes to All**. Click **Close** to return to the Control Panel.

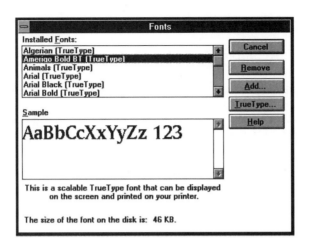

Murdering fonts in Windows 3.1.

To delete some fonts under Windows 95, click on the **Start** button, select **Settings**, and then select **Control Panel**. Now, double-click on the **Fonts** icon.

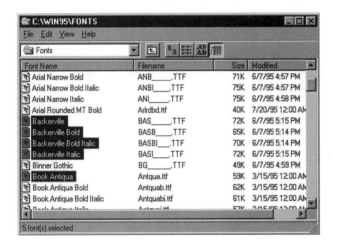

Murdering fonts in Windows 95.

Select the fonts you want to bump off, open the **File** menu, and select **Delete**. Again, a warning appears. Click **Yes**, and Windows 95 zaps the files. If you make a mistake, put on your "I'm sorry" face and restore the files from the Recycle Bin.

The Least You Need to Know

There's a lot you need to know before you decide to switch to Windows 95. Here's a quick run-down:

➤ Yep, when you get Windows 95, you don't see Program Manager or File Manager anymore.

➤ Windows 95 replaces the Program Manager with the taskbar, a Start button, and tons of menus. Explorer replaces the File Manager.

➤ You can really use long filenames in Windows 95 (up to 255 characters, in fact).

➤ If you delete files in Windows 95, they aren't destroyed. Instead, they get *recycled*—so you can get them back later if you need them.

➤ To switch to Windows 95, your PC should have at least 8 M of RAM and about 85 M of free hard disk space. You might also want to add a CD-ROM drive, fax modem, tape backup, and sound card while you're at it.

➤ If you need to live with Windows 3.1 for a while, you can make your life easier by whipping your PC into shape.

➤ The best upgrade you can make for either version of Windows is to add memory.

➤ If you use Windows 3.1, you can speed it up by creating a permanent swap file. If you use Windows 95, the swap file is already as fast as it's gonna get.

➤ Also, if you use Windows 3.1 or Windows 95, you can speed things up by using your Startup group wisely. In addition, delete any fonts that you never use to add a little extra speed.

Chapter 7

Examining Your Alternatives

In This Chapter

➤ Get more use out of your RAM with MemMaker

➤ Double your PC's hard disk space with DriveSpace or DoubleSpace

➤ Make your hard disk smarter with SMARTDrive

➤ Reorganize your files with DEFRAG

Just because you can't afford to upgrade, that won't stop you from wanting your PC to run just a little bit better. In this chapter, you'll learn some tricks you can try to stretch your existing resources and keep your money from the upgrade man just a little longer.

There are a lot of things you can do to improve the performance of your PC without actually upgrading, as you'll learn in this chapter. However, a lot of those methods depend on you having one of the latest DOS versions. Upgrading DOS is a simple and relatively inexpensive venture, and it's certainly worth your time because of the extra benefits.

The latest version of DOS is 6.22. You will need at least version 6.21 to use DriveSpace to compress your hard drive. If you have version 6.0 or 6.2, you will use DoubleSpace instead.

How Can I Tell What DOS Version I Have?

Well, if you have Windows 95, you have the latest, so you won't need to update anything. Other than that, you can't be too sure, because Windows 3.1 will run on anything that's at least DOS 3.1. To tell what DOS version you have, type **VER** at the DOS prompt and press **Enter**.

For information on upgrading to DOS 6.2, see Que's *MS-DOS 6.2 QuickStart*. For information on upgrading to DOS 6.22, see *Peter Norton's Complete Guide to DOS 6.22* (Sams). But if you're an Internet user, you can check out Que's Web page (http://www.mcp.com/que/new_users/DOS622.html), which gives you the complete scoop on how to upgrade DOS.

Making the Most Out of Memory with MemMaker

RAM is one of your PC's most precious resources, because it's the area in which your PC works. When you want to work on something at your desk, you get it out of a drawer (or off the floor) and place it on your desktop. DOS does basically the same thing; it retrieves files off of the hard disk (or a diskette or a CD-ROM), then places the files on its "desktop," which is called RAM. Once the files are in RAM, DOS can begin processing them.

All programs need memory in order to run—some programs need quite a lot of memory. Not having enough memory affects the way your programs work and can even prevent some programs from starting. So it's just good sense to make the most of what RAM you've got.

How to Use MemMaker If You Have One of the DOS 6-Somethings

If you have one of the DOS 6-somethings (DOS 6, 6.2, 6.21, or 6.22) then you can use a utility called MemMaker to *optimize* (improve) your system's use of memory automatically, making it "be all that it can be." If you're using Windows 95, then you have essentially DOS 7, so you can also join in on the MemMaker merriment.

To begin to optimize your system, exit all programs, then type **CD\DOS** and press **Enter**. Then type **MEMMAKER** and press **Enter**. A message appears, asking you to choose between Express (for real people like us) and Custom optimization (for geeks). To use Express, just press **Enter**. Then you're asked if you use any programs that require expanded memory. If you're not sure, pick **No**, because you can always rerun MemMaker and change it later.

A message appears, asking you to press **Enter** so MemMaker can restart your PC. Do it, and MemMaker analyzes your system and makes changes to your AUTOEXEC.BAT and CONFIG.SYS files. Press **Enter**, and MemMaker tests your new configuration.

MemMaker will then ask if your new configuration is **OK**. Basically, if your PC didn't blow up during reboot, then your new configuration is OK. Press **Enter** for *Yes* if the computer restarted okay, or press the **Spacebar** and then **Enter** to answer *No* (and continue testing different configurations).

Finally, MemMaker shows you all the fine work it's done and takes a bow. Press **Enter** to exit MemMaker.

What to Do If You Have Windows

If you're using Windows 3.1, no problemo, as long as you also have one of the DOS 6-somethings (DOS 6, 6.2, 6.21, or 6.22). Just exit Windows 3.1 before you do your MemMaker stuff.

If you're using Windows 95, you can restart your PC with DOS, and then run MemMaker. Just click on the **Start** button, select **Shut down**, and then select **Restart** the computer with DOS. Once you get the friendly prompt, follow the MemMaker steps given earlier.

Double Your Hard Disk

If you're running out of space on your PC's hard disk, but you can't afford to add an additional hard disk right now, there may be a way for you to live with the situation a while longer—by doubling your disk.

With disk doubling, a *disk compression* program "shrinks" your files using a kind of "computer shorthand" that enables it to store those same files in less space than dumb ol' DOS and even Windows—actually, a little more than half the space. Which is why compressing your hard disk is called *doubling*, because you end up with almost twice as much space for files! After you compress the hard disk, you can still open, save, copy, and delete files just like you did before—your hard disk handles the compression process invisibly, so you don't have to worry about how it works—it just does.

The only potentially bad news here is that you have to have at least DOS version 6.0 in order to get disk compression for free. If you have DOS 6.0 or 6.2, then you get a program called DoubleSpace with which you can compress your hard disk. If you have DOS 6.21 or 6.22, then you get DriveSpace instead.

Check Before You Run a New Utility

Once you compress the hard disk, you can safely use any of the utilities that come with DOS (such as SMARTDrive or DEFRAG) without any problems at all. But if you want to use some other utility such as a disk repair utility, a memory manager, or an anti-virus program on your compressed drive, make sure that it's compatible with DoubleSpace or DriveSpace first.

Compressing a Hard Disk Under Windows 3.1 and DOS

Regardless of whether you use DoubleSpace or DriveSpace, follow these steps to compress your hard disk—but remember, you have to have at least DOS 6-something to do this. (If you use Windows 95, skip ahead to the Windows 95 steps.)

First, exit all programs, including Windows. Then come to a screeching halt as you stop to do a complete system backup. If something goes wrong here, you'll have to get back your data. So do a backup now.

Finally, at the C:\> prompt-thing, type **CD\DOS** and press **Enter**. Now, type **DBLSPACE** or **DRVSPACE** and then press **Enter**. You see a message touting all the benefits of compressing a drive. Choose **Express setup**.

Now, keep in mind that some portion of your drive remains undoubled (uncompressed); the operating system recognizes this portion as if it were a new drive and assigns it a brand new letter. If you want this uncompressed not-really-a-disk-drive to be called anything other than drive H:, type a different drive letter now. Press **Enter**.

This compression stuff takes about one minute per megabyte to compress, regardless of how fast your computer is. Click on **Continue** (which completes the compression process) or press **Esc** to exit (which stops it). After the disk compression is complete, a summary displays, showing information about the compressed drive. Press **Enter**, and your system restarts with the compressed drive active and ready to use.

Compressing a Hard Disk under Windows 95

If you use Windows 95 and you haven't compressed your hard disk yet, this section shows you how to do it. (Uh, if you have a really large hard disk, DriveSpace will force you to divide it into smaller portions such as a drive C, D, E, and so on. Before you start, see the sidebar coming up for info on a Plus! pack that can help.)

First, click on the **Start** menu. Select **Programs**, select **System Tools**, and then select **DriveSpace**. Whew!

Now, select the drive you want to compress from the list. I'm guessing that it's probably drive C. Open the **Drive** menu and select **Compress**. Okay, so far.

Click on **Start**. You see a message telling you to do a backup. If you haven't done a backup lately, it's a good idea to do one now, so click on **Back Up Files**. Just do as it says, and no one gets hurt. (And have a pile of diskettes handy.)

Once you complete the backup, you end up back where you started (well, practically). Click on **Compress Now**. Keep in mind that this compression stuff takes about one minute per megabyte to do, so go get a cup of coffee and a good magazine.

At some point, DriveSpace tries to restart your computer. If it needs help, click **Yes** when you see a prompt asking you if you want to restart the computer.

Converting a DoubleSpaced Drive to DriveSpace

If you've recently upgraded to DOS 6.21 or 6.22 and you compressed your hard disk with DoubleSpace, you can leave it as it is, or convert it to DriveSpace compression. Why bother? Well, the conversion doesn't take very long, and your hard disk will run better with DriveSpace. (If you're using Windows 95, you don't have to convert your hard disk at all; it can use either DoubleSpace or DriveSpace compression. But if you want to convert the drive, just start the DriveSpace utility by selecting it from the **System Tools** menu—select **Programs**, **Accessories** to see the System Tools menu option—and then follow the on-screen prompts.)

Make Way for DriveSpace!

DriveSpace needs some elbow space in which to work. Make sure that you have at least .6 M free on drive H: (the uncompressed drive) and around 4 M free on drive C: (the compressed drive). If you don't have enough free space, remove some not-often-used files to make room and then convert the drive.

Back up your files first; then, in case something goes wrong, you can at least get your data back. Then when you're ready, type **DRVSPACE** at the DOS prompt and press **Enter**. You see a message warning you to do a backup. Since you've already done one, just laugh and press **Enter** to continue.

DriveSpace runs a scan to check your disk, and then it starts converting the drive. When DriveSpace is done, press **Enter** to restart your system with a DriveSpace drive.

Use your newly converted DriveSpace drive as you did before; there aren't many differences between DoubleSpace and DriveSpace, certainly none that you can see.

Pump Up the Hard Disk with SMARTDrive!

The hard disk in your computer subscribes to the "turtle principle": it figures that nobody's going to remember how slow it is if it still finishes the race and coughs up a file.

But if you'd rather fly than crawl, you can make your hard disk faster by making it *smarter*. All you need is a bit of RAM and a little fella called SMARTDrive. Don't lose any sleep wondering how it works—it just does.

Anyway, chances are that you may not have to actually *install* SMARTDrive, because it is probably installed for you, if you have Windows 3.1. If you use Windows 95, it handles SMARTDrive internally, without the help of the AUTOEXEC.BAT, so don't even worry about it anymore.

If you don't use Windows but you have at least DOS 6, again, SMARTDrive is probably installed for you, so you can just sit back and relax. If you want to be sure, type **SMARTDRV /S** at the DOS prompt and press **Enter**. If SMARTDrive is installed, you see a message telling you so, followed by some parameters and settings.

If it's not installed, then type **EDIT C:\AUTOEXEC.BAT** at the DOS prompt and press **Enter**. The contents of the AUTOEXEC.BAT file appear on-screen, for all to see.

Error! If you get the error message: Bad command or file name, take two steps back, type **PATH=C:\DOS** and press **Enter**. Now, try again.

Press **Ctrl+End** to move to the end of the file and type C:\DOS\SMARTDRV.EXE. Save your work by opening the **File** menu and clicking on **Save**. Now you can get out of here. Just open the **File** menu and click on **Exit**.

Now you need to add something to your CONFIG.SYS file as well. Type **EDIT C:\CONFIG.SYS** and press **Enter**. Look for the line, C:\DOS\HIMEM.SYS, at the beginning of the file. If you don't see it, press **Enter** to create a blank line, use the up arrow key to back up to it, and add the darn thing— **C:\DOS\HIMEM.SYS**—yourself.

Save the file and exit as before. Once you see the C:\> prompt thing, restart your system by pressing **Ctrl+Alt+Delete** to make SMARTDrive active.

Reorganize the Hard Disk

DOS is not a very good housekeeper; in fact, it's pretty sloppy when it comes to organizing files on the hard disk. When you (or some program you're running) tell DOS to save or copy a file to the hard disk, DOS begins saving the file at the first unused portion of the disk that it finds. More often than not, DOS finds out in mid-save that the unused portion is smaller than the file it's trying to save; so DOS breaks that file up into tiny bite-size pieces which it then scatters all over the hard disk, in whatever spots seem the most convenient.

Although all of these goofy antics may make DOS seem all the more endearing, this sloppiness makes your PC work harder to locate the files you need. It can also mean that, although it appears that you have several megabytes of free space, you can't save a 150K file because DOS's hard disk space is in too many tiny pieces. So if you've been noticing that it seems to take a long time (in PC-time, meaning more than a couple of seconds) for your PC to open documents for you, you can speed up things a bit by reorganizing the hard disk.

If you're using one of the DOS 6-somethings (you know, DOS 6.0, 6.2, 6.21, or 6.22) or if you have Windows 95, then you're in luck because they come with a handy tool called DEFRAG, which you can use to *defragment* (nerd word for reorganize) your hard disk. If you don't have one of the DOS 6-somethings, then you can upgrade your DOS version (you'll find help earlier in this chapter), or you can buy a set of utilities such as Norton Utilities or PC Tools.

Reorganizing a Non-Compressed Disk

A compressed hard disk holds about twice as much data as its non-compressed brother. If you have a compressed disk, then the way you reorganize its files (defrag) is a bit different. Skip to the next section for help. (If you use Windows 95, skip to the Windows 95 section.)

Defragging takes a while for your PC to complete, so you may want to start this at the end of the workday and let it run overnight. *Just follow these steps if you use Windows 3.1 or DOS*: Exit all programs, including Windows; at the C:\> prompt thing, type **DEFRAG**, press the **Spacebar**, and type the letter of the drive you want to defrag, followed by a colon (for example, type **C:**).

The whole thing now looks something like this:

    DEFRAG C:

Bad Command or File Name?
If you get the error message: Bad command or file name, type **PATH=C:\DOS**, press **Enter**, and try it again.

Now, press **Enter**.

DEFRAG takes a look at your hard disk and then comes up with a recommendation for the best way to reorganize it. If it tells you that your hard disk is pretty well organized already, then just press **Esc** to skip the whole thing. If it recommends optimization, then get on with it by clicking on **Optimize**.

DEFRAG does its thing and beeps at you when it's done, telling you, "Optimization complete—go home now." If you want to defrag another hard disk, click on **Another Drive**. Otherwise, just click on **Exit DEFRAG**. Once you land back at the prompt, press **Ctrl+Alt+Delete** to restart the PC. This makes sure that the picture of your hard disk that's kept in memory is current.

May I recommend red wine with your DEFRAG?

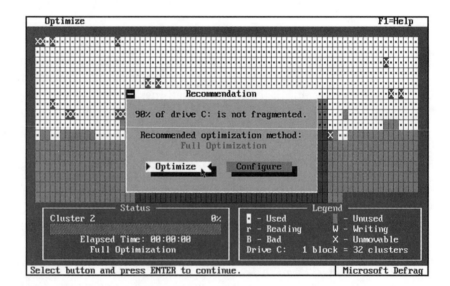

Reorganizing a Compressed Disk

If you read the first part of this chapter, you already know that a compressed disk stores more files in the same space than a non-compressed disk because it's smarter. What makes the disk smarter? Well, a compression utility such as DoubleSpace or DriveSpace takes over the file management from DOS, using a kind of "shorthand" that enables it to squeeze the same data into a smaller space. Because disk compression uses this special shorthand business, you need to follow these steps to reorganize its files (to defrag the disk).

Now, Microsoft is going to warn you that defragging a compressed drive may not be worth the trouble. That's because a compressed drive organizes its files differently from the way a normal non-compressed drive does. All you usually get with defragging is a compressed drive with a bit more room on it—but it isn't any faster. All this will lead you to believe that defragging your compressed disk is not worth the bother. Au contraire—if you don't defrag your disk every once in a while, it will eventually get so disorganized that even DOS won't want to deal with it. So eat your vegetables and defrag every month or two.

When you're ready to defrag, follow these steps if you're using Windows 3.1 or DOS (if you're using Windows 95, again, skip to the next section). Just keep in mind that the defragging thing takes a while to complete, so don't start this in the middle of the day unless you're looking for a way to go home early.

This Doesn't Work for Stacker-Compressed Drives

If you compressed your hard disk using some other utility such as Stacker or SuperStor, then you need to follow its directions to reorganize your files. The steps here are only for DoubleSpace or DriveSpace users.

Exit all your programs, including Windows. Then type **DRVSPACE** or **DBLSPACE** and press **Enter**. Choose the drive you want to defrag; hint: this is probably drive C. Now, open the **Tools** menu and select **Defragment**.

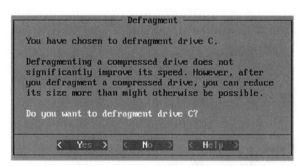

Warning, warning.

You see a warning similar to the one in the figure above, telling you that this may not be worth doing. We've already determined that you're stubborn, so simply ignore all the warnings by clicking **Yes**. If you've changed your mind, press **Esc** instead.

This takes a while, as defragging reorganizes your files and restarts the PC a couple of times. When it's finally done, the Optimization menu is left open for you. Just select **Exit**, and you're through.

Why Do it?

If there's not a lot of benefit in defragging a compressed drive, why is there an option for it? Well, although the compressed drive isn't faster, you may gain a little more room on the drive by reorganizing it. Also, as I discussed earlier, DOS will have an easier time finding a file on an organized compressed disk, rather than a disorganized one. (This means it'll be faster.)

Reorganizing a Disk with Windows 95

With Windows 95, it doesn't matter whether or not you're trying to defrag a compressed or non-compressed disk; Windows 95 handles both the same way. Also, in Windows 95, you can keep working while you defragment your hard disk (but your boss doesn't have to know that).

Just click on the **Start** menu and choose **Programs**. Select **Accessories** and then select **System Tools**. Now, after ten minutes of seemingly endless menus, you can finally choose **Disk Defragmenter**.

Select the drive you want to defrag and then click on **OK**. The Disk Torturer (OK, Defragmenter) takes a look at your hard disk and gives you a recommendation for the best way to reorganize it. If it says that your hard disk is pretty well organized, just click **Exit** to forget the whole thing. If it says that you need to organize things, then get on with it by clicking **Start**.

To defrag or not to defrag?

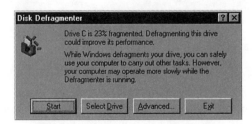

Now, although you can keep on working while Disk Defragmenter does its thing, you may not want to, because everything will be a bit slower. If you want to pause the Disk Defragmenter while it's running, just click on the **Pause** button.

When it's done, you see a message telling you "Defragmentation complete—go away now." If you want to defrag another hard disk, click **No**, (I Don't Want to Go Away). Otherwise, just click on **Yes**. That's it.

Create More Space on Your Hard Disk with ScanDisk and CHKDSK

When DOS deletes a file, it does a pretty sloppy job of it, leaving bits of old deleted files sitting around in the DOS junkyard, trading stories and hubcaps. If you want to know why DOS is so sloppy, read the sidebar coming up. Anyway, these little unused bits of old files that were never actually deleted are called *lost clusters* or *lost chains*. There are several commands that come with DOS to help you get rid of these old files and free up otherwise-unused disk space. Which one of these commands you use depends on your DOS version.

The Truth Behind Why DOS Is a Slob

When you delete a file, DOS doesn't really delete it. Instead, it erases the *reference* to that file and marks the spaces it used to occupy as "available." The next time you save a file to disk, DOS may place it in one of these available spots, overwriting the deleted file and reclaiming the space for use.

Sometimes DOS erases the reference to the file, but forgets to mark all the spaces that the file was using as "available." That results in little parts of old file spaces not being reused because DOS goofed. These dusty parts of old files are called *lost clusters* or *lost chains*.

If You've Got DOS 6.2 or Higher

If you've got an earlier DOS, such as DOS 6.0, DOS 5.0, or DOS 3.3, then skip to the next section for help. Now, before you use ScanDisk, you must exit out of any programs, such as Windows. Type **SCANDISK C:** and press **Enter**.

ScanDisk entertains you with a magnificent display of check marks as it looks for problems. If ScanDisk uncovers a problem, an error message appears. Should ScanDisk uncover lost data, press **Enter** to save the lost data in a file, or press **L** to delete it (which is what I normally do, because it's usually data from some old deleted file I don't even want anymore). If you're asked to create an Undo diskette, you can stick a blank disk in drive A and press **Enter**. An Undo diskette allows you to change your mind and undo what

ScanDisk does. But take it from me, Undo diskettes are risky, like jumping off the tight-rope in hopes there's a net below. You can skip Undo by pressing **S**.

Network Users, Beware!
Do not use ScanDisk on a network drive, such as drive F. If you do, your network administrator may hang you up by your keyboard, and believe me, it's not a pretty sight.

ScanDisk also checks out your hard disk for physical problems with a surface scan (you should probably do one of these about once a month or so). This is a bit noisy, so if you decide to do it, don't get too worried when it starts crankin'. Just press **Enter** when prompted, or press **N** to bypass this step. Logical problems with your files are rarely the result of a physical defect in your disk; however, if the problems you're having don't seem logical (OK, what problem ever does?), a surface scan may be in order.

After the scan is complete, you can view a log of the results by pressing **V**. Press **X** anytime to exit.

If You've Got DOS 6.0 or Below

If you have a DOS version earlier than DOS 6.2 (such as DOS 6, DOS 5, or DOS 4), you don't have a SCANDISK command. Instead, you'll use CHKDSK to clear away all those lost clusters and lost chains.

A couple of warnings first: exit all programs before you use CHKDSK, including Windows. Also, *don't try to use CHKDSK on a network drive, such as drive F.* OK, now type **CHKDSK C: /F** and press **Enter**.

What's That /F Thing For?

If you forget the /F switch, CHKDSK will pretend that it's fixing the problem, but when you run CHKDSK again, the problem will still be there. The /F switch tells DOS to write the changes to the disk. If you get a message like this:

> Errors found, F parameter not specified
> Corrections will not be written to disk

then you have forgotten to type /F. Retype the command and be sure to include the /F switch.

If CHKDSK finds an unused part of a deleted file, it displays something like this:

> 2 lost allocation units found in 1 chains.
> 8192 bytes disk space would be freed.

You have lost clusters or chains, so press **Y** to convert them to usable space. DOS creates a file to contain the data that was in each lost cluster. The data is probably unusable because it's part of an old file. To delete the files, type **DEL C:\FILE????.CHK** and press **Enter**.

Running ScanDisk with Windows 95

Unlike running ScanDisk under DOS, you don't have to exit out of any programs to run ScanDisk in Windows 95. To run ScanDisk in Windows 95, click on the **Start** button, select **Programs**, select **Accessories**, select **System Tools**, and then finally, select **ScanDisk**.

Under **Type of Text**, click on **Standard**. The other option, Thorough, actually tests the hard disk itself, and that's a bit much for today, thank you (you may want to run the test some other time, though). Click **Automatically fix errors**.

Click **Start**. ScanDisk does its thing, cleaning up after little lost clusters. When it's done, it proudly displays the results. Click **Close**.

The Least You Need to Know

Upgrading is no fun. There's the money for the parts, and of course, the time it takes to install each part once you get it. Nevermind the terror some upgrades instill. So if you can avoid an upgrade while keeping your sanity and your productivity, so much the better. Here are some ways to do just that:

➤ Upgrade to a recent version of DOS (6.0 or later) to take advantage of its compression and speed features.

➤ Double the space on your hard disk with either DoubleSpace or DriveSpace. If you're using DOS version 6.0 or 6.2, then you use DoubleSpace to compress your disk. If you're using DOS version 6.21 or 6.22, you use DriveSpace instead.

➤ You can make your hard disk faster with SMARTDrive. SMARTDrive creates a disk cache out of memory for storing your most-often-used data. Since memory is faster than the hard disk, SMARTDrive helps your computer reach the files it needs more quickly.

➤ Because your operating system splits files into bits and places them on the hard disk willy-nilly, occasionally you need to get them back in some kind of order so that your computer can run faster.

➤ You can reorganize the files on your hard disk with DEFRAG.

When Upgrading Was Not Your Idea

Your computer's acting strange. Before you panic, it's important to realize that this doesn't always mean that you'll have to replace something. There are several solutions you can try, including turning the darn thing off and walking away.

After your return, you may want to turn the PC back on and see if it's still acting strange. If it is, try some of the solutions in this chapter. If they don't fix the problem and you decide you need to replace a part, well, it just so happens that the rest of this book covers that very thing.

When Your PC's Acting Weird

It's hard to define weird. Computers, after all, are pretty strange creatures, even when they're well. If your PC is making strange noises, flipping strange little zigzags across the screen, or generally acting very uncooperative, then try some of these things:

➤ The first thing to check is the cables, to make sure that none of them is loose. If you find a guilty party, plug it back in and then get a screwdriver to stick it in place permanently. If you have one of those cases where two cables are supposed to plug in right next to each other, but the engineers didn't leave enough room for both cable ends to co-exist, consider a trick that the pros use: Attach an extension cable to one of the ends, even if you have enough cable anyway. For some reason, the connectors on extension cables are thinner than the connectors on standard cables.

➤ Next, try turning the PC off, waiting three seconds, and then turning it back on again. This forces the computer to clear all its gook out of memory (RAM). It's amazing how often this can make the weirdos go away—especially if you usually never turn off the computer.

➤ With the computer turned off, remove all your cables and inspect the little pins—whether they're in the cable end or the connector end. Are any of them bent over to one side? If so, you can take a pair of needle-nose pliers and carefully bend the pin back in place. Don't yank, though; it's only wire and therefore, very cheap and easily broken.

➤ Are you working at home? If so, do you have a fairly big-screen, color TV or a high-wattage stereo set? If so, don't just turn it off but unplug it. Sometimes high-power receiving equipment generates what geeks who love the alphabet like to call "RF interference," which cuts right into the electronic signals going on in your computer's bus. (Sound unlikely? Actually, your PC is more likely to catch RF interference than a computer virus.)

➤ Is your surge protector making noise? If it is, its fuse may be about to burn out. No big deal here, just replace the burned out fuse. (Of course, if the surge protector only cost you $20 or less, then toss it and get a new one instead.) You see, burning out fuses is exactly what surge protectors are designed to do, before something burns out your computer. (Uh, you do have a surge protector, don't you?)

➤ Do you keep anything large and magnetic close to your monitor, like, say, a magnet? You're not using your monitor as a catch-all for old sticky notes clamped together with a magnetic clamp, are you? In any case, put anything the least bit magnetic out of the way of your monitor.

➤ Is the weirdness centered around the mouse? If so, then try giving it a spring cleaning. Flip the mouse over and open the latch that holds the trackball. Use something dry and non-metallic like a toothpick to scrape all the gook off the rollers. Don't use your fingernails; your fingers deposit oils that cause the type of grime that makes it easy for the mouse ball rollers to pick up gunk off your desktop or mouse pad. That's why I say to use something dry and non-metallic. If this doesn't fix the problem, try borrowing a mouse that's the same brand and see if the problem goes away. If your friend's mouse works, then that will tell you there's nothing wrong with your PC, but there is something wrong with your mouse. See Chapter 10 for help.

➤ Try using an anti-virus utility to check the hard disk for viruses. A virus is a program that can wreak havoc on your PC, destroying files and rendering your computer useless. A mild virus may only display an annoying message. A virus can get on your computer through an infected diskette, or an infected file downloaded from an online service or bulletin board. Don't panic—most computer weirdness has nothing to do with a virus, but you should at least eliminate that possibility. If the utility does find a virus, it can usually remove the bugger with no problems.

➤ If you try all of these things and the PC refuses to start acting normal, you may want to call for help. Before you do, however, make sure that you can help your helper by giving him this information:

> **Can you duplicate the problem?**   Does the weirdness happen when you attempt some particular task, or is it a one-time thing? Is the weirdness related to a particular program? If so, try backing up your program's data and reinstalling the program—this usually fixes the problem.

> **What have you changed lately?**   If you just installed a new part, there are probably some additional things you need to do before you can use it. (See "Part 5: Getting Your PC to Figure Out What You've Done.") These "additional things" involve making changes to the configuration files, CONFIG.SYS and AUTOEXEC.BAT. Also, if you've just installed a new program, it's likely that the program itself also made changes to your files.

> If you suspect that the setup program for your new application or your new part has made changes to the configuration files that are causing your weirdness, use your emergency diskette to copy the original versions of your files back onto the hard disk and restart the PC. After you get your PC back, try making the changes to your configuration files one at a time, so you can isolate the one that caused the weirdness.

When Your PC Won't Start

Although this one is pretty scary, try not to panic—it doesn't necessarily mean that you've killed the PC. Check these things:

➤ First, start with the cables. If you find one trying to escape, guide the loose cable back to its plug. Then screw it in place to prevent another episode.

➤ Next, make sure that the PC is getting power. Take a lamp or other convenient appliance and stick it into the socket you normally use for your computer's plug. Does it work?

➤ If you use a surge protector with your PC, it might have gone off. If necessary, reset the surge protector by pressing its **Reset** button. An inexpensive surge protector doesn't usually have one, which means that it just burns itself out to save your PC. Give it a nice burial and buy a new one.

➤ If you've plugged in the computer, and the power is on, the next thing to check is the monitor. Is it getting power? If so, are you turning it on? If the monitor is on, fiddle with the brightness and contrast knobs for a while.

➤ If you use your emergency diskette (see Chapter 12), can you get the PC to start? If so, there may be a problem with the hard disk. See the next section for help.

When Your PC's Locked Up

If you're working away at the computer and you suddenly realize that the PC's no longer paying attention, it might be locked up. Here are some things you can do to get its attention.

➤ First, try pressing **Esc**. This is the universal get-me-out-of-here key, and it may just awaken your sleeping beauty.

➤ Next, try pressing **Ctrl+C** (or **Ctrl+Break**).

➤ If you're working in Windows 3.1, then press **Ctrl+Esc** to display the Task List. Select the rotten program (the program you were using when the PC decided to freeze up) from the list and click on **Delete** to end it.

➤ If you're using Windows 95 instead, then try to get back to the taskbar. (You may have to minimize a window or press **Ctrl+Esc** to get back to it.) Once the taskbar is visible, right click on the problem program and select **Close** from the pop-up menu. This terminates the darn thing.

➤ If everything else fails, you may have to restart your PC to get its attention. Do this by pressing **Ctrl+Alt+Delete**. But be warned! Restarting your PC in this manner causes you to lose any work you haven't already saved. Sorry, but that's the way it goes. If you're using Windows 3.1, you see a message asking you if you want to terminate the program that's gone to sleep on you. Click **Yes**. Windows terminates only the one program, so your other work should be OK. If you're using Windows 95, you see the **End Program** list appear when you press **Ctrl+Alt+Delete**. Select the bad program and click **End Task** to terminate it. Again, this should not affect your other programs.

➤ As a last resort, turn off your PC, wait a bit, and turn it back on. This certainly gets the PC's attention, but it also causes the computer to close everything down. Keep in mind that if you had been working on something and you haven't saved it yet, it will be lost when you turn off your PC.

Keep in mind that turning your PC off and on a lot doesn't do much for its delicate parts, which will heat up, cool down, then heat up again when you turn it back on. Better to leave the PC on all day until you go home, except in cases like this, where you have to turn the thing off just to get its attention.

Save Early, Save Often!

At one time or another, no matter how careful you are, your PC is going to lock up on you, and anything you haven't saved will be lost. So be sure to save your work often. Most programs offer an automatic save feature, which saves your work at timed intervals, such as every ten minutes. In some cases, you need to turn this feature on for it to work. Check the program's manual for help.

When Your Hard Disk Plays Hide and Seek

If your PC won't start normally, but it starts when you use your emergency diskette, then something is probably wrong with the hard disk. Try these things:

➤ First of all, did you (or some new program) make changes to the configuration files, CONFIG.SYS or AUTOEXEC.BAT, recently? If so, you may have accidently deleted a *device driver* file, which the PC uses to access data on the hard disk. For example, if you compressed your hard disk in Chapter 7, then you may have deleted the device driver file which starts DoubleSpace or DriveSpace. Or, if you have a large hard drive and you use a DOS version earlier than DOS 4.0, you may have deleted the device driver file that your DOS uses to access large disks.

In any case, if you suspect that you (or some installation program) changed the contents of your configuration files, then copy them back to drive C from your emergency diskette and restart the computer.

➤ Your CMOS may be damaged, or incorrect. CMOS, you may remember, is a chip inside your PC that stores important information such as how large your hard disk is. If you've recently changed your computer's battery, or if you've added some other major part, such as a new floppy disk or more RAM, then you may need to update the CMOS info. See Chapter 24 for help.

➤ Think back. Has your hard drive been giving you trouble for the past few months? Has it had trouble reading files, or saving them? If so, you may have a real problem. In order to figure out what might be wrong, check the hard disk first with a good utility program such as Norton Utilities, PC Tools, or Mace Utilities. You don't have to have one of these already installed on your dead hard disk in order to rescue it—you can run out and buy a good utility program and run it from a diskette. If you decide to get some help, be sure to tell your rescuer what's been going on.

When Your Mouse Has Gone to Disneyland

If you've suddenly lost the use of your mouse, or it's acting funny, try some of these tricks:

➤ Has your mouse gotten loose? Its tail (the cable) needs to be connected to the back of the PC. If you're not sure where to plug it in, check out Chapter 2.

➤ If you find a loose mouse and you plug it back in, you need to restart the PC for it to start working again. Of course, before you restart your PC, use keyboard commands to save your file and exit the program. You remember them, don't you? To open a menu for example, you press **Alt** plus the menu's first letter. So to save a file, press **Alt+F** to open the File menu and then **S** to choose Save.

➤ Are you using a program that supports a mouse? In other words, are you expecting to see a mouse pointer where one doesn't belong, such as at the DOS prompt? Try going into a program which you know for sure supports a mouse. Windows is a good example. Do you see the mouse pointer?

➤ Is the mouse playing hide and seek with you? It's easy to hide a mouse pointer at the edges of your screen. So move the mouse around and see if its pointer pops out of its hiding place.

➤ Have you cleaned your mouse lately? If not, it probably needs it. Open the hatch on the back that holds the trackball and use a toothpick to clean the rollers.

➤ Is the mouse driver installed? If you start your PC and end up with a missing mouse, then the driver (the program that enables the PC to talk to the mouse) isn't loaded.

Someone (or some setup program) was probably fiddling with your AUTOEXEC.BAT file. Use EDIT to open the AUTOEXEC.BAT file and add the command, which is usually something like this: C:\DOS\MOUSE, to get the mouse working.

➤ Does your PC insist that you load the Microsoft Mouse driver after you install a Microsoft program? You may encounter this problem if you use a different brand of mouse (and driver). Make a quick edit of the AUTOEXEC.BAT file to fix the problem.

When Your Coffee Meets Your Keyboard

Uh, oh. Well, follow these steps to get your keyboard back in working order:

1. First, turn the PC off.

2. Get a clean cloth or a paper towel and dab up what you can.

3. Turn the keyboard over to let the gunk drain out.

4. Spray a cleaner on a cloth and then use the cloth to wipe down the keyboard if needed.

The Truth about H2O

If the spill is really bad, you can douse your keyboard in water—it won't ruin anything as long as you unplug the keyboard before you douse it. Use distilled water though, because it's free of minerals that can gunk up the keyboard's components. And of course, make sure the entire keyboard is dry, dry, dry before you try to plug it back in again.

5. If several keys are sticky, you can pop them off to clean them. It's okay; the keys are built to snap off and on. Just be careful, because some keys (such as the Spacebar and the Enter key) are trickier than others to get back on. They generally have hidden levers on their lower edges (the sides facing you). You can reach these levers with a flat-head screwdriver.

6. Leave the keyboard alone for a day or so, so that it can dry thoroughly. You can use a hair dryer to dry it more quickly if needed, but make sure that the keyboard is thoroughly dry before you try to use it!

When Your Diskettes Suddenly Become Unreadable

If your computer is having trouble lately reading or copying files to a diskette, ask yourself these questions before you try to replace the drive:

➤ First, check to see if the drive can read any other diskettes. If so, then the problem is with the one diskette that can't be read, and not with the drive.

➤ Second, if you're trying to save something to the diskette, make sure that its write-protection is turned off.

➤ If the drive is having trouble reading a particular diskette, try removing the diskette and giving it a light tap on the side. This hopefully realigns the disk inside, so that the drive can read it more easily.

➤ Still having trouble? Make sure you formatted the diskette properly, and that it's the proper density for the drive you're trying to use it in. For example, if your PC has a double-density drive, you can only use double-density diskettes in it. If the drive is high-density, this isn't a problem because this type of drive can read both high- and double-density diskettes. Also, if this is a new diskette, you have to format it before you can use it.

When Your Printer's Acting Funky

Before you replace your funky printer, try these things:

➤ First, make sure that the printer is on, and *online*. If you're unsure if the printer is online or not, look for a button marked **Online**, and, if it isn't lit up, press it.

➤ Next, check the cable. If it's loose, plug it back in. (Unlike when a mouse gets loose, you *don't* have to restart the PC at this point.)

➤ The next thing you can do is to reset the printer by turning it off and then back on. Sometimes, this is all you have to do.

➤ If the printer still isn't responding, it's time for some serious testing. First, exit all programs and get to a DOS prompt. Press the **Print Screen** key and see if anything happens. You can also try printing a file by typing **PRINT C:\AUTOEXEC.BAT** and pressing **Enter**. You may see a message asking you what list device to use. Just ignore it and press **Enter** again.

➤ Now, go back into your program and try printing. If it doesn't work, try running the program's Setup and installing your printer again. Be sure to install the exact brand of printer that you have. If you don't see your particular printer listed, then try Epson FX-80 if your printer is a dot-matrix, or HP LaserJet if your printer's a laser, or if all else fails and there is no "Text Only" choice, look for Diablo 630.

➤ Another way to tell if it's your program that's the problem is to try to print from some other application. If you can find an application that works with your printer, check its Setup to see what type of printer you installed. Now, install that same brand in the program that's not working.

➤ If you're using Windows 3.1, open up **Print Manager** in the Main group and check to see if the document is there, waiting to print. If so, select it and click on **Retry**. If Print Manager has trouble printing the document, it may be that you're low on memory. Exit as many programs as you can and try printing the document again.

➤ If you're using Windows 95, click on the **Start** button, select **Settings**, and then select **Printers**. Double-click on your printer's icon. This displays your document's place in line as it's waiting to print (also known in geek circles as the print queue). Open the **Printer** menu and make sure that the **Pause Printing** option is not selected. If the document's status says Paused, select the document, open the **Document** menu, and deselect the **Pause Printing** option.

When Your Modem's on the Fritz

When your modem refuses to cooperate (communicate) try some of these tricks:

➤ First, dumb questions: Is the modem on, and is it plugged in? Also, is there a phone line running from the modem to a phone jack?

Check This Out...

Beware Digital Phone Line Jacks If only a digital phone works in the jack, then don't try to use that particular phone line for your modem, because it carries extra digital gook that can interfere with modem communications.

➤ Have you ever used this particular phone jack before? To test a phone jack, plug a regular phone (not one of those digital read-out things) into it and see if it works.

➤ Can you hear the modem dialing? If not, first check the preferences in your communications program to see if it's turning off your modem's internal speaker, or at least turning it down so low that you can't hear it. If that's not the problem, the computer may be having trouble locating the modem. This usually happens when you select the wrong communications (COM) port during setup. Select a different one and retry the modem.

➤ Does the modem have a COM switch? Older modems have a switch that sets the COM port, and this switch must match the setting you choose during setup. Check the modem's manual for help. Also, the communications program you want to use needs to use the same COM port the modem is on, or they won't find each other.

➤ Does the modem answer at the other end? If you're not sure that the number you're trying to use is a valid one, dial it using a regular phone. Be sure that the modem is dialing a "9" if it's needed in order to get an outside line. For most modems, you can add that 9 to the number you're dialing by separating it with a comma, as in "9,5551212"—this tells the modem to pause a second to access the outside line.

101

➤ Do you have call waiting installed? If so, you need to disable it before using your modem, or the modem will disconnect you if another call comes in. The best solution is to have separate phone and modem lines. In the meantime, add * 70 in front of the phone number you want to call, like this: *70,355-9089. If you use an old-fashioned rotary (pulse) system, then add 1170 instead, like this: 1170,355-9089.

➤ If you get connected and *then* the modem acts funny, the settings may be off. If you're seeing garbage on-screen, make sure that the speed (baud rate) you're using is set *equal to* or *lower than* the modem you're calling. For example, if the modem you're calling is set to 2400 baud, don't dial in at 9600 baud or higher. Also, make sure that the terminal emulation is set to the same thing that the receiving modem is set to.

➤ If you're typing a message and you can't see what you're typing on-screen, then turn on local echo. There may be some menu command for this, or you can type **ATE1** and press **Enter**.

➤ If you're seeing double (two of everything you type), then change to full duplex and turn off local echo.

➤ If you can't get the modem to hang up, try typing the command **ATH** and pressing **Enter**. If that doesn't work, try pressing **Ctrl+H** (for hang up) and then **Ctrl+X** (to exit). Next, try exiting your communications program, and turning off an external modem. As a final resort, reboot your PC.

The Least You Need to Know

If there's one lesson for you to learn in this chapter, it's that it's never over 'til it's over. In other words, don't jump to the conclusion that something's broken when it's not. Here are some other tidbits to remember:

➤ If something starts acting funny, such as the printer, the monitor, or your mouse, check the simple things first, such as making sure the item is plugged in and powered up.

➤ Remember that there are some very useful utility programs that can help in times like these. My favorites include Norton Utilities, PC Tools, and Mace Utilities.

➤ Your best insurance against total disaster is a good backup. Your second best insurance against disaster is to save your work often.

➤ Sometimes the easiest way to get something to work again is to turn it off and then back on again.

➤ Before real trouble strikes, make sure that you create an emergency diskette and keep it current. See Chapter 12 for help.

Part 2
Easy Upgrades

Got a klunky keyboard, a malfunctioning mouse, or a pain-in-the-neck printer? Well, in this section, you'll learn some quick fixes for what ails them.

If kicking, punching, and pleading don't work, you can always toss the darn things out and replace them with something that does. Even if you've never attempted to upgrade or replace anything on your PC before, you'll find these upgrades the easiest to try.

Dealing with a Funky Keyboard

Keyboards don't usually die, but they can wear out. When a keyboard is on its last legs, the keys stick, you type G and get GGGGGGGGGGGG, and theSpacebardoesn'twork anymore. However, there are other things that can go wrong with a keyboard without it necessarily meaning it's time for a replacement.

In this chapter, you'll learn how to fix an ailing keyboard, even if one or more of the keys aren't working at all. If you learn that your keyboard's a goner, you can easily replace it with the instructions at the end of this chapter.

How to Tell When It's Time to Say Goodbye

Don't assume that you have to replace any computer part just because it's acting funny. The problem may simply be that you haven't dusted in a while, or something just as silly. You see, modern keyboard mechanisms use as few moving parts as possible; most don't even have springs anymore. While this makes keyboards easier to make, it also tends to cause them to wear out easier.

Beep! Beep! Beep!

If your keyboard beeps at you every time you press a key, the problem is not with the keyboard, but with the PC. What's happened is that your computer's gone into a tizzy over something, and it's locked itself up. Every key you press at this point simply goes unheard, which is why you're hearing the beeps. Restart your PC and everything should be all right again. (Keep in mind that when you restart your PC, you lose any work you haven't already saved. Use your mouse to save your work if you can.)

For example, if you start your PC one day and get this message: Keyboard not found. Press F1 to continue, don't assume that your keyboard's still out on an all-nighter with the mouse. This message is simply telling you that the PC can't communicate with the keyboard, and that's usually because the keyboard cable is loose. So return the wayward plug back to its socket, and restart the PC.

Spilled Coffee and Other Common Disasters

If you spill something on your keyboard, don't panic—there may still be a chance to save the patient. Turn off the PC and use a dry cloth to wipe up what you can. Flip the keyboard over to let it drain for about a day. You can dry the keyboard with a hair dryer if you want, but wait about a day before you try to use the keyboard. After a day or so, plug the keyboard back in, cross your fingers, and turn on the PC.

If that doesn't work, you can do a more thorough job of cleaning by removing the keys with a small flat-head screwdriver. Using the screwdriver as a kind of lever, gently pry up along the bottom edge of each key to remove it. Once you get the keys off, use a dry cloth to clean as much as you can. Some keys, such as the Spacebar and the Enter key, are real buggers to get back on, so don't bother to remove them. Clean up what you can and try the keyboard again. If you've made a big mess, you can give the keyboard a bath in soapy water—but make absolutely sure that everything is dry, dry, dry, before you plug it back in. Also, make sure that you use distilled water for the bath (the minerals in regular water can corrode the keyboard's parts). If it still doesn't work, you need to replace it.

Sticky Keys?

Perhaps you didn't spill anything on it, but your keyboard has developed a few sticky keys anyway. Before you decide to replace your keyboard, try cleaning some of the sticky keys and see if that helps. Gently pry off the gummy key using a small flat-head screwdriver. If the key is located in the middle or top of the keyboard, feel free to pry off a few extra keys from the lower rows so you can easily get to the gummy key. Once you have the key off, clean its socket with a dry cloth sprayed with some type of cleanser. *If you spray anything on the keyboard itself, make sure that the keyboard is bone dry before you try to use it again.* Replace the key and test it to see if it acts a little better. Don't forget where the keys belong; you'll really fool yourself later if you forget.

Other Ways to Bust the Dust

You can clear a lot of dust bunnies out of your keyboard with a can of compressed air with dust-eating cleaner added or a computer vacuum. The can of air runs about $10, while the vacuum costs about $30—either one is a good investment.

When You Can't Tell What the Keys Are For

If some of the letters on your keyboard are worn off, it's no big deal—unless you're a hunt-and-peck typist. Now, if you're like me, then you probably hate to spend hard-earned bucks replacing something that still works at least 75 percent…okay, 60 percent of the time. If you can get your hands on a used keyboard somewhere, you can pry the keys off that you need and use them on your keyboard. Some mail order shops sell replacement keycaps—get a copy of *Computer Shopper*, and you can locate hundreds of mail-order sources for all sorts of items, not just keycaps. Before you go overboard about a few missing letters, keep in mind that replacing a keyboard is easy, and it only costs between $50 and $100.

What to Do When Your Puppy Attacks the Keyboard Cable

You may also encounter a problem with the keyboard cable wearing out. Usually the trouble is pretty easy to spot—the keyboard stops working or every key you press results in an error. Although you can replace the keyboard cable, it's not a good idea to try because you can only take the keyboard apart so much before you are literally showered with springs, clips, and keycaps. If you're careful, you can do it, but if you accidently loosen the wrong screw, blammo! So in a case like this, just replace the keyboard rather than spending your life putting it back together.

Shopping for a New Keyboard

Once you decide to replace your old keyboard, you'll have to make quite a few choices. For the most part, your choice of keyboard is one of personal preference, and this section describes your various options.

First, Make Sure You Buy the Right Connector Type

One part of your decision that you can't control is the type of connector your keyboard uses. There are only two types: the larger, five-pin DIN connector, or the smaller, "PS/2" six-pin DIN connector.

You Can Get an Adapter...

There's not a lot of difference between these two connectors, except their size. In fact, you can use an adapter to convert one type of connector to the other. That is, if you can find someone who carries the adapter. In most cases, you're better off getting a keyboard with the right kind of connector for your PC though.

The right connections.

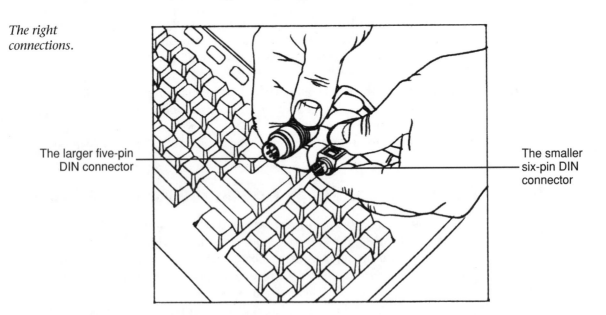

The larger five-pin DIN connector

The smaller six-pin DIN connector

How Does Your Keyboard Talk?

Once you learn which keyboard type and connector to use with your PC, you'll still find yourself with a lot of choices. Another part of your choice that you can't control is the *type* of keyboard your PC uses. By type, I don't mean something that you can see. Instead, I'm talking about the way in which your keyboard communicates with your PC. There are only two keyboard types: the XT-style and the AT-style. You can't really tell one type from the other just by looking, because the difference doesn't depend on the number of keys, but rather, on the internal electronics. But the original XT keyboards have only 83 keys, and they are missing the fancy running lights of modern keyboards.

So how will you know which keyboard type to buy? Well, all modern keyboards are AT-style, so it shouldn't be an issue unless your PC was built prior to 1981. If you do buy the wrong keyboard type, most new keyboards come with a switch on the bottom for changing from AT-style to XT-style, so you can just flip the switch to make the keyboard compatible with your PC. If you're in doubt about the age of your computer, make sure that the replacement keyboard you buy has this switch, so the type isn't a problem.

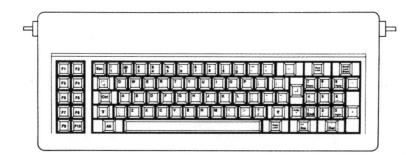

The granddaddy of them all, the old XT keyboard.

The original AT keyboard has 84 keys. The extra key is the Sys Req key, put there by some evil mainframe programmer at IBM who was out to protect his job by stopping the PC revolution in its tracks with a key that confuses people.

Again, you probably won't find an old AT keyboard anywhere except in a museum. That's because they're not sold today, although they are electronically compatible with modern PCs. (Well, kinda. You can connect an AT keyboard to your PC, but it may or may not be able to talk to a modern PC, depending on the PC's BIOS.) You'll notice that besides the extra key, the layout is quite different from the original XT keyboard. The AT keyboard accommodated users who wanted a friendlier keyboard, with a larger Enter key, a separate Numeric keypad, and indicator lights for the Num Lock, Caps Lock, and Scroll Lock status.

The AT keyboard added one whole key.

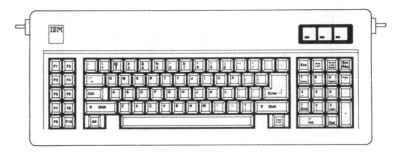

The most popular keyboard today is the Enhanced 101-key keyboard. Notice that there are two more function keys, and that they're lined up at the top of the keyboard. The Enter key is smaller, though, but the backslash key is in a more convenient spot. A few keyboard manufacturers from some other planet put the backslash key to the left of the Spacebar. Some manufacturers have added a few more keys around the Spacebar, bringing the total to 104. These extra keys are great if you plan on using the keyboard more than the mouse to control Windows 95.

The Enhanced keyboard.

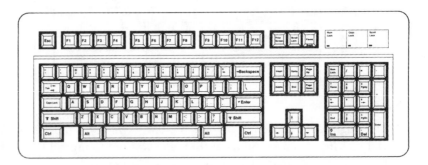

Other manufacturers restored the larger Enter key from the old AT keyboard to their version of the Enhanced keyboard. You lose the convenient placement of the backslash key, but hey, if you don't use DOS, who cares?

Can You Say Er-go-nom-ic?

Another popular version of the Enhanced keyboard is the *ergonomic* keyboard. The premise of ergonomic keyboards is that they are supposed to be gentle on your hands; *ergo*, it reduces the stress normally placed on the hands when they try to twist themselves into position to type on a regular keyboard. The design enables your wrists to stay level with the floor as you type, thereby avoiding *repetitive stress injuries* such as carpal tunnel syndrome. Ergonomic keyboards arrange the keys into two sets, dividing the middle by a blank space. Some models enable you to adjust the degree of this space. The better models (including Microsoft's version) position each key at the medically prescribed inclination for each finger and at the proper angle for your wrist. In addition, the Spacebar is sometimes (but not always) hacked in two, giving you one Spacebar for each set of keys. Don't fall for a cheap keyboard—make sure that the design fits the way you work by typing on it before you buy it.

Microsoft's version of an ergonomic keyboard.

Other Cool Features

Another feature you may find on your keyboard is *mapping*, which enables the keyboard to mix up the purpose of the keys. For example, you can make the F1 key act like the Escape key if you want. I find this feature incredibly annoying, because it is ever so easy to accidently map a key when you don't want to. I once mapped the Tab key on my Gateway keyboard when a book fell on it. To get out of the mess, I had to press this bizarre key combination: Ctrl+Alt+Suspend Macro, which told the keyboard to return to its original non-confused state. If this ever happens to you, check out your computer manual for help in getting the keyboard back to normal.

Built-in Mouse
Another feature to look for is a built-in mouse, which may take the form of a button or trackball, or a flexible key which you can bend in the direction to which you want the mouse pointer to move. There are many ways to marry a mouse to the keyboard, and frankly, I find most of them too funky to use. Try them out and judge for yourself

If you look hard enough, you can find just about any type of keyboard, including a multicolored one designed for kids, a collapsible one for those of us who work in a closet, and a sound keyboard for musician-wannabees that includes speakers, a microphone, and a volume control.

Regardless of which keyboard you choose, remember that you're going to live with this decision for a while. The main thing you do with a keyboard is type, so why not test out the typing on the same keyboard you plan to buy? Spend a little time trying out your new friend before you decide to take it home. What you're looking for here is a keyboard that feels comfortable, which usually means that its keys are not too smooshy and not too hard. If there's a mouse or trackball included with the keyboard, try it out too.

Let's Go Shopping

Here's what to look for when buying a new keyboard:

➤ Look for one which is the same type (XT or AT) as the keyboard you're using now, or look for a keyboard with the XT-AT switch on the bottom.

➤ Make sure you get a keyboard with the same type of connector as the one you currently own.

➤ Test out your keyboard by typing a long passage and making sure you like the way the keys feel.

➤ Check out the size of the Enter key, keeping in mind that a larger Enter key causes the backslash key to turn up in inconvenient places.

➤ Consider an ergonomic keyboard if you type a lot.

➤ If you need to replace your mouse, look for a keyboard that includes one or a mouse substitute, such as a built-in trackball or a touchpad.

➤ You may want to see if your keyboard supports *mapping*, and, if it does, make sure the key that maps the other keys is located in a hard-to-bump-when-you-don't-really-want-to mess-up-your-keyboard kind of place.

Check This Out...

Help for Heavy-Duty Typists

If you're concerned about carpal tunnel syndrome, make sure you buy a wrist rest with your ergonomic keyboard. A wrist rest is a soft pad which sits in front of the keyboard, on which you can rest your wrists. A mouse rest is nice, too. For ergonomic keyboard designs that have a curved bottom edge, you need a wrist rest that's curved to fit—or the wrist rest may be built-in.

Replacing the Keyboard (Uh, Even Your Mother Could Do This)

Once you purchase your keyboard, it's pretty simple to connect it. Start by exiting all programs and turning your PC off. You should never plug or unplug anything from your PC while it's on. If you do, something bad can happen—for example, the nerd police might show up at your door.

Disconnect your old keyboard. Keep the thing in a box labeled "Spare PC Parts," for the time when your new keyboard's keys, cable, or whatever starts wearing out. My box of spare parts has helped me more times (and saved me more moola) than you can imagine.

Reconnect the new keyboard. Don't worry—the plug only fits one way, with the little dent on the top of the connector facing up. If you accidently bought a keyboard with the wrong connector, you can exchange it or buy a convertor.

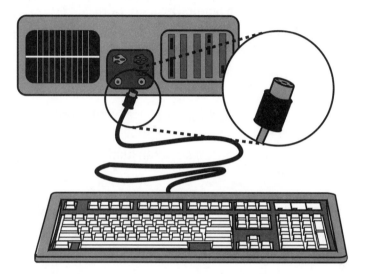

Connecting a new keyboard is easy.

Turn the PC back on. The computer wakes up and searches for the keyboard. If something's wrong, you see an error message. Check out the next section for help. Otherwise, you're home free.

What Could Go Wrong

If you get an error message when you try out your new keyboard, turn the PC off and check the cable again. Turn the PC back on. If the problem doesn't go away, try these things:

➤ You may be trying to use an AT-type keyboard on an XT-type PC. If your new keyboard has an XT-AT switch, flip it to XT and try the keyboard again.

➤ You may have accidently bent one of the pins in the connector when you plugged it in. If so, try to bend it back *gently* and then try the keyboard again.

If neither of these tricks coaxes your new keyboard into working, you may want to return it. If the new one has the same problem, then take your PC in for a checkup; there may be something wrong with the keyboard controller chip.

The Least You Need to Know

Chances are good that you won't have to replace your keyboard just 'cause it's acting funny, especially if you keep these things in mind:

➤ First thing, check the keyboard's cable. If it's loose, then plug it back in and restart the PC.

➤ If your keyboard has sticky keys, or if you spill something on it, you can clean it by removing keys and wiping up the liquid with a dry cloth.

➤ A can of compressed air (with added dust-busting cleaners) is a handy fellow to have around when you're trying to get your keyboard clean.

➤ If some of the keys are worn down, you may be able to salvage replacements from an old keyboard.

➤ Replacing the internal parts of a keyboard is generally not worth it, because taking a keyboard apart sends keys, springs, and clips flying.

➤ If you decide to replace your keyboard, make sure that you test it out first, to see if you like the feel of the keys.

➤ If you're concerned about carpal tunnel syndrome and you spend a lot of time on your PC, you may want to consider an ergonomic keyboard or a wrist rest.

➤ To replace your keyboard, turn the PC off, unplug your old keyboard, plug your new keyboard in, and turn the PC back on.

➤ If you have trouble with your keyboard, it's usually a loose cable. So check the cable, replace it if necessary, and restart the computer.

Chapter 10

Mousing Around

In This Chapter

➤ Giving your old mouse a new lease on life

➤ Replacing your old mouse with a new one

➤ Adding a mouse to a mouseless system

➤ Installing your new mouse without pain

A mouse is a piece of plastic about the size of a bar of soap that attaches to your PC by its "tail," or cord. Underneath, the mouse contains a trackball that helps it sense the direction in which you move the mouse. You point to objects on-screen by shoving the mouse in the correct direction. Cute idea, but if you push your mouse around and nothing happens, you've got a problem.

Or do you? Well, in this chapter, you'll learn how to cure an ailing mouse, or if needed, replace it.

How to Tell When It's Time to Say Good-bye

If you've had your mouse for a while and it suddenly starts acting weird, chances are all that you need to do is clean it. You see, there's a roller ball on the underside of the mouse that just loves to grab dust, dirt, hair, and any other disgusting thing on which it can get its, uh, hands.

Gutting a Standard Mouse

First, exit all programs and turn off the PC so it doesn't go nuts with all the screwy signals it'll receive during the cleaning process. Flip your mouse over on its back and open the hatch that holds the trackball in place. (You see an arrow telling you which way to twist or push the hatch to get it to open.)

Watch the dust balls fly.

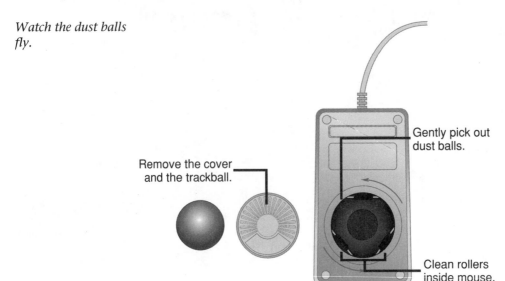

Remove the cover and the trackball.

Gently pick out dust balls.

Clean rollers inside mouse.

Remove the trackball. Now, take a toothpick and gently scrape the gook off of the two or three rollers you find inside the mouse. You can dip the toothpick in rubbing alcohol if you like, but not anything that's oily (like acetone) because this does more harm than good. Someone may tell you to use a Q-tip for this, but Q-tips leave their own fuzz behind as well.

Use a lint-free cloth or warm soap and water to clean the trackball, too. Don't use rubbing alcohol on the rubber—it'll mess it up. When you finish cleaning, put the whole thing back together and try it out.

Maintaining a Cordless Mouse

If your cordless mouse starts acting strange, it's probably low on batteries. The batteries go either in the mouse itself, or in the receiving thingie (the box that's attached to the PC, which receives the mouse signals from the cordless wonder). Your cordless mouse works just like the remote to the VCR. If you've got tons of tapes piled up in front of the

VCR, the remote doesn't work; same thing with your cordless mouse—if it keeps cutting out, it's probably because you've got tons of junk piled up in front of the receiving unit. Just move the junk, and your mouse should be fine. If you're still having trouble, the problem may be your monitor—it may put out too much RF interference (see Chapter 16) and hamper reception.

Maybe It Was Something I Did?

Has your mouse been working fine up to now, but suddenly it stops working right after you install some kind of serial device such as a modem, joystick, scanner, or serial printer? The problem is that the new device and your mouse duked it out over a COM port, and the mouse lost.

You see, all serial devices communicate with the PC through a COM (communications) port. Each serial device needs its own COM port, or it gets mucked up and doesn't work. So if your mouse and some new serial device are messing with each other over the same COM port, you have to switch one of them to a different port. See Chapter 24, "Fiddling with COM Ports, IRQs, Addresses, and Such," for more help.

Choices, Choices, Choices

A new mouse costs between $15 and $150, depending on how picky you are. My mouse, a Logitech MouseMan, cost about $50. A Microsoft Mouse costs about $55. You may also want to invest in a new mouse pad if yours is trashed—look for one with a built-in wrist rest. (If you're new to this mouse business, a mouse pad is a small foam or plastic pad where a mouse hangs out, rather than running around on your desktop and picking up all the crud you keep there.)

Before you run out to get your new mouse, keep in mind that they come with one of three connectors: bus, serial, or PS/2. Look at your old mouse, and get the same type of connector for your new mouse. If you're adding a mouse to your system, make sure you get one that fits an open connector. For example, if your PC comes with a PS/2 mouse port, then by all means, get a PS/2 style mouse. Otherwise, get a serial mouse—however, if you don't have an open serial port, then you'll need to get an I/O card too, which will add both a serial and a parallel port to your PC. Bus type mice are difficult to find, so if you're adding a mouse where none has gone before, don't bother with them.

The picture here shows a serial connector and a PS/2 connector. (Bus connectors vary by manufacturer. However, a lot of them look suspiciously like PS/2 connectors, only skinnier.)

Choose a replacement that matches your old mouse type.

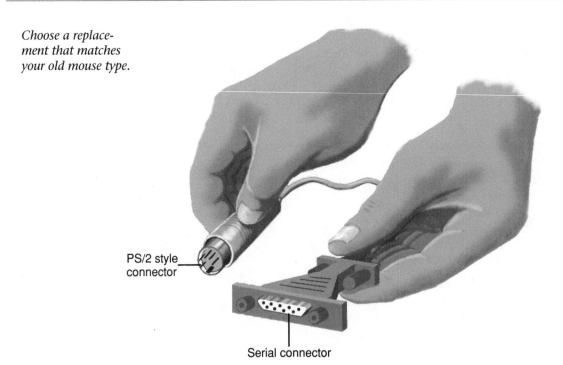

PS/2 style connector

Serial connector

Bus Mouse

It's unlikely that you'll add a bus mouse to a mouseless system, because they're kinda hard to find. However, if your PC already uses a bus mouse and you need to replace it, you'll find it easier to get another bus mouse (provided you can find one.) How can you tell if you have one of these critters? Well, a bus mouse connects to a special card in your PC, which takes up one of the expansion slots. Unlike a serial mouse, a bus mouse doesn't communicate with the PC through a COM port; instead, it uses the expansion bus just like any other expansion card. This means that if you use a bus mouse, you may still have conflicts with other devices through the IRQ setting, but you won't run into the problem of not having a free serial (COM) port into which to plug the mouse. If your computer is one of the slower models, you may notice the bus mouse is somewhat faster than a serial mouse; however, you won't notice any difference at all with modern computers.

The bus mouse connects to the PC through the plug on the bus card; the type of plug varies by manufacturer, so be sure to get the same kind you were using. A bus mouse is rare, so you may run into a problem locating the exact brand and model of mouse you had before. Take it with you to your local computer store to see if it can help you order a replacement mouse.

What's an IRQ?

To get somebody's attention, you wave your hand, whistle, or yell, "Hey, you!" The devices you connect to your PC can't whistle or yell, but they do need some way to communicate, so they use an IRQ. An IRQ is like a special "message box" in the CPU. When a device needs to get the CPU's attention, it leaves an urgent message in its own IRQ. For example, when you punch the keyboard, it leaves a message in IRQ 1. The CPU constantly checks the IRQs, so it gets the message right away.

Most PCs have 16 IRQs, but many of them have already been assigned to normal devices, such as the keyboard, hard disk, floppy drives, and the COM and LPT ports. If you connect a mouse to your PC, you have to assign an available IRQ to it. A serial mouse is connected through a COM port, so it uses the same IRQ that the COM port uses. If you choose a bus or a PS/2 mouse, you'll save a COM port (a connector), but you'll use up another IRQ.

This whole IRQ business can get real nasty; if you run into a problem after installing your new mouse, you can turn to Chapter 24, "Fiddling with Ports, IRQs, Addresses, and Such," for help.

Serial Mouse

A serial mouse plugs into one of the serial (COM) ports on the back of your PC. There's usually two, so using one for your mouse may or may not be a problem, depending on what other things you're trying to connect. Other serial devices include modems, serial printers, joysticks, and scanners, among others. A serial mouse is the most common type of mouse available, but it usually comes with a connector that fits a nine-pin serial port. If you're going to connect your serial mouse to a fat 25-pin port, be sure to buy a 9-to-25-pin adapter if your new mouse doesn't come with one.

Serial Ports

Your mouse plugs right into the serial port—at least, most of the time. (If you have a bus or a PS/2 mouse, it'll plug into its own connector.) A serial port is easy to identify because it has pins; the mouse connector has an equal number of holes. Serial ports come in two sizes, 9- or 25-pin. Mouse connectors come in only one size—with only nine holes.

PS/2 Mouse

A PS/2 mouse connects to your PC through a special PS/2-style mouse port. Even if you don't own an IBM PS/2, your PC may have one of these ports; they're usually marked with a cute mouse icon. One warning: be careful not to plug a bus mouse into one of these ports; the silly thing could damage the motherboard. You must plug a bus mouse into its own bus card.

Choosing a Brand and Model

Even though you now know the type of mouse connector you need to shop for, you still face a truckload of choices. Logitech, Microsoft, and Kensington are among the leading mouse manufacturers; you'll find that they and scores of smaller companies offer lots of variety.

Nice mice.

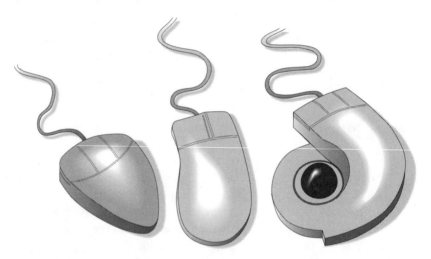

Don't Leave Home Without It Take your old mouse with you when you shop. This makes it easier for the salesperson to help you locate a compatible replacement.

Mice come in all shapes and colors. They even come in lefty and righty varieties. Before you get overwhelmed by all the special mouse features, remember that one of the most important factors is how the mouse *feels*. If possible, try out your new mouse before you buy it and see if it fits comfortably in your hand. Also, check its weight. Some of the cheaper brands are just that—cheaply made, lightweight, and flimsy.

Some mice have three buttons—some programs ask you to use that third (middle) button for something. Most of the time, you'll use the left and right buttons, so don't jump for a third button unless you know that you have a program that requires it for something. (Even so, most of these programs let you get away with using a two-button mouse if you don't opt for three.) Logitech mice (all of which have three buttons) come complete with a nifty setup which enables you to program the middle button for your choice of things, such as Help, automatic click-and-hold, or single-click double-clicking. Even though I use a Logitech mouse, I still end up ignoring the middle button most of the time. Not that there's anything wrong with having extra buttons—the PowerMouse/70 comes with 17 buttons which you can program for common functions like cut, copy, and paste.

If you're tired of moving your mouse around, or if you're limited on space, you might want to consider a stationary mouse, otherwise known to its friends as the *trackball*. A trackball is kind of like an upside-down mouse—the ball is on top. With a trackball, the mouse stays still; you move the mouse pointer by moving the trackball itself. Buttons on the trackball enable you to click, double-click, and drag.

A cordless mouse is a good choice if you do a lot of multimedia presentations with your PC, or if you simply hate it when the mouse cord gets tangled on all the junk on your desk. The receiving unit plugs into your PC's serial or PS/2 port; you wiggle the hand-held mouse in your palm or on a far-away desktop to move the mouse pointer.

Installing the Thing

Before you install your new or replacement mouse, get a small flathead screwdriver. Unless you're installing a PS/2 style mouse, you need the screwdriver to screw the mouse connector in place. But I'm ahead of myself.

First, turn off your computer and remove your old mouse. Next, if you're replacing your old mouse with a mouse of the same type, simply plug your new mouse into the old mouse's connector. If you're adding a mouse, or replacing your old mouse with a new type, then plug your new mouse into the appropriate connector. For example, plug a serial mouse into an available serial connector.

Plug your mouse into the appropriate connector.

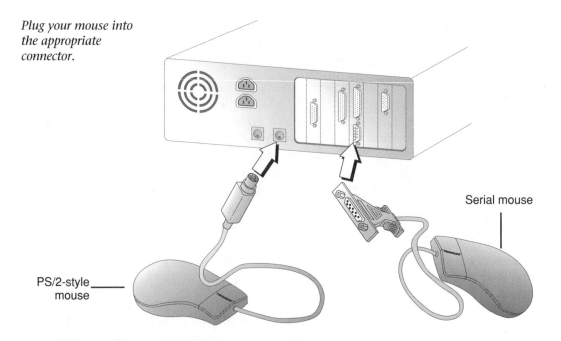

Serial mouse

PS/2-style mouse

The Nitty-Gritty About Connectors

Now, a couple of comments about mouse connectors:

Serial ports   Your PC probably has two of these; your mouse can use either one. A serial port is easy to identify; it's the one with *pins*. If the free port has nine pins, fine. Your mouse connector plugs right in.

If the free port has 25 pins, plug your 9-to-25-pin adapter into the mouse connector and then plug the whole contraption into the free serial port. Sometimes these adapter things are called DB25 to DB9 connectors—but whatever the name, you won't have any trouble finding one at your local computer store.

PS/2 ports   A PS/2 port (usually called simply the "mouse port") is small, round, and has six small holes. The mouse connector has pins arranged in a small ring that fits right into the PS/2 mouse port.

Bus ports   The bus port is located on the bus card. If you're adding a bus card to your PC, you have to open up the system unit. Before you do, read the instructions in Chapter 12 to avoid messing something up.

Once you connect your mouse, use your screwdriver to lock it in place. Some mouse connectors use thumb screws instead, and some have no screws at all.

No Open Ports

If you need to add a new serial port because your computer has only one and you're already using it, get yourself a so-called "multifunction" I/O (input/output) card. It only costs about $30, and you get an extra parallel port in the bargain. To install it, see Chapter 12 for help.

If your PC has two serial ports and you're using both, you need to get a bus mouse because you've reached the limit on serial ports, partner. (Here's hoping your PC has a free expansion slot to put it in.) The bus card provides the port into which you can plug your new mouse. Again, see Chapter 12 for help installing the bus card.

Announcing the New Guest

Now, before you can use your new mouse, you need to tell your PC how to communicate with it. This involves running the mouse's Setup program to install a *mouse driver*.

A mouse driver is a computer program that tells your PC exactly how to talk with your particular brand of mouse. Think of it as a kind of translator specializing in mouse-speak. You should run the Setup program even if you replace your old mouse with a similar brand; it updates your mouse driver to the latest and greatest. If you plan on using the mouse with Windows, you need to run the special Windows Setup too. Check out Chapter 23 for more help.

Don't Forget that Emergency Diskette! Be sure to update your emergency diskette before you run any Setup program. See Chapter 12 for help.

The Setup program asks you a lot of questions, including what COM port your mouse is using. If you're using a bus or PS/2 mouse, you won't be asked this because, uh, it doesn't use a COM port. If you use a serial mouse, and you used the larger 25-pin port built into your PC, then it's probably using COM2. If you plugged the mouse into the smaller 9-pin port, then it's probably using COM1. Don't ask how I know—it's a real science. After the Setup program's done, you need to restart the PC to bring your new mouse to life.

What Could Go Wrong

If your PC uses several serial devices, such as a mouse, a scanner, modem, or a joystick, the problem may be that they're all trying to talk over the same COM (serial) port. You see, even though your PC can handle up to four COM ports, only two can be active at any one time. This is pretty head-grinding stuff; so jump to Chapter 24, "Fiddling with Ports, IRQs, Addresses, and Such," for help in sorting it out.

If your mouse works in DOS programs but not in Windows, it's probably because you didn't run the Windows Setup for your Windows mouse driver. See Chapter 23 for help in that department. If your mouse works in Windows but not in DOS, see Chapter 22 instead. (Remember, even though your mouse works in DOS, it won't work in Windows until you install some kind of Windows mouse driver.)

If you're having trouble using your mouse in a particular program, then you may have to check the program's configuration to make sure that you selected the right mouse. You won't have to do this with any Windows program, because Windows handles the mouse's talking. A lot of DOS programs don't require you to choose a particular mouse, because they just let device driver do the talking. But there are a handful of DOS programs that require you to pick your mouse brand from some kind of setup list (WordPerfect 5.1 is one of them). If you don't find your brand listed, then choose Microsoft Mouse (it's the most generic kind of mouse driver, and it probably works with whatever kind of mouse you own).

The Least You Need to Know

Installing a new mouse is not usually difficult, but there are some things you should remember:

➤ Before you replace your mouse, clean it well and see if that doesn't perk it up.

➤ There are lots of mice you can choose from. You have your choice in shape, color, number of buttons, and left-handed or right-handed.

➤ Your new mouse has one of three possible connectors: bus, serial, or PS/2. Get a replacement mouse with the same type of connector that your old mouse used.

➤ To install a mouse, turn your PC off and then plug the new mouse in. Turn the PC back on and run the mouse's Setup program. Run the Windows Setup program if you plan on using the mouse under Windows.

➤ If you run into problems with your new mouse, more than likely there's some kind of COM port/IRQ conflict. See Chapter 24, "Fiddling with Ports, IRQs, Addresses and Such," for the mind-numbing explanation on what to do.

Chapter 11

Painless Printing

In This Chapter

➤ Turning a turtle printer into a rabbit

➤ Fixing those nasty printer problems

➤ Replacing the ribbon, inkjet cartridge, toner cartridge, and the kitchen sink

➤ Shopping for and installing a new printer

Printers are handy little fellows. After you work hard all day creating the perfect letter, presentation, worksheet, or graphic, your printer enables you to create a handy hard copy so you can bother people far and wide with your creativity. That is, when your printer works. In this chapter, you'll find out how to fix an ailing printer, and if you can't fix it, what you should look for in a replacement.

Can I Save My Old, Slow Printer?

If your printer is a turtle, you can easily speed it up without replacing it. A printer by nature is slower than your computer, which means that the PC can easily send data to the printer faster than the printer can print it. What happens in most cases is a bottleneck: the stuff you send to the printer creates a logjam back at the computer end, waiting for the printer to catch up.

While your computer waits around feeding your printer a page to print every so often, you wait in frustration for your PC to start paying more attention to you. To solve this problem, get yourself a print spooler program. When you print something, the computer tosses stuff over to the print spooler and gets on with its life. The print spooler then takes over the boringly slow job of feeding the printer.

If you have Windows 3.1 or Windows 95, then you already have a print spooler since it's built-in (in Windows 3.1, the print spooler is called Print Manager. In Windows 95, the spooler doesn't have a name, but it's accessible through your printer icon). But if you're just using DOS, adding a print spooler program really makes a difference. Getting a DOS-based print spooler is quite a pickle, because most people carry only a limited amount of DOS programs (everything's Windows, don't ya know). If you insist on using DOS, it's worth your time to locate a good DOS utilities package such as Norton Utilities or Mace Utilities, which includes a terrific DOS-based print spooler.

Another way to speed up a slow printer is to add a print buffer. A print buffer acts as a holding spot for stuff you send to the printer, just like the print spooler. But unlike a spooler (which is a program), a buffer is a series of RAM chips, which means that it's faster. If you have a laser printer, then it has a print buffer built-in. There's a good chance, however, that the amount of RAM your printer comes with is minimal—such as 512K. Don't get sad; you can easily increase the speed of your printer by adding more buffer RAM. Also, some printer sharing devices (commonly called A/B switches) come with their own print buffers. So if you're stuck sharing a printer with someone, get one of these A/B switches with lots of buffer RAM built-in; it's worth the extra investment.

Solving Printer Problems

Now, if speed is not your main concern right now because the printer's giving you a problem, there's a chance you can easily fix the bugger.

My Printer Doesn't Print!

If the printer doesn't print at all, make sure that it's on, and that it's on line ("on line" here means that its communication channel to the computer is open). To put a printer online, press its **On Line** button or switch.

If the printer's on but not responding, check for paper jams. Also, make sure it's not out of paper. If your cheap boss is making you share your printer with a coworker through one of those switch boxes, make sure that the switch is set to your PC. If everything else checks out, you should try printing with another program. If that works, then the first program is set up with the wrong printer. Use the **File**, **Print** or **File**, **Printer Setup** command to change the designated printer.

One Last Thing

Sometimes when your printer won't print, the villain is the printer cable. It's sad, but sometimes your cable will just go bad. So before you chuck your printer, consider replacing the cable instead. Or better yet, borrow a cable from a friend and see if your printer works with it.

My Printer Keeps Jamming!

If you're having problems with paper jams, there are several possible explanations. If your dot-matrix printer jams, you might be using paper that's too thick. If you're using regular tractor-feed paper, the problem could be that you've got the paper too taut (or too loose). Tractor-feed paper guides are those two rubber things with the pins that look like tank treads and hold on to your paper. If they're not stationary, then readjust the position of the guides so that your paper doesn't appear to have any warps or buckles in it, and that the paper is aligned correctly. Another possible problem with tractor-feed is that the paper guides may be gumming up. Be careful here: household oil such as 4-In-1 fixes the gumming up problem, but it can oil up your paper if you use too much.

A Problem That Looks Like a Paper Jam but Might Not Be

Now, if the document you sent to the printer prints on one line so that an entire page looks like one long very, very black stripe, you may think you have a paper jam when you don't. You see, when a dot-matrix printer reaches the end of a line, it waits for a signal telling it to drop down to the next line. The techies call this "line feed at carriage return," or CR/LF for short. The CR/LF signal can come from the printer, or from the computer, depending on how both devices are set up. If that signal doesn't come at all, then the dumb printer keeps printing over the same line. Likewise, if it comes from both the computer and the printer, then you get double-spaced print when you don't want it.

To solve the problem, adjust the line feed settings, both for your printer and for the program you're using. Your printer may have a line feed switch marked "CR/LF," or it may have a series of DIP switches (generally either in the back of the printer or below the print carriage). A DIP switch looks like a tiny light switch; push it up for on, or down for off. Look for help with the DIPs in Chapter 24, "Fiddling with Ports, IRQs, Addresses, and Such." In any case, once you change the line feed setting, you need to turn off your printer and then wake it back up again before it'll realize that you've changed anything. Now don't change the line feed unless you're sure you have a problem, because, well, your nice printer will suddenly start printing weird. If the printer only prints goofy in one program, then the printer setup in that program is probably the guilty party.

Laser Printer Jams

If you're having printer jams on a laser or inkjet printer, then again, the problem might be that the paper is too thick. If you're trying to use copier paper, don't. Laser paper is specially treated so that the printer can grip it properly. When buying reams of paper, look for thirty-pound bond (written "30# bond") or greater.

Also, there's a right way and a wrong way to load laser paper into your printer. When paper is pressed at the factory, it goes through hot rollers in one direction; the best path for that paper through the printer is the same direction. Check the package end for the arrow that tells you which direction you should load your paper. In addition, keep your laser paper in a dry, cool place—not in your damp basement.

I'm Having Trouble Printing My Envelopes and Labels!

If you're trying to print an envelope through your laser printer, read the manual. There's usually some short paper path you can use so your envelope doesn't come out looking like your dog chewed it. This paper path may be located above the regular path, or you may simply have to throw some switch to turn the regular path into a shortened one. Also, if you're trying to print labels on your laser printer, make sure that you get a style of blank labels that's specifically designed for laser printing, or else the labels will peel off and stick inside your printer. Also, just like envelopes, use the shorter print path for your labels.

You may also be wondering "which way is up"—in other words, should you put the envelope in face up, or face down? Well, the answer to that quandary is in your owner's manual. If it helps, my laser makes me put envelopes face up along the left-hand side of the paper feed.

The Printout Is Garbled!

If your printout looks as illegible as a doctor's prescription, the problem may be the cable. First of all, you want to be sure to place your printer only a short distance from your PC. Longer distances (and longer cables) tend to garble up the data unless that data's boosted by a printer-helper (otherwise known as a parallel line extender).

If your printer cable's loose, remove it. Check all the pins; if one of them is bent, gently bend it back. Then replace the cable and try printing again.

Another thing you might want to check when the printout is goofy is whether or not you selected the correct printer for your program. In most programs, you can get to the printer selection screen through the **Print** or **Printer Setup** command on the **File** menu. Just change the printer to the exact brand you're using and then try printing again. In Windows 3.1, you can change the default printer though the **Printer** icon in the **Control Panel**. In Windows 95, open the **Start** menu, select **Settings**, and then select **Printers**. To add a new printer, double-click on the **Add Printer** icon. To make an existing printer the default one, right-click on the printer's icon and select **Set As Default**.

If you have a PostScript laser printer, disregard anything you've ever read that told you that there's only one PostScript version. There are actually well over 12,000 or so versions. If your program has both a listing for your particular brand of printer and another listing for "PostScript printer," by all means choose your particular brand for your printer driver. Don't choose the latest and greatest PostScript driver on hand because you think it will improve your PostScript printing. In other words, only choose the new HP LaserJet 4 driver if you own a LaserJet 4; if you own an old Apple LaserWriter Plus, don't install the HP drivers.

If the only choice your program gives you is "PostScript," and your sparkling new PostScript laser printer is goofing up pages, you may need to check whether your printer has a "step-down" emulation mode for an older edition of PostScript. If that's the case, set it into emulation mode and choose the appropriate driver. For example, if your printer emulates an HP LaserJet III, then set it in emulation mode and choose the HP driver. Of course, if you've invested big bucks in a fancy schmancy page printer, you won't want to step it down to a lower mode just to get the thing to print. Solution: get the right PostScript driver for your printer from the manufacturer, an online service, BBS, or the Internet.

I Can Hardly Read My Printout!

If your printout is getting light, it may be time to change the printer's ribbon, inkjet, or toner cartridge. You can try increasing the print density setting in your program or printer driver before you replace your ribbon or other ink source. This makes your printouts darker, but if it's really time to change the ribbon, inkjet, or toner cartridge, then you won't see much improvement.

On the other hand, if even the lightest subject matter prints too dark, try decreasing the print density setting. If it's down to almost nothing and things are still dark, the problem may be that your program isn't properly creating gray-scale graphics for your printer. Word processors are especially prone to this problem whenever there is a graphic on the page. Make sure your program is properly configured to handle gray-scales. (If you're printing with PostScript, you should not have this problem under any circumstance, unless something's really, really wrong—like a toner leak.)

After you change the toner cartridge on a laser printer (this is best done in the dark, to avoid damaging the developer drum unit), use a dry, soft toothbrush or similar instrument to sweep off any loose toner from the components. In any event, your documents will be streaked for a while—this is just spilled toner dust working its way out. It's always a good idea to have the printer run a couple of test pattern pages to get the streaks out of the system. If your printouts are streaked after you've had the toner in for a long while, there may be a problem with the toner. Check to see if your cartridge is the type that you can reseal, and if it is, then try resealing the cartridge and changing it again. If that doesn't make a dent in the problem, your print drum may be going out, and you'll need to take your printer in to a registered service center for the necessary surgery.

My Printout Is Only Half There!

If your non-PostScript laser printer only prints part of your document, then you may be asking it to do too much. You see, for a laser printer to print a page, it first has to cram the image for that entire page into its memory. The imaging system has to have access to the whole page, otherwise nothing works. For most plain text pages, you only use a trickle of the printer's memory when you print these pages because the image is not very complex. Add a few fancy fonts, and it gets harder. Add a couple of fancy graphics, and it gets harder still.

Your only fix here is to either simplify your document by using less graphics and only one or two fonts, or by adding more memory to the printer. For some printers, this is about as fun as at-home ulcer surgery, so have your registered service representative take care of it for you.

If your PostScript laser printer only prints part of your document, then your problem may not be in your computer or your printer, but rather in the document itself. Try ejecting the page manually. If the page is incomplete, or the text is in 1200-point type rather than 12-point, then as a test, try printing out something else—anything other than the same document again. If that something else prints just fine, your problem may be with the PostScript instructions that your program is sending to your printer for that one document. This is a good time to see if there are any other types of PostScript drivers that work with your brand of printer.

Replacing a Ribbon in a Dot-Matrix Printer

If you need to replace the ribbon in your dot-matrix printer, first trot down to the computer store and buy one. Be sure to get the exact type that matches your printer. There are lots of differences here, so double-check the box before you buy. Don't take the old ribbon with you, because it's pretty messy and not really necessary as long as you know which brand of printer you have. Just jot down the ribbon's part number on a piece of paper and ask for that specific part number. If the store doesn't have your printer's own brand of ribbon, you can perhaps use another brand that's listed as a replacement for that specific part number.

The way you should replace your ribbon varies a bit from printer to printer, but here are the basic steps:

Printer Ribbon Types Vary...

Really old printers, such as a Star NX-10, don't have self-contained ribbon cartridges like modern printers. Instead, the ribbon is a simple spool; in fact, it's the same spool that's used in an IBM Selectric I *typewriter*. You thread one of these printer ribbons like you'd thread a reel-to-reel tape recorder.

Old printers aren't the only ones with ribbon installation instructions that vary from the following general directions. For example, the newer Epson Stylus uses an ink cartridge/print head combo kinda like an inkjet cartridge. To remove it, you flip a little lever which pops the whole gizmo out. You then replace it with another ink cartridge/print head combo, so you get a new print head every time you replace the cartridge.

1. First, lay out a couple of pieces of paper. Now, rip open the plastic bag and take the new ribbon out. Lay your new ribbon on the paper and save the bag for later.

2. Next, turn off the printer. You may be tempted to move the print head out of the way, but don't. Moving the print head manually can cause big, expensive problems—just check your printer's manual before you try it.

3. If there's a ribbon-release lever, flip it. Then press and hold the funny clips on either side of the ribbon and lift the ribbon out of the printer. Some models, such as certain Okidata printers, have a cartridge that is bolted down with three screws. Anyway, unlock the ribbon and take it out. Put the old inky thing into the bag you saved from the new ribbon.

Press the retaining clips and remove the old ribbon.

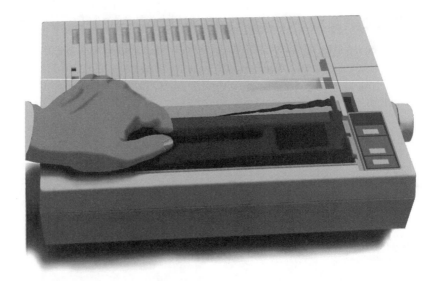

4. Position your new ribbon in place, but don't lock it in just yet. Thread the ribbon between the print head and the print shield.

5. Push down to lock the ribbon cartridge in place. If there are any retaining clips, make sure they snap in place too. Now, turn on the printer and test it out. If it doesn't work, take the ribbon out and start over. If it does work, go wash your hands; you've probably got lots of ink on them.

Make sure you insert the ribbon between the print head and the shield.

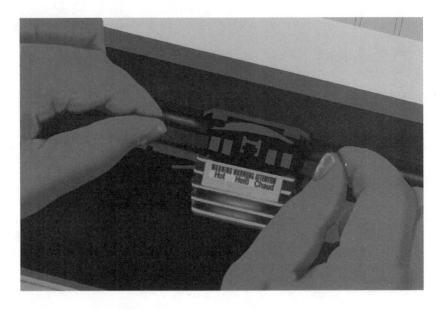

Replacing an Ink Jet Cartridge

Replacing an ink jet cartridge is not as messy as it sounds:

1. To replace the cartridge on your ink jet printer, you need to first unpack the cartridge itself. Then remove the seal that covers the bronze print head.

2. Lay out a piece of paper. Remove the old cartridge by pulling backwards at the top of the cartridge, away from the green dot on the cartridge holder. It should snap loose. Put the old inky cartridge on the paper for now.

Color Printers

If you have a color inkjet printer, its cartridges are contained in a single unit. Press the release clips and pop the cover, and you can replace individual cartridges as needed. You'll find that the black ink goes out more quickly than the other colors. Keep in mind that you don't have to replace all the colors each time; just replace empty cartridges as needed.

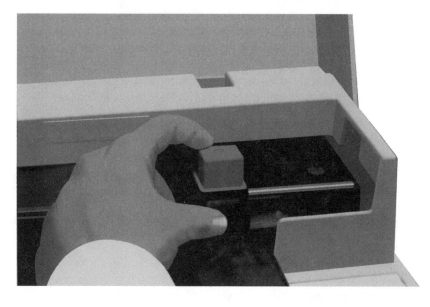

Remove the old cartridge by pulling from the top.

3. Take the new cartridge and position it so that the arrow points forward, toward the green dot on the holder.

4. Slide the cartridge into the holder and use your thumb to snap it into place.

5. Throw away your old cartridge.

Installing a Totally New Toner Cartridge

Most every laser printer manufactured today uses toner cartridges, rather than the old toner reservoirs the owner had to fill manually through a bottle and a straw. Installing a toner cartridge is kinda messy, but fairly simple.

1. First, lay out a few pieces of paper. Open the front or top of the printer. (Check in your printer's manual for the exact steps for opening your printer—there's usually some kind of "hood release" button.)

2. Grab the tab on the old cartridge and lift it up and out. Put the old icky cartridge on the paper for now. Take this opportunity to clean any dust you see inside the printer with a clean cloth and a bit of rubbing alcohol. Most manufacturers recommend cleaning the corona wire each time you change the toner—that's the wire that heats or "sets" the toner onto the paper as it comes out of the printer. Some manufacturers even give you a special brush just for that purpose that's kept on a conspicuous clip inside the printer. Also, some manufacturers expect you to change other parts near the toner, such as a felt filter. Check in the manual for how-tos, because this procedure varies a lot. Also, while you're working in there, don't touch anything that's still hot—if you're not sure what's okay to touch, check the manual.

3. The old, charred, burned-out toner powder is generally collected in a little bottle or reservoir. With newer toner cartridges, this reservoir is part of the cartridge itself; but with older printer models, the bottle actually rests in its own, separate cradle. If that's the case, lift out the bottle now, carefully. There should be a cap clipped to the side of the bottle. Peel off this cap and use it to close the bottle. Throw the bottle away and replace it with a new one from your toner cartridge kit.

4. Now for the truly yucky part. Open the foil wrapper holding your new toner cartridge. Some manufacturers make you reuse the distributor unit, so you may have to unsnap yours from the old toner cartridge and snap it onto the new one. Once you get the whole rigmarole together, continue with the next step.

5. Hold your toner cartridge at either end and gently rock the cartridge back and forth to distribute the toner gunk. Don't turn the thing upside down unless you don't mind wasting some toner to create a designer floor pattern.

6. Remove the seal that holds the toner in place. Slide the cartridge into the printer until it snaps into place. If there's a retaining thumb screw, twist until it's snug but not too tight. Close the panel. Turn your printer on and print a few test pages. Don't be surprised if you see some streaking; if you spilled a bit of toner earlier, it'll take a while to work itself out. Printing a few test pages usually takes care of the problem.

Slide the new cartridge in place.

Adding More Memory

Adding more memory to your laser printer keeps it from choking on the big complex graphics and fancy fonts in your documents. To add more memory to your laser printer, you first have to figure out whether or not it will fit. In other words, do you have an empty memory slot into which you can put more RAM? For example, my laser can take up to 4 M of RAM, but it only has one more slot to put it in. So if I try to upgrade from my current 2 M, I can either upgrade to a total of 3 M by buying the 1 M upgrade board, or to 4 M by buying the 2 M board instead. I can't buy 1 M now and another 1 M when I can afford it. Ugh.

The second thing you need to figure out is how to insert the RAM. Some laser RAM comes in nice, easy-to-insert SIMMs, while others come in funky hard-to-deal-with DRAM chips. And some (I'm not kidding here) actually come on boards that you need to *solder* to the printer's motherboard. Ugh.

So you better buy the exact RAM upgrade kit for the brand of printer you own, or you'll be stuck with a bunch of junk you can't do anything with. Don't try to steal RAM out of your PC to use in your printer—it just won't work.

The method for inserting your new printer RAM obviously varies by printer, but you'll find general information on inserting various RAM chips in Chapter 15.

But I Want a New Printer!

There are basically three different types of printers you can buy: dot-matrix, inkjet, or laser. Most printers print only in black and white, but color versions of all three types are available. Dot-matrix is the least expensive kind of printer to buy, and lasers are the most expensive. Keep in mind though that as the price goes up, so does the output quality.

Printers come in three basic types.

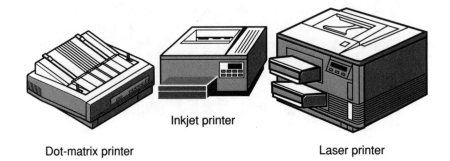

Inkjet printer

Dot-matrix printer

Laser printer

Shopping for a Dot-Matrix Printer

A dot-matrix prints by firing a series of pins against a ribbon, which in turn deposits tiny dots of ink on paper. These dots form images of letters, numbers, or graphics.

The quality of the output of a dot-matrix printer depends on the number of pins it uses. The more pins, the closer the dots, and the better the image. Dot-matrix printers use either 9- or 24-pin print heads. Get a printer with a 24-pin print head unless you really can't afford the extra $50 it'll cost you. (A 9-pin dot-matrix printer will cost around $140; a 24-pin dot-matrix printer will cost from $180 to $600.)

You can usually put your dot-matrix printer into *near letter quality* (NLQ) mode, where it will print somewhat better output than the regular *draft* mode, but this takes more than twice the time. In NLQ mode, your printed characters will look more like fonts than something on a football scoreboard. To compare print speeds between printers, compare the CPS (characters per second) speeds. They'll range anywhere from 250 CPS to over 1,000 CPS. Remember, though, these speeds are measured for draft quality; NLQ mode can slow things down to a range of 50 to 250 CPS.

Dot-matrix printers come in three sizes: standard width, mid-carriage, and wide carriage. Get a wide carriage only if you plan on printing really wide worksheets from Lotus 1-2-3 or Excel. A mid-carriage printer may be a bargain for you if you ever find yourself needing to print on a sheet of letter-size paper sideways (called "landscape mode" by those who are paid to name things poetically). You can also get dot-matrix printers that print in color, which is useful for graphs and presentations. Some so-called "color-capable" printers give you the option of buying them as black-and-white now, and upgrading them to full-color later with an upgrade kit that costs about $100.

Most dot-matrix printers use a tractor-feed—the paper you'll use comes with tiny holes along each side that fit onto rollers which feed the paper through the printer. For using stationery or ordinary paper, you'll want a printer that has a friction feeder built-in, which grips ordinary paper like a typewriter. You can generally switch between tractor-feed and friction-feed modes whenever you need to. Some dot-matrix printers—especially wide-carriage models—offer a cut sheet feeder option that works like the paper cartridge in a laser printer. A cut sheet feeder will hold half a ream of paper and feed it into the friction feeder automatically.

Dot-matrix printers don't produce high-quality work, but they're cheap, easy to use, and inexpensive to operate. On the downside, they aren't really great (actually, they're lousy) at printing graphics. However, if you need to print multi-part forms or, better yet, payroll checks, they're champs.

Shopping for an Inkjet Printer

An inkjet printer prints by spraying ink through a series of jets, forming tiny dots of ink on paper. Like a dot-matrix printer, these dots form printed characters or graphics.

Inkjet printers offer printout quality that's only slightly less classy than that of a laser printer, but for a few hundred dollars less. (Inkjets cost anywhere from $200 for mono-chrome to $600 for color.) They're also generally whisper-quiet. On the downside, they are slow and expensive to use—especially the brands that require you to buy specially coated paper.

The quality of the output of an inkjet printer is measured in dpi, or *dots per inch*. For a black-and-white inkjet printer, the resolution ranges from 300 to 600 dpi, depending on the brand you buy. A color printer usually has a higher resolution (for which you pay dearly) of around 720 dpi. The speed of an inkjet printer ranges from slow to slower: 3 ppm (*pages per minute*) to 6 ppm. (By comparison, laser printers print from 6 ppm to 17 ppm.)

Some inkjet printers can print in color. Others allow you to purchase a color upgrade kit later on. In addition, some inkjet printers, just like laser printers, come with built-in fonts. The advantage here is that when you use a built-in font, your PC doesn't have to download it to the printer. This saves time and allows your printer to handle more fonts and graphics on the same page without running out of memory.

How Much Memory Does It Come With?

When shopping for an inkjet printer, be sure to check out the amount of memory (RAM) it comes with—if any. Just like a laser printer, an inkjet printer will print faster if it has more on-board memory. Another handy option to consider is a sheet feeder that handles envelopes.

Shopping for a Laser Printer

A laser printer prints one page at a time. First, the printer assembles the page in memory and then uses its laser to "burn" an image of that page onto a drum. The drum rotates into the toner, picking up ink in the pattern of the image. The drum then brushes against the paper, transferring the inked image onto it. The paper passes near a heated wire on its way out, drying the ink and making the image permanent.

Sounds like science fiction, right? Well, expect to pay a bit more for all that technology. Still, non-color lasers are surprisingly affordable (from $350 to $1,000).

Printer Languages

Some laser printers come with *PostScript* capability; others are *HP-PCL-compatible*. PostScript is a printer language that translates a page into a series of math equations much harder than the ones that stumped you in high school. This enables PostScript printers to print scalable fonts and cool graphics without breaking a sweat.

HP-PCL is a printer control language created by Hewlett Packard, the leader in laser printers. Although not nearly as complex as PostScript, nor as adaptable to heavy-duty graphics, PCL's advantage is its speed. If you get an HP-PCL printer, you can sometimes add PostScript capability (if you need it) through a special expansion card, or through software.

Software-based PostScript interpreters such as GhostScript (available via the Internet) may substitute for a PostScript interpreter in your printer, giving you much nicer print quality and greater graphics capability. The downside of these interpreters is that you have to pretty much lead them by the hand all the way through the print process.

Like inkjet printers, the quality of a laser printout is measured in dpi, or *dots per inch*. Laser quality ranges from 600 to 1200 dpi. Laser printers have inkjet printers beat not only in quality but also in speed, which, like inkjet printers, is measured in ppm, or *pages per minute*. Laser print speed ranges from 6 ppm to 17 ppm.

If you want color, you might want to consider your proximity to a printing shop before you start shopping for a laser printer. That's because only big shots can afford color laser printers. However, some of the latest models by Hewlett Packard can be had for around $1,200, which is not as bad as the $10,000 price tag of the first color laser printers. Still, the average color laser printer price is around $3,000.

Like inkjet printers, laser printers also come with built-in fonts. You see, when you use a built-in font, the PC doesn't have to waste time downloading it from your PC. Also, using built-in fonts allows your printer to handle more fonts and graphics on the same page without running out of memory.

By the way, laser printers come in two types: parallel and serial, which describe not only how they transmit data to the PC, but also the kind of port to which you should connect them. Most printers use a parallel port, so you probably have one free—this makes a parallel printer your best choice. If you fall in love with a serial printer, just make sure that you have a serial port open so you can connect the printer once you get it home.

Installing Your New Printer

First, disconnect your old printer. Start by turning it off and removing any paper. Disconnect the cable and the power cord. Next, remove your new printer from its box. Be sure to look inside the printer and remove any shipping materials such as those silly foam peanuts—sometimes they're placed there in order to keep delicate parts from moving during shipping. But if you don't remove them all and you turn on the printer...well, you get the ugly picture.

Follow the steps earlier in this chapter for inserting the ribbon, inkjet, or toner cartridge. Follow the manufacturer's directions for inserting any other miscellaneous parts. For example, when I got my new laser, I had to insert the drum unit (yech).

Connect the printer cable to the back of the printer. Connect the other end to your PC, to the port with 25 holes in it (the parallel port). If your printer has a serial cable, connect the printer to the port with 25 pins at the back of your PC. With an adapter, you can connect it to a 9-pin serial port instead.

Connect your printer to the PC.

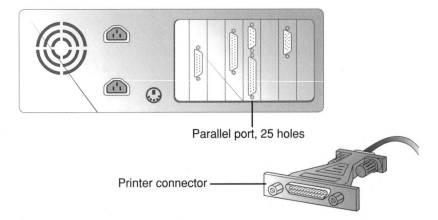

Parallel port, 25 holes

Printer connector ————

Some Setup Stuff

If you have a laser printer with a serial port (and that's the one you're using rather than the parallel port), then you'll probably have to push lots of buttons on its control panel to set nasty things like the baud rate, data bits, and parity. You'll find the control panel on the front of the printer. On a serial dot-matrix printer, you'll probably have to set at least the data bits and parity with DIP switches. (Baud rate is usually fixed.)

In any case, you'll need to make sure that Windows knows the COM port (serial port) into which you plugged your printer. See Chapter 24 for help. Also, if you plan on using your printer with DOS programs, you'll have to add the following two commands to one of your PC's configuration files, something called the AUTOEXEC.BAT:

> MODE *baud, parity, data bits, stop bit,* P
> MODE LPT1=*com port*

For example, if your printer prints at 9600 baud, with 8 data bits, 1 stop bit, and no parity on COM2, then your two commands would look like this:

> MODE 9600,N,8,1,P
> MODE LPT1=COM2

For help in dealing with the AUTOEXEC.BAT, see Chapter 22.

Plug the power cord in. Add paper and turn your printer on. Use the self-test mechanism to test your printer (that is, if it has one). This usually involves pressing several buttons on the printer's control panel at the same time. What you'll get is a page full of numbers and letters. If your printer doesn't have a self-test mode, don't fret; all it does is test whether the printer works at *all*, not whether it's set up to work with your computer. That'll come in a minute.

Once you connect your printer, you'll need to run its Setup program to install the printer *driver*. A driver, you may remember, is a program that helps your PC talk to a specific part, such as the printer. Run the Setup program even if you have the same kind of printer you had before; it'll update your printer driver to the latest version.

If you use any DOS programs and you've changed printer models, you'll need to change the printer selection in those programs in order to print from them correctly. In most cases, you can change the printer selection with the **File**, **Print** or **File**, **Printer Setup** command. Some programs make you rerun their setup to install a new printer, so check the manual for the program if you run into problems. If you plan on using the printer in Windows, you'll need to run the Windows Setup too. Turn to Chapters 22 and 23 for help. After you set up your printer, be sure to open one of your programs and print something as a test.

Emergency Diskette Alert! Get your emergency diskette in order before you run any setup program. See Chapter 12 for help.

Check This Out...

What Could Go Wrong

If the printer doesn't print at all, don't forget to turn it on and hit the **On Line** button.

If the printer chokes on your printouts from one program but not another, then you forgot to select the correct printer in the program with which you're having printing problems. Redo your setup process to select the right printer this time.

The Least You Need to Know

When your printer starts giving you problems, you don't always need to replace it. Instead, try these fixes:

➤ Free your PC from the burden of a slow printer by adding a print spooler or a print buffer.

➤ If your printer isn't printing, make sure that it's on and on line. Check for printer jams and make sure that the printer's not out of paper.

➤ If everything prints on one line, or if your printer prints double-spaced text, the line feed setting is either off or wrong.

➤ To print envelopes or labels on a laser printer, select the short print path. Also, be sure to get labels designed for use in a laser printer.

➤ If your printouts come out garbled, check the pins in the printer cable. If one of them is bent, gently bend it back. If your printer's garbling printouts in only one program, then you selected the wrong printer during the setup.

➤ If the printout is light, you may need to change the ribbon, inkjet, or toner. Sometimes you can adjust the print density to darken an image.

➤ To share a printer with several PCs, buy a switch box.

➤ If your printer refuses to print a document, or only prints part of it and then chokes, it may be that you're running out of printer memory. Add more memory to your printer if you can, or make the document simpler by removing excess fonts, using the fonts built into your printer (if there are any), or removing large graphics.

Part 3
Really Revving Up Your PC

In Part 2, you got your feet wet with some easy upgrades—things that don't require you to actually open up the PC. In this part, I'll lead you through what is otherwise the scary process of checking out what lurks below your PC's cover.

The pain will be worth it though, because in this part I'll show you how to rev up your PC with a new CPU, add another hard disk, add more memory, upgrade your video, add another floppy drive, and upgrade the power supply. Along the way, I'll show you the tricks that will keep you from frying yourself or your PC in the process.

Chapter 12

Before You Open That Box

In This Chapter

➤ Preparing for the fifth disaster of the day

➤ Backing up important stuff

➤ Getting ready for the big moment

➤ Uncovering your PC's innards

I'm not really much of a mechanic, but given enough time, I can usually take something apart and put it back together with only a few miscellaneous parts left over. For me, opening up a PC and playing around with its guts is about as much fun as getting my teeth cleaned. But when I absolutely have to, I perform upgrades to my PC, and even if you're not much of a mechanic either, you can too.

If you've upgraded a few things on your PC already, you probably started the same way I did—with some of the easy upgrades such as replacing your keyboard, mouse, or printer. If you want to upgrade anything else, the chances are pretty high that you'll need to actually open up your PC, and that can be pretty scary.

In this chapter, you'll learn how to do just that without frying either your PC or your nerves.

Don't Leave Home Without Your Emergency Diskette

Before you upgrade anything on your PC (or install a new program, for that matter), you should update your emergency diskette. With an emergency diskette, you'll be able to restart your PC should something (such as a bungled upgrade) prevent you from doing so. If something happens to prevent your PC from starting normally, just slip the emergency diskette into drive A and restart your PC from it.

What Do I Put on It?

An emergency diskette contains a copy of your operating system (DOS), the AUTOEXEC.BAT file, and the CONFIG.SYS file. When your PC first starts, it checks drive A for a copy of the operating system and the configuration files. If there isn't a diskette in drive A, then your PC boots with the copy of the operating system and configuration files that it finds on the hard disk. If something you do during your upgrade (such as changing the configuration files) accidently causes the hard disk not to work, you can put your emergency disk in drive A and start the computer that way.

Some newer PCs like to check both drive A and B for a copy of the operating system before going onto the hard disk. (How rude!) In any case, your emergency diskette will work on these PCs, too.

How to Create Your Emergency Diskette

To create an emergency diskette, grab a disk that fits drive A. Then format it by typing **FORMAT A: /S** at the DOS prompt.

After a bit of thinking, DOS copies the operating system to it and then asks you to supply a volume name for the diskette. This is the name that comes up when you list the contents of a directory, in the line that starts **Volume in drive A is...**, type something like **EMERGENCY** and press **Enter**. When DOS asks if you want to format another diskette, press **N** for No, thanks.

After you format the diskette, copy the configuration files onto it. If you're using DOS, just type these two commands, pressing **Enter** after each one:

```
COPY C:\AUTOEXEC.BAT A:
COPY C:\CONFIG.SYS A:
```

Check This Out...

Formatting Disks with Windows

If you use Windows, you don't have to jog out to a DOS prompt just to format a diskette.

If you have Windows 3.1: In File Manager, open the **Disk** menu and select **Format Disk**. Then click on the **Make System Disk** check box and let 'er rip.

If you have Windows 95: Open the Explorer, right-click on drive A, and select **Format**. Then, under **Other** options, click **Copy system files** and click **Start**.

Time Out! Check Your Config Files

Check your configuration files before you copy them to your emergency diskette. Use EDIT (or, if you're in Windows, use Notepad) to view the contents of the AUTOEXEC.BAT and CONFIG.SYS files. Make sure that all the programs, drivers, and files use a complete path, with a *drive letter* and *directory name*. For example, if you have this command in your AUTOEXEC.BAT:

MOUSE

and you boot your PC from drive A, DOS wouldn't be able to find the mouse driver because it assumes that the driver is located on the diskette (that is in drive A). The driver is actually hiding out in the root directory of the C drive. To fix all this confusion, you simply add the complete path (with the drive letter and the directory) to the MOUSE command, like this:

C:\MOUSE

By adding a complete path to all the programs and drivers in the AUTOEXEC.BAT and CONFIG.SYS files, DOS will be able to find all of them when you boot from drive A.

The other way to help your computer find all your drivers when you boot from drive A is to copy the necessary driver files to your emergency diskette in the first place. It's a bit more trouble than simply editing AUTOEXEC.BAT and CONFIG.SYS, but at least if your hard drive goes completely down, you may be able to restore some parts of your system (like your mouse). On the other hand, most of those drivers are of no use to you if the hard drive's down anyway, so you may not want to bother copying them to the emergency diskette. I copy the drivers to the diskette as long as I have the room.

Now, Back to Creating that Disk...

If you've compressed your hard disk using DriveSpace, use this command to copy that file onto the diskette as well:

> COPY C:\DOS\DRVSPACE.BIN A:

If you used DoubleSpace (the older version of the drive compression program) instead, well, use *this* command:

> COPY C:\DOS\DBLSPACE.BIN A:

If you use Windows, better save these files too:

> COPY C:\WINDOWS\WIN.INI A:
> COPY C:\WINDOWS\SYSTEM.INI A:

Finally, add these handy commands to your emergency diskette. If you replace your hard disk at any time, you'll need the FDISK and FORMAT commands to finish the job. The MEM command helps you check RAM, while SCANDISK helps you check the hard disk. MSD you already know; it's a diagnostic tool. RESTORE and UNDELETE can help you if an important file gets trashed, and SYS can restore your system should your hard disk become corrupted. The MSAV command helps you check for viruses when you suspect that they may be the reason your PC won't boot correctly.

> COPY C:\DOS\FDISK.EXE A:
> COPY C:\DOS\FORMAT.COM A:
> COPY C:\DOS\MEM.EXE
> COPY C:\DOS\SCANDISK.* A:
> COPY C:\DOS\MSD.* A:
> COPY C:\DOS\RESTORE.EXE A:
> COPY C:\DOS\UNDELETE.EXE A:
> COPY C:\DOS\SYS.COM A:
> COPY C:\DOS\MSAV.EXE A:

Check This Out...

Having Two Disks Is OK If you run out of space on your emergency disk, you can put the last set of files on another disk. You don't have to update these files ever, so having them on a separate diskette won't hurt.

Keep your emergency diskette in some handy place, where you can get to it quickly when you need it. No, not on top of your computer—it'll just get warped by the heat. Put it in your top desk drawer, or in your file cabinet.

Now That I Have One, What Do I Do with the Darn Thing?

To be useful, you have to keep *updating* your emergency disk. For example, when you install something new, such as a new CD-ROM drive or a new program, it'll probably make changes to your configuration files. So, this is what you do:

➤ *Before* you install a new program or a new toy, update your emergency diskette. Just use these commands (uh, they'll look vaguely familiar):

> COPY C:\AUTOEXEC.BAT A:
> COPY C:\CONFIG.SYS A:
>
> COPY C:\DOS\DRVSPACE.BIN A:
>
> COPY C:\WINDOWS\WIN.INI A:
> COPY C:\WINDOWS\SYSTEM.INI A:

> **Zip That Lip!** Don't compress (zip) the files to make them fit onto one diskette. You can't use compressed files unless you unzip them, which you won't be able to do if your hard disk is damaged and you're trying to use your emergency diskette to get out of your mess.

Techno Talk

➤ Now that you have an updated emergency diskette, install your new toy and then run its setup program. The setup will probably make changes to the configuration files to add a driver program, for example. Once the setup program is done, you should restart the PC so that any changes it might have made to the configuration files will be activated.

➤ If the changes caused by the setup program end up wrecking your life (and your PC), then undo them by copying your good, older versions of the configuration files from your emergency diskette back onto the hard disk. Use these commands:

> COPY A:\AUTOEXEC.BAT C:\
> COPY A:\CONFIG.SYS C:\
>
> COPY A:\DRVSPACE.BIN C:\DOS
>
> COPY A:\WIN.INI C:\WINDOWS
> COPY A:\SYSTEM.INI C:\WINDOWS

➤ If, on the other hand, the changes made by the setup program seem to work fine (your new toy is happy, you can still run all your programs) then repeat these commands to copy your updated CONFIG.SYS, AUTOEXEC.BAT, DRVSPACE.BIN, WIN.INI, and SYSTEM.INI onto your diskette.

```
COPY C:\AUTOEXEC.BAT A:
COPY C:\CONFIG.SYS A:

COPY C:\DOS\DRVSPACE.BIN A:

COPY C:\WINDOWS\WIN.INI A:
COPY C:\WINDOWS\SYSTEM.INI A:
```

Go Back and Get the CMOS

If you skipped over Chapter 4, go back and print out a copy of your CMOS information—you know, the stuff that tells your computer where and what your hard drive is—before you continue. Not having this could literally cripple your computer if the CMOS ever gets lost.

Now, Back Up Your Data

Making a backup of your data is like wearing a seat belt when you drive. It's uncomfortable, and sometimes you can get by without one, but if you ever slam into a wall at 60 mph, you'll be glad you took the time to buckle up.

So before you perform any surgery on your system, make sure that you've got backup copies of your important data, such as important reports, letters to your lawyer, tax filings, and so on. That way, if the patient dies on the table, you can always restore the important parts once you get the body working again.

Backing Up with DOS

To back up all your data using a DOS version prior to DOS 6 (such as DOS 3.3, 4.0, or 5.0), type this at the prompt:

```
BACKUP C:\*.* A: /S /L
```

and press **Enter**. You see a prompt to insert a diskette into drive A. Do that and press **Enter** again. Eventually, DOS asks you for another diskette, and so on. Make sure you actually insert a different diskette; if you keep the same one in the drive, DOS will write over the top of its data and ruin the whole backup. While DOS is doing its thing, amuse yourself by labeling each diskette as you go along.

Bummer

Make sure that you have enough diskettes to finish the job. Even though DOS will format diskettes for you as it goes along, this adds an enormous amount of time to an already tedious task. So get your diskettes ready by formatting them before you start.

How many will you need? That depends on how large your hard disk is, and on how many of its files you're planning on backing up. But if you're using high-density diskettes, they'll hold about a megabyte or so.

If you have at least DOS 6.0, then there's an easier way to go about this. At the prompt, type **MSBACKUP** and press **Enter**. If you've never done a backup before (shame, shame), MS Backup will perform some tests; get yourself two diskettes of the same size and density as the ones you'll be using for the big backup. Just do whatever it says, and, when it's done, you end up at the main screen. Click on **Backup**.

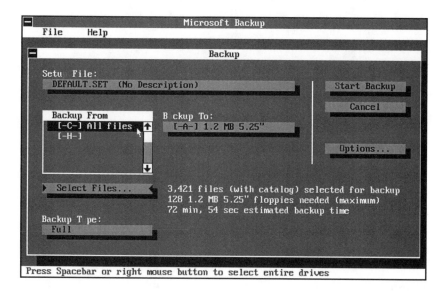

MS Backup makes it easy to select what you want to back up.

From here, you can select what you want to back up and skip over things you already have copies of, such as your programs (which you still have on installation diskettes). Start by clicking on drive **C** in the Backup From box. Select the drive you want to backup to (such as drive A) in the Backup To drop-down list box. If you don't want to back up certain directories, just click the **Select Files** button and then click on the files you don't want to back up. (A check mark indicates the ones you will back up.) Click **OK** to return to the Backup screen and then click **Start Backup**. You do the diskette shuffle with MS Backup too—just pop in diskettes when it asks for them.

Backing Up with Windows 95

If you use Windows 95, open the **Start** menu, select **Programs**, select **Accessories**, select **System Tools**, and then finally, select **Backup**. (If you didn't install Backup when you installed Windows 95, then hang your head and go install it. Then come back here to do your backup.) Again, if this is the first time you've done a backup, you'll have to get past a bunch of rigmarole (just do what the screen tells you to do) before you finally get here:

Using MS Backup with Windows 95.

To back up everything, open the **File** menu and select **Open File Set**. Then select the **Full System Backup Set** and click **Open**.

If you don't want to waste time backing up silly program files, double-click on the check box in front of the drive you want to back up. This takes a while; Windows has to go through and put a check mark in front of all the files. You can tell Windows which files to ignore by clicking on them one at a time to remove the check mark.

When you're done selecting files, click **Next Step>**. Click on the drive you want to back up to (such as drive A or if you're lucky, your tape drive) and click **Start Backup**. If it asks, type in a name for your backup set, like **Important Files Only**, and click **OK** to finally get the backup under way. Every so often, while you're backing up to diskettes, MS Backup will ask you to switch diskettes in the drive; each time

Sole Heir If you don't like Windows 95's Backup program, you can buy Arcadia Backup for Windows 95, the one and only alternative.

you do, you don't have to hit Enter, just let it go. Of course, if you're backing up to tape, then you won't have to switch diskettes. When it's done (in a year or two), click **OK**.

The Tools of the Trade

Before you attempt an upgrade, you'll need to gather some tools together so you can successfully get your PC apart. You'll need a small flat-head screwdriver as well as small and medium Phillips-head screwdrivers.

If you don't mind looking a little nerdy, get yourself a set of cool computer tools. You can find them at any computer store. They include extra tools for removing chips and retrieving dropped screws—and, at about $20, they won't break your wallet. They generally include those strange foreign "nuthead" screwdrivers (yes, that's what they're really called) that look like a combination screwdriver and mini-socket wrench. For some PC tower cases, you may need a nuthead screwdriver to take the cover off or maybe just a nutty head. Make sure that your tools have non-conducting handles made of hard plastic, PVC, or ceramic.

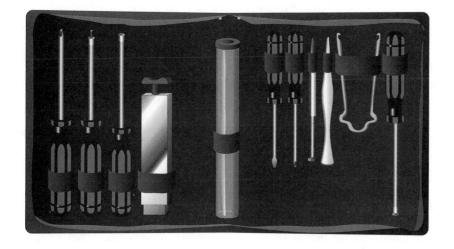

Get yourself a set of cool tools.

Grab a couple of empty pill bottles, 35mm film cans, or even an old egg carton; any of these containers makes a great gathering place for the various screws you'll encounter.

You may also want to grab a flashlight (it gets pretty dark in there), a box (for storing spare computer parts), and a can of compressed air or dust remover. (Hey, while it's open, you might as well do some cleaning.)

One thing you'll find pretty indispensable is paper and a pencil. You can write down the switch and jumper settings of any card you remove in case your fingers fumble at some point and accidently change one of them. A switch, by the way, is like a tiny light switch, and a jumper is a set of pins connected by a removable gizmo called a shunt. You'll learn how to set switches and jumpers in Chapter 24. Paper's also handy for writing down part numbers, cable orientation and placement, or any other info you find important. (I've saved some space along the margins here for you...)

Opening Pandora's Box Without Frying Yourself or Your PC

Opening your PC's system unit for the first time is a bit like digging up Al Capone's vaults. There's a lot of anticipation, maybe a little fear, and just when you begin to think you should put on something bulletproof, you find out there's nothing in there that can kill you. All this fuss over nothing may ruin your image among friends; that can happen—just ask Geraldo. You'll soon learn that being a bit scared (and therefore, a bit more careful) is better in the long run than tons of confidence.

To open up your PC successfully, all you really need is a few screwdrivers and a bit of common sense.

The 12 Steps to Success

1. **Prepare for disaster** Before you do anything, I mean anything, you should back up your data and update your emergency diskette. Remember, anything you don't save, you should be prepared to *lose*. Also, make sure you have a copy of your PC's CMOS data. See Chapter 4 for help.

2. **Read the instructions that came with your new part** The documentation may actually give you some real information, such as how to get your exact brand of PC to talk to your new part. If it tells you to check out a text file on an enclosed diskette, then do it. Type **TYPE A:README.TXT | MORE** at the DOS prompt to read the file. (The TYPE command tells DOS to display the contents of the README.TXT file, and MORE tells it to pause when a screen is full so you can actually read it. Press **Enter** to move to the next page of the file.)

3. **Turn off your PC and unplug it** No, it's not enough to just turn the darn thing off. Un-plugging the PC from the wall ensures that there's absolutely no possible way that you could plug something into the computer while it's on. And believe me, you really don't want to do that.

You Can Print It If you'd rather print out the README.TXT file, type this at the DOS prompt instead: TYPE A:README.TXT > PRN.

Also, remove any other plugs, such as the one that connects your monitor, modem, or printer to the PC. (You'll probably have to unscrew it first.)

4. **Clear the area** All those parts have got to go somewhere, so make room on your desk for them before you find yourself struggling to keep your hold on a 20 pound monitor. Use all the magic at your disposal to remove excess electricity from your workplace: stand on a static free tile or linoleum floor, use a wooden desktop to work on, touch a doorknob to remove your own static, and so on. Also, place both your PC and yourself on some surface that doesn't conduct static electricity, such as a wood, formica, concrete, plastic, or linoleum. Don't stand (or put the PC) on carpet!

5. **Unscrew the cover** You probably need a screwdriver for this, and your film cans, egg carton, or whatever other clever device you plan on using to corral the screws. Be sure to only undo the screws holding the cover on. Don't do like I did one time and accidently unscrew the power supply. Just stick to the screws along the outer edge of the cover. This figure helps:

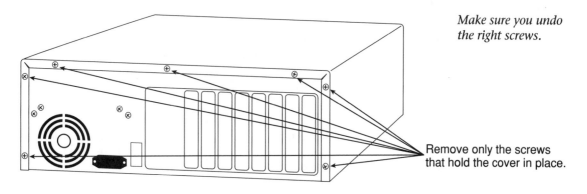

Make sure you undo the right screws.

Remove only the screws that hold the cover in place.

6. **Remove the cover** To pull off most desktop unit covers, you simply slide the cover backwards and then lift it straight up. With some other PCs, you may have to do the exact opposite—slide the cover forward and then lift it up. For some of the older IBM-brand PCs, there may be hinges so that the cover doesn't actually come off but instead lifts up. On a tower unit, either one side comes off, or the entire "n" shaped

155

cover lifts straight off. You may have to tug a little, but be careful not to pull any cords loose while you're tugging. Put the case somewhere where you won't trip over it. There may be a plastic back panel on your tower PC that you can pull off first—there are no screws to it, so it should just snap right off.

Check for Hatch Releases or Locks

A hatch release secures some covers; you press this hatch release in order to remove the cover. Keys lock other covers; you have to turn the key to the "unlock" symbol (which looks kinda like an open padlock) in order to remove the cover.

7. **Ground yourself** Touch something metal, such as your PC's cover, to discharge static electricity. Don't dance (or otherwise move your feet) while you're working. *Don't touch anything inside the PC until you're sure that you're grounded.* After you discharge yourself, no matter how nervous you get, don't scratch your head or shuffle your feet. It takes a minimal amount of static to zap just about any part of your PC—I'm talking less static than it takes to zap a friend—so don't move when working on a PC, or, just before touching something inside the PC, discharge any static by touching a file cabinet, a coworker, or whatever.

Sure-Fire Static Protection

Some computer stores sell a "ground wire" that you place over your wrist to prevent you from building up any static while you work. You can also buy a static mat that does the same thing; you just stand on it to avoid static build up.

8. **Get that dust outta there** Big, flaky, dusty things in your expansion ports can literally short them out if you plug something new in and push them deep into the connector pins. Don't use furniture polish or anything you ordinarily use to dust your candelabra and other valuables. Don't use a cloth either. Instead, go to your local computer store and pick up a can of dust-blasting spray. It has one of those thin straws like on a WD-40 can; but rather than squirting lubricant, this straw blasts a powerful spray of air that literally eats dust without touching it. It's not terribly expensive, but replacing your motherboard is.

   You may also want to clean the edge connector of any new expansion card you want to install. Use some rubbing alcohol and a Q-tip.

9. **Out with the old, in with the new**   To remove an expansion card, unplug any cables attaching it to the motherboard or to any of your peripherals. Unscrew the retaining screw and put the little guy somewhere where he can't roll away. (Nuthead screwdrivers take off retaining screws in a flash.) Grip the card at the top with both hands and pull straight up.

To install a new expansion card, find an open slot that's of the proper type. (Confused about expansion slots? See Chapter 3.) Unscrew the retaining screw holding the slot cover in place. Again, put the screw somewhere where you won't lose it. Remove the slot cover and hang it as a decoration in your cubicle. (Don't throw it away; if you ever take the card back out, you need it again.) Hold the card at the top with both hands and gently position the edge connectors on the bottom of the card over their slots. Gently rock the card until it slips into place. You may have to apply just the right amount of downward pressure to insert it.

Retaining screw

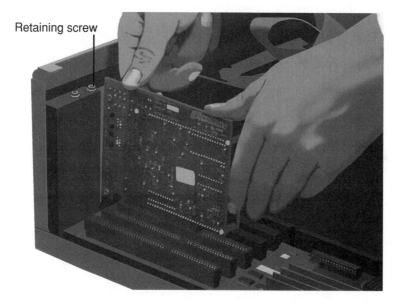

Push the expansion card gently into place.

If you're installing a chip instead, such as a RAM chip, make sure that the little guy's legs are straight, and not bent. Then position the chip's legs over the corresponding holes on its holder. Gently press the chip into place, but don't force it—you could break one of its legs.

10. **With the cover still off, plug the PC back in, turn it on, and check to see if your new toy works**   Yes, with the cover *off*, you should test to see if you properly connected the new part, so you can quickly correct it if it isn't, *before you put the cover back on*. If something's wrong, you'll usually hear a few beeps. If that happens,

157

turn the PC off, unplug it again, reconnect things, and then fire it back up to test your adjustments.

11. **Close up the box**   Repeat step 6, only backwards. Once the Humpty Dumpty's back together again, plug everything back in and start up the PC.

12. **Introduce the computer and your new toy to each other**   With most new parts, you'll have to run some kind of setup program which comes on some diskette. The setup will make changes to the configuration files so that your computer can talk to the new part. See Chapter 22 for help.

    If you run Windows, see Chapter 23 for additional setup things you may have to do, as well.

What Could Go Wrong

Here's a quick checklist of things to watch out for:

➤ Before you begin work, remove potential disasters from your work area such as cups of coffee or cans of soda.

➤ Unplug your PC and ground yourself before you touch anything.

➤ Unlike a mattress tag, no one's going to arrest you if you remove a tags on any chips that you find, but if you do, you may lose some irreplaceable bit of information. Also, some tags are actually put there to *protect* a chip from damage.

➤ Even if you bought your new CD-ROM and sound card together, you should only try to install one thing and get it to work before you attempt to install something else.

Chapter 13

Getting Your PC to Go Fast

In This Chapter

➤ Replacing your PC's brain

➤ Adding a math nerd

➤ Chucking the whole thing and replacing the motherboard instead

➤ Jump-starting a dead battery

➤ Updating your old BIOS

Sometimes the only thing wrong with an old PC is its speed. Well, the speed of a PC is largely controlled by its "brain" or CPU. So by upgrading the CPU, you can make your PC "think" faster.

In this chapter, you'll learn how to do just that, along with other "mind-boggling" operations such as adding a math coprocessor and upgrading your BIOS.

Okay, What Am I Getting Myself Into?

You'll learn about the various types of CPUs available in just a minute, but first, I thought I'd let you in on exactly what you can expect with a CPU upgrade. To upgrade, you'll either remove the old CPU and actually replace it with the new chip, or (if the CPU is a surface-mounted CPU and can't be removed) you'll snap the upgrade chip on top of your old chip. Sometimes your motherboard includes what's known as an OverDrive socket, into which you push your new OverDrive chip—here, you don't touch the original CPU at all.

There are a few things that threaten to limit your upgrade parade. First, you have to find an upgrade chip that's compatible with your current CPU. Most upgrade chips are made to replace old Intel or AMD chips, so if your PC uses something different, it may be more difficult to find a compatible CPU upgrade.

Also, there are limits to what a CPU upgrade can accomplish. For example, you can upgrade a 286 PC to a 486, but not to a Pentium, or even the fastest version of a 486. You see, your CPU sends data back and forth over a bus—a kind of electronic highway that the PC uses to send data back and forth. The size and speed of this bus limits what even a faster CPU can do in your PC. In other words, your CPU can think fast, but it still talks to real slow, real stupid PC parts. So don't expect a CPU upgrade to take your 286 or even a 386 up to a Pentium level.

Some computers are equipped to make upgrading a CPU easy; there may be a quick release lever so getting the old CPU out is simple, or an extra socket for the upgrade chip. Other PCs are made to make upgrading darn near impossible, with a soldered in or surface-mounted CPU chip that you can't get out at all. With these, if you're lucky, you can find a compatible CPU upgrade chip such as the Evergreen REV to 486 chip, which will snap over the top of the existing CPU. If you can't find a compatible upgrade and your CPU is soldered to the motherboard, you may be forced to upgrade the motherboard itself (complete with a fast CPU). This isn't as horrible as it sounds, because upgrading the motherboard also upgrades the bus, resulting in a PC that is much faster overall.

Also, when you upgrade a CPU chip, you may have problems with overheating, especially if you upgrade to a Pentium. Consider adding an extra fan—there are plenty that snap on top of the CPU itself, cooling it as it works.

Controlling the Heat

Many chips have protruding clips on top called heat sinks. They dissipate the heat generated by fast chips so they don't overheat. You may need to attach a heat sink to your new upgrade chip, that is, if the manufacturer recommends it. In other cases, you may want to get a fan card (an expansion card that's basically a fan) to help with the heat problem. When you order your CPU upgrade, just ask what the dealer recommends.

Finally, some systems don't take a clock-doubling upgrade very well, because it throws off the timing of their BIOS. You remember clock doubling from Chapter 3, don't you? That's where the CPU has an internal clock that runs twice as fast as the motherboard clock. Sometimes this doubling-thing doesn't match up too well with the internal clock, so an upgrade fails. Fortunately, upgrading your clock chip and the BIOS fixes this problem.

Um, Do I Need a Math Coprocessor, Too?

Hardly anyone *likes* to do math, or at least, if they do, they don't like to admit it. Well, math is not a lot of fun for your CPU either. You see, when a CPU stops to do some math calculation, it usually takes a long time. For this reason, a special chip called a *math coprocessor* was designed to take the burden of heavy math calculations off of the CPU. This math coprocessor was placed into a special slot next to the CPU.

In the old days, hardly any PCs came with a math coprocessor already installed; you usually had to fork out the extra bucks (about $70) for one and put it in yourself. So if you own a PC with a 286, 386, or 486SX CPU and you do large spreadsheets, keep giant databases, or play around with complex graphics (which take tons of math calculations to display), then adding a math coprocessor is worth the trouble. (Yes, in case you're wondering, there is a math coprocessor for even a lowly 8088 CPU, but if that's what you've got, you shouldn't bother upgrading the PC at all.)

One piece of good news, though: if your PC has a 486DX (not SX) or a Pentium CPU, you don't have to worry about this math coprocessor business. That's because Intel and the other CPU makers finally got smart and built the math coprocessor function into their CPU chips. The built-in math coprocessor still handles math separately from the main functions of the CPU so it doesn't slow anything down, but you no longer have to buy a separate chip.

Just What Coprocessor Do I Need?

If you want to add a math coprocessor, here's the number of the chip you'll need to get:

Your CPU	Math Coprocessor That Goes with It
8086	8087*
8088	8087*
286	287
386SX	387SX
386DX	387DX
386SL	387SL
486SX	487SX (now called the DX2/OverDrive chip)

* If your PC has an 8086 or an 8088 CPU, don't bother adding a math coprocessor, because upgrading such a PC is mostly a waste of time. Consider starting over with a new PC—it'll be cheaper and easier in the long run, and you'll be happier with the result.

By the way, you won't be able to walk into a computer store and just pick up a math coprocessor. Most computer stores don't stock them. So you'll probably have to order it. Just be sure to tell the clerk what CPU you have now, and its speed.

Mind the Megahertz!

It doesn't do any good if your math coprocessor goes nuts and starts calculating its head off at a speed that's too fast for your CPU. So if your CPU is a 386 25MHz, then you'll need to match it with a 25MHz 387 math coprocessor. If a 25 MHz 387 math coprocessor isn't available, you can use a faster math coprocessor in a pinch—although I don't know why you'd bother, because the CPU can't take advantage of the fact that the math coprocessor is faster. However, *under no circumstances can you try to use one that's slower*. So if a 387 25MHz isn't available, you cannot substitute a 20 MHz one instead. Check the package when your math coprocessor arrives to make sure that you ordered the right one.

Shopping for a New Brain

Back in Chapter 3, you learned about the various types of CPUs and how fast they don't go. Here's a recap:

CPU	Comment
8088, 8086	These two chips are so old, they're practically dead.
80286	Found in old AT-type PCs.
80386	Found in second-generation AT-type PCs, dating from 1985 to 1991.
80386DX	A true 386.
80386SX	Slower version of a 386, built for AT motherboards
80386SL	386 designed for laptops.
80486	Found in third-generation AT-type PCs, dating from 1989 to present.
80486DX	A true 486.
80486SX	Slower version of a 486.
80486DX2	Clock doubler; double the speed of equivalent 486. If sold as an upgrade, then Intel calls it an OverDrive chip.
80486DX4	Three times the speed of equivalent 486

CPU	Comment
80486SL	486 designed for a laptop; no longer sold. New 486 chips destined for laptops are billed as "SL-enhanced."
80586	Intel calls their version of this chip the Pentium. Introduced in 1993.
Pentium OverDrive	Upgrades a 486 to a Pentium (586).
Pentium Pro	To be introduced late 1995. The sixth generation in the series (formerly called "P6").

Popular makers of upgrade CPUs include Intel, Cyrix, Evergreen, Kingston, and Improv Technologies (creators of the Make-It 486 chips). CPU upgrades are available for 286, 386, 486, and even Pentium chips. (For an IBM PS/2, you'll need an IBM-brand upgrade chip.) The kind of upgrade chip you can get is limited by the original chip with which you're starting. That's because the replacement chip needs to fit in the same

What's the Cost? A new CPU costs anywhere from $125 to $350. Most cost about $200.

slot and work with the parts already in your PC. So you need to shop for a replacement chip specifically rated for your original CPU. For example, the chip you need to upgrade from a 386DX 33 MHz is different than the one you need to upgrade from a 386SX 33 MHz or even a 386 DX50 MHz CPU. You should also make a note of the brand of CPU your PC is using, because upgrade chips are designed to replace specific brands, such as Intel or AMD. So before you go shopping, you better know *exactly* what kind of CPU your PC actually has: its brand (such as Intel), its type (such as 386), and its speed (such as 20 MHz.)

When you look at your CPU, note how it is mounted. Some CPUs are mounted (kinda glued) to the mother-board. This makes upgrading difficult, if not impossible—don't give up hope, because there are a limited number of upgrade chips designed to clip onto surface-mounted CPUs. Thankfully, most CPUs have tiny pins on the bottom that fit exactly into tiny holes in a black square holder-thing on the motherboard. To upgrade these babies, you just pull them out and replace them with a chip that fits. By the way, do you see two extra rows of holes around your CPU? If so, then your 486 CPU is fitted

What's a 586? Chip manufacturers other than Intel aren't allowed to use its registered "Pentium" trademark, so their "fifth-generation" upgrade chips are instead called 586 chips.

with a socket for a Pentium chip. This is good to know. If you don't see the extra rows of holes, do you see an empty blue socket nearby? That's an OverDrive socket, designed for an OverDrive upgrade chip. If you don't have one, then you can't upgrade with the OverDrive brand of chips.

If you have to open up your PC to tell for sure, then you should do that. However, most manufacturers paste the PC's type of CPU on the front of the system unit, such as Gateway 2000 4DX-66, which means that your CPU is a 486DX 66MHz.

Performing Brain Surgery (Replacing the CPU)

Replacing the CPU in your PC is relatively easy, that is, if you try not to think about all the things that can go wrong. First of all, make sure that you buy the right chip! Using the wrong upgrade chip can damage your PC. So open up your computer and take a real long look at the CPU (see Chapter 12 if you need help getting it open). It's usually the largest chip on the motherboard, marked with something like 80386 across the top. Intel-brand CPUs have the big lower-case "i," if not the word "intel" itself written on them. Some old 286 chips look just like everything else, so if you need help locating the thing, pull out your good old manual. It should show you the CPU's exact location.

Uh, My CPU Seems to Be Glued In Place

While you have the computer apart, check the CPU carefully. If it is soldered permanently to the motherboard, or if it's surface-mounted so all you see is chip and no socket, you probably can't upgrade it. True, Evergreen Technologies does offer a few chips designed to clip onto a surface-mounted CPU, so there's hope. But in a lot of cases, your best bet is to see if you can get a replacement motherboard that will fit your PC's case and work with all your other parts. Actually, replacing the motherboard isn't hard, but it's also not a lot of fun because you have to take all the things off it and then reconnect them to the new motherboard—feel free to have someone at a service center replace the motherboard for you if you're feeling at all uneasy about doing it. If you're game to try it yourself, I give you how-tos later in this chapter.

Next, write down the chip's name and manufacturer. You also need to make a note of the chip's speed, such as 33 MHz. (The chip label won't have the little "MHz," but the speed is generally the last few digits of the chip title.) Take this information with you when you go to the computer store to get your upgrade chip. Make the salesperson swear a thousand times that you've got the right chip. Then go find somebody else and make them swear, too.

Once you have the right chip, follow the steps in Chapter 12 for opening your PC. *Follow all the steps,* such as backing up your data, copying down your CMOS information, and updating your emergency diskette. Remove any parts that stand in the way of the CPU. Make a note of what you remove and where the cables go, so you can get everything back together again. A perfectly safe thing to do is mark on the ribbon cables with a magic marker—something simple like "HD" and an arrow pointing to the hard drive—before you unplug any cables.

Put It in OverDrive!

Keep in mind that some 486 and Pentium PCs come with a blue OverDrive socket which sits next to the CPU. If that's the case, you won't have to worry about actually removing the old CPU. Just leave it there; the new CPU will override it electronically.

Also, some other chips are designed to plug into the top of your existing surface-mounted chip, thereby overriding it. The instructions that come with these kinds of chips will provide additional details on how to clip it onto your existing chip.

Now, before you touch your old CPU, *make sure you discharge any static electricity!* Touch your coworker, a metal table, or whatever, then stand still so you don't build up any more static. Before you begin to remove the CPU, take a minute to look at it. You'll see a notch or a dot at one corner. Use your pencil and paper to make a note of the orientation of this notch. You'll see why in a minute.

If your PC comes with a ZIF (zero insertion force) socket, thank your lucky stars, because all you have to do to get the old chip out is to pull the lever back.

Careful...
Don't touch the CPU's legs (connector pins) because that can damage the chip, and if you ever needed to reuse the CPU someday, you wouldn't be able to.

If your PC doesn't have a ZIF socket, then it'll take a little more work to get the old CPU out. Your upgrade kit probably came with a tool, called a chip remover, for prying the CPU out. If your kit didn't come with a chip remover, then use a small flat-head non-magnetic screwdriver. With your tool, gently pry up each side of the CPU *just a tiny bit.* Don't try to remove the socket, which is flat against the motherboard; just remove the CPU, which sits inside the socket. Repeat this process several times, lifting the CPU just a little bit higher with each pass. Eventually, you'll be able to lift the CPU out of its socket. Don't be tempted to rush this process; doing so will damage the CPU and possibly the socket.

It's Wired!

If your CPU uses an LCC socket (Leadless Chip Carrier—you know, for CPUs that don't use pins but instead have tiny gold leads on the bottom), then you'll find two funny wires holding it in place. Remove one wire at a time by placing one hand at each end and gently pushing the wire to the closest edge. Remove the second wire the same way, and you can lift the chip right out.

With a ZIF socket, removing a CPU is easy.

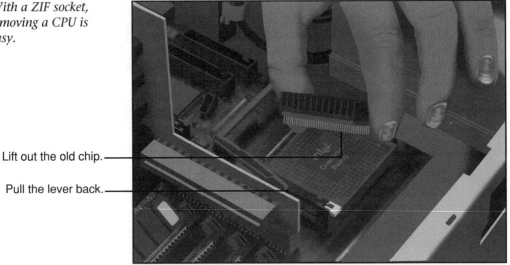

Lift out the old chip.

Pull the lever back.

Once you remove your old CPU, it's time to put in the new one. First, take a good look at the empty socket. One corner of the socket will be notched or beveled in some way, to indicate the location of pin 1. You have to match the notch or bevel on the replacement chip with the notch on the socket.

Once you correctly align the chip, make sure that you line up all the pins with all the holes. Press down on the chip very carefully. If your PC has a ZIF socket, the chip should fit in pretty easily. If you have a regular socket, then you'll have to press down pretty hard to get the chip in, but be careful not to bend your motherboard—you could break it. Put something like a magazine or a stack of newspaper under the motherboard to absorb some of the shock if needed. (That's right, there's actually some space between the bottom of the motherboard and the bottom of the PC case. Just slip a few sheets of newspaper in there to "stiffen" the motherboard so it won't bend down if you press too hard to get the CPU in.) If you feel like you're pressing too hard and that you might break the motherboard, you can always stop and take the thing into a service center for somebody else to finish.

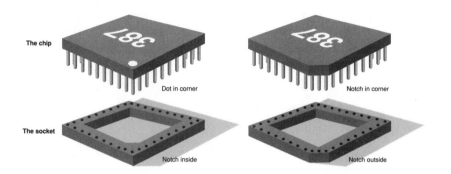

The chip

Dot in corner   Notch in corner

The socket

Notch inside   Notch outside

Match up the notch on the socket with the one on your CPU.

If you have a ZIF socket, be sure to swing the lever back into its original position. Then plug your PC back in; it's time to test the new CPU.

What Could Go Wrong

If your new CPU doesn't work, turn the PC off and check for any stray legs hanging out of the socket. If so, remove the CPU, gently bend the leg back, and try inserting it again.

Techno Talk
blah blah
blah bla
ah bl
b

Upgrade Software

Some chips come with upgrade software that you must run to make the chip work. Your PC should boot fine, but then you'll need to run the software to test the chip and upgrade your system. Follow the steps in the upgrade packet, and you should be okay.

If the PC starts with a boot diskette, but you've lost your hard drive (in other words, you can't switch to C:), you'll have to reenter your CMOS info. See Chapter 24, "Fiddling with Ports, IRQs, Addresses, and Such," for help.

Once you're sure you've got everything right, put your PC back together and get back to your life.

167

Helping Your PC Cheat at Math—Adding a Math Coprocessor

Compared with replacing your CPU, adding a math coprocessor is relatively easy. First, make sure that you get the right coprocessor for your system. If you need to, open up your PC and check out the exact type of CPU that you have and then get the math coprocessor that matches that model. You do have a choice of brands here, but not of types; there's only one that works with your installed CPU (see the section "Just What Coprocessor Do I Need?," earlier in this chapter, to find out which one to buy).

When you're ready, open up your PC, following all the steps in Chapter 12. Be sure to back up your data, update your emergency diskette, and so on.

Look around and locate the empty socket for the math coprocessor. It is probably the only empty socket on the board. You may find other empty sockets—in pairs—for extra ROM chips. Ignore these imposters. You're looking for a single empty socket, usually very close to the CPU.

If you have to remove a thing or two to clear a path to the coprocessor socket, go ahead. If you need help removing something, check out the appropriate chapter in this book. As you whack your way through the PC forest, take a second to make a note about what you're removing and where it goes. Also note any switch settings on the part before you remove it, in case you accidently knock the switches out of position.

Now, before you touch the coprocessor, discharge any static you may have built up by touching a door knob, a file cabinet, or a coworker. Don't touch the computer—that's not where you want the static to go.

Examine the chip and make sure that its little legs are bent at a 90 degree angle to the chip. If you need to, gently realign any lazy legs. An easy way to do this is to gently press one side of the chip against the top of your desk. Flip the chip over and repeat.

Line up the notch or blunt corner on the chip with the same notch, corner, or dot on the processor socket. Some sockets have an extra row of holes that run all the way around the chip. Just make sure that the chip doesn't go in so that two rows end up on one side of the chip. Now, gently press the chip into its socket.

Check the chip to make sure that none of its legs are hanging out. If so, remove the chip, bend the leg back in place, and replace it. Once you've got the chip in right, turn your PC back on.

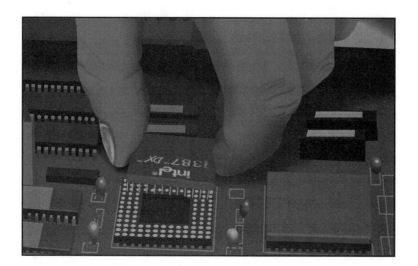

Line up the chip's pins over the holes correctly.

What Could Go Wrong

The easiest way to tell whether your new math coprocessor is working okay is to run MSD (Microsoft System Diagnostics). At the DOS prompt, type **MSD** and press **Enter**.

Click on the **Computer** button and check the math coprocessor status. If MSD doesn't think that you have a math coprocessor, then you'll have to check a bit further.

If your new coprocessor came with software, you'll have to run it to upgrade your system. If not, you'll probably need to flip some switch somewhere or change your CMOS to tell your PC all about the new math coprocessor. See Chapter 24, "Fiddling with Ports, IRQs, Addresses, and Such," for help. Once you're set, put your PC back together and go math-crazy.

Replacing the Motherboard Instead

If you're considering replacing your motherboard, take a couple of steps back. The problem with adding a new motherboard to your PC is that, as a general rule, you won't be able to get away with replacing just your motherboard without replacing something else along with it. If your PC is pretty old, most of your existing stuff probably won't work with a new motherboard. For example, the memory chips on an old 286 just won't keep up with newer 486 technology. Of course, throwing away those old memory chips won't result in a big loss—usually about $20 to $30 worth. And just because your PC's not that old, don't think that you can reuse the RAM chips. I had to replace my barely worn

72-pin SIMMs for 30-pin SIMMs when I had to replace my 486 motherboard just last year. Also, in most cases when you upgrade the motherboard, you'll probably need a new power supply.

Does It Fit Your System?

The next problem you face with a motherboard replacement is finding one that fits your system. For most PCs, this is easy, but some manufacturers use strange sizes of motherboards in order to make their PCs smaller. If you run into a big problem, consider buying a new system case, too. Cases are surprisingly inexpensive.

When you're out looking, make sure that you get a motherboard that's compatible with the type of expansion cards you use. (See Chapter 3 for a description of various expansion slot types.) Also, make sure that the holes on the motherboard that screw it into place in your PC's case line up with the same holes on your existing motherboard. If you decide to buy a new case with your new motherboard, make sure that your disk drives will fit into it okay.

If you're still determined to try this, keep in mind that you'll have to disconnect every darned thing from the motherboard and reconnect every darned thing to the new one—usually in different locations. Also, a motherboard is easy to break accidently if you shove it too hard, or if you're not careful of the leads on the bottom.

Doing the Deed

Well, if you're ready, I guess I am. First, back up your data, write down your CMOS, and update your emergency diskette as usual. *You must write down the CMOS information because your new motherboard isn't going to know any of it.* See Chapter 4 for help.

Before you start taking things apart, you may want to use masking tape to mark your cables and other parts of your PC, so you can remember what they're connected to. Discharge your static electricity on something metal, but don't use the PC.

Unplug the two cables to your power supply, the speaker cable, system lock, reset and turbo switches, lights on the front of your PC, and battery.

Disconnect the cables at the end of any expansion cards and unscrew the retaining screw holding them in. Lift each card out and place them on a static free surface, such as a wooden or plastic desk (not metal). You may want to make a note of the order of your expansion cards—they don't have to be put back in the same order, but why risk it?

Unplug your memory chips and put them on a static-free surface, too. Even if you can't reuse them, you may be able to trade them in for a reduction in the cost of new RAM chips.

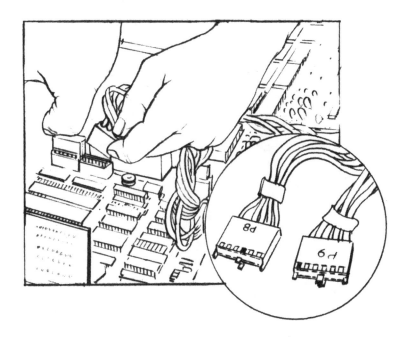

Disconnect the cables that connect to the motherboard.

Now that you've got everything off of your old motherboard, remove the screws holding it in place. Don't be surprised if there's only two or three. Again, make a note of where they go. Your motherboard's probably loose at this point, but not completely free. You probably need to move the motherboard to the left just a bit to release the spacers underneath. Again, discharge yourself so you can lift the thing out (just be sure to hold the board by the sides to limit the chance of shorting anything out).

Get yourself a pair of tweezers and remove the spacers from the old motherboard. Just pinch the top of each spacer and push it back down through its hole.

Discharge any static again and unpack your new motherboard. Look for damage, such as broken wires and such. Snap the spacers up from the bottom into identical positions on your new motherboard. Transfer the salvaged memory chips from your old motherboard (that is, if you can recycle them). If your old RAM chips, SIMMs, or SIPPs don't fit in the new motherboard, install your new memory chips now before you do anything else—see Chapter 15 for help. Next, place your motherboard in the same spot from which you lifted the old one out. Make sure that the spacers line up with their slots in the PC case. Move the motherboard to the right until the screw holes line up and screw it in place— but not too hard—you may bend or crack it.

Remove the spacers from your old motherboard.

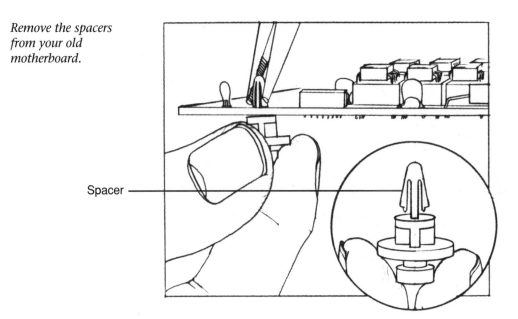

Spacer

Replace the cables to your power supply (commonly called the P8 and P9 connectors)—make sure that the two black wires on each cable go next to each other. Next, replace the cables connecting your speaker, system lock, reset and turbo switches, lights on the front of your PC, and battery. Keep in mind that you need to align the red wire on a cable with pin 1 on the connector.

Put your expansion cards back in the same order in which you had them originally and screw them in. Don't drop any screws! Screws that are accidently forgotten can ruin your new motherboard when you turn it back on. Plug each card's cable back in (if any).

Plug your PC back in and turn it on. Do you get a response, doctor? If so, congrats on a successful surgery. Put your PC's case back together.

What Could Go Wrong

If something's wrong, it's probably because you need to change the default CMOS settings for your new motherboard to match some of the ones from your old system. Good thing you wrote them down! See Chapter 24, "Fiddling with Ports, IRQs, Addresses, and Such," for help getting them into the CMOS of your new motherboard.

You might also want to turn the PC off and recheck all the connections. If you have a problem with a particular part, check the appropriate chapter for help.

Replacing a Dead Battery

The battery in your PC keeps the CMOS chip charged so that it can remember important stuff such as what day it is and what kind of hard disk your PC is supposed to be running. This battery is not the same as the power supply, which converts AC current into DC current to feed hungry PC parts. So when the battery starts to die, the data in CMOS is lost, and as a result your PC gets a bad case of amnesia. When this happens, your PC will cry out, "Where am I?" with a message that looks like this:

Invalid system settings—Run Setup

In short, the battery is dead, and you're going to have to replace it. After that, you have to reenter the data that was in CMOS. Hopefully, back in Chapter 4, you copied down that data—because without it, there's a good chance your PC's going to be in a coma for a long, long time.

To replace the battery successfully, you've got to find the right kind of replacement. First, open up your PC; then, locate the battery. Sounds easy, but most of the time it's not because PC manufacturers are often ingenious at disguising things. If your computer is an old PC or XT, then the battery is on the clock card. Otherwise, look for something attached to the power supply. You're looking for one of these things: a set of AA or similar sized batteries, two cylinders sealed in a red plastic sheath, a black and red box, a silver disk like a watch battery, or even a silver cube. If you don't find it near the power supply, check close to the keyboard connection.

If you can't find the battery anywhere, you may need to look for a chip instead. Try to find something called Dallas, which is short for Dallas Real Time—it'll have a cute picture of a clock on it.

Once you find the battery, or the chip, take a good look at it. Jot down a note about the way it's positioned—for example, which way the plus (+) and the minus (-) ends face. If the battery connects to the motherboard with small wires, make a note of their positions, too. You'll have to replace the battery *so that it faces the exact same way*, or you'll blow up the CMOS chip. (And, since it's soldered to the motherboard, you'll have to replace the motherboard to fix it.) So take a good, long look.

When you're ready, make sure you discharge any static electricity by touching something like a file cabinet or a coworker. Now, remove the battery, or chip, and take it with you to the computer store so you can ask the clerk to get you another one just like it. Take the new battery or chip back to your dead PC and replace it so that it faces the exact same way as the old battery or chip. If the cable connecting the battery to the motherboard comes loose, replace it too, but make sure that you position it in the exact same way as it was before.

Put your PC back together and turn it on. Don't expect fireworks—you're not through yet. You still need to enter the CMOS info that was lost. See Chapter 24, "Fiddling with Ports, IRQs, Addresses, and Such," for help.

Yes, You Too Can Replace Your BIOS!

The BIOS is like the PC's butler—performing the lowly tasks that the computer doesn't want to waste its time doing. This includes basic input and output stuff such as paying attention to the keyboard or the mouse, reading and writing files, or displaying information on the monitor.

One or two chips on the motherboard contain this BIOS. You don't normally have to upgrade your BIOS—that's because it contains all the information it needs to run all the input and output devices in your system. What it doesn't know, it learns through *device drivers*, which supplement its language skills, as it were. For example, if you add a CD-ROM drive to your computer, you need to add a device driver as well, so that the BIOS can "talk" to it. Other devices that might cause you to upgrade your BIOS include 3 1/2-inch diskette drives, large hard disks, CD-ROM drives, tape backups, and SVGA monitors.

If you have an older system, you may notice when you add a fancy new part that its technology is so advanced that the old pokey BIOS just can't keep up. If you're told that you must upgrade the BIOS to get something to work right, then this section shows you how.

It's Not a Speed Thang

Keep in mind that replacing your old BIOS won't make your PC faster. It just enables it to talk to some new fancy gadget such as a 3 1/2-inch diskette drive, large hard disks, IDE anything, SVGA cards, CD-ROM drives, and tape backups. A new set of BIOS chips, by the way, will cost between $30 and $100.

First, you've got to get the correct BIOS chips. Start with your PC's manufacturer. If they can't help you, you need to tell the guy at the computer store exactly what kind of BIOS you currently have so he can help you get the right chips. One way to learn more about your PC's BIOS is to use MSD (Microsoft Diagnostics). Just type **MSD** at the DOS prompt and press **Enter**. Click on **Computer**, and you see a screen telling you what you need to know. Make a note of the BIOS's manufacturer, version, and date. Of course, you have to have DOS version 6-something or Windows in order for MSD to be present.

Another way to discover what kind of BIOS your PC uses is to simply open it up and look. You're looking for anywhere from two to four chips located together, hopefully marked with something useful such as AMI BIOS. Sometimes the label on the chips match what MSD told you about the BIOS. You may discover a single BIOS chip all by its lonesome, but that's not what you're looking for—it's probably the video or the keyboard BIOS chip, not the system BIOS chip (yes, they're different).

Once you have your new chips, take the usual precautions (backing up, upgrading your emergency diskette, and so on) and open your PC. Locate your old BIOS chips. Make a careful note about which chip goes into which socket, and which way each one faces—because you have to put your replacement chips back in the exact same way.

Once you've written down everything you can about your existing BIOS chips and how they fit, you can remove them. First, check your static level by touching something metal. Now, if your upgrade kit included a chip puller (a large set of tweezers), use it to remove each chip. Otherwise, use a small flathead screwdriver to gently pry up one side of the chip a small amount. Then pry up the other side a small amount. Repeat until the chip comes loose. Don't play macho chip puller and try to remove the things in one step—you'll likely break off one of the legs. Just go slow and easy, and you should be fine.

Use your notes to help you place each chip in the right slot, facing the right direction. Line up the notch on one end of the chip with the same kind of notch on the chip's socket. To insert a chip, line up its little legs with the corresponding holes on the socket and apply a gentle downward pressure. You may want to straighten the legs out by pressing one side of the chip against your desktop before you insert the chip. Flip it over and press the other side against the desktop as well. This lines up all the legs so they are perpendicular to the chip.

Flash BIOS
If you have a really fancy-schmancy PC, it may have something called *flash BIOS*, which means that you simply run a software program to upgrade it. Check for a diskette that came with your PC, such as one marked Setup.

The errant leg

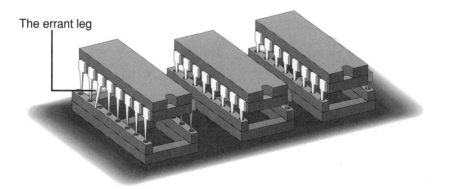

When inserting a chip, make sure that you don't leave a leg hanging out.

What Could Go Wrong

Once you have the chips in, just plug in the PC and start it up. You see a message during startup displaying the name and date of your new BIOS. If anything funky happens, turn the PC off and check the legs on each chip. One of them is probably sticking out. If so, remove the chip and gently bend the naughty leg back in place. Try inserting the chip again. If you still run into a problem, then you may have inserted the chips into the wrong sockets. One BIOS chip is the leader, and the other is the follower. Switch their places and try again.

The Least You Need to Know

Before you begin upgrading the thinking parts of your PC, consider these things:

➤ To replace your old CPU, you have to get a *compatible* upgrade chip.

➤ Keep in mind that your faster CPU has to work with all your old, slow components.

➤ You only need a math coprocessor if you use programs that do a lot of math, such as CAD (Computer-Aided Design) programs, huge spreadsheets, or large databases. A math coprocessor also speeds up some graphics-intensive programs.

➤ Your new math coprocessor needs to match the type of CPU you use.

➤ A math coprocessor is built into 486DX and Pentium chips.

➤ Replacing the motherboard upgrades the CPU and BIOS at the same time, but you may end up replacing other things as well so that they are compatible with the new motherboard—such as your RAM chips and video card.

➤ To replace a dead battery, you need to know your PC's CMOS information.

➤ Replacing a PC's BIOS is only necessary when your old one isn't compatible with new technology such as 3 1/2-inch diskette drives, large hard disks, IDE anything, SVGA cards, CD-ROM drives, and tape backups.

Chapter 14

Solving a Hard Disk Problem

In This Chapter

➤ IDE, SCSI, ESDI, and all the kids

➤ What to look for in a new hard disk

➤ Performing open PC surgery

➤ CMOSing, partitioning, and formatting a new drive

I married my husband, and we moved into a nice two bedroom apartment. Nice, that is, until we started to stuff all our things into it. If your hard disk is starting to look like my apartment, chances are that you need to add more space. Before you hire an architect to design your new addition, try compressing your drive, as you learned how to do in Chapter 7.

If you still feel like you need to "add on," then this chapter will lead you through the scary business of picking out a new hard disk and stuffing it into your PC.

What Am I Getting Myself Into?

First, if you're adding a second drive, you have to find a drive that works well with your first drive. If you don't mind ditching your first drive, you open up more options, but you still have to find one that's compatible with your PC. More on shopping for your hard drive in a moment.

Now, assuming that you find a hard drive you can use, what do you have to go through to get the thing to work in your PC? Well, if you're replacing your old hard drive, you have to take the old drive out, of course. This usually means removing some other stuff so that you have enough room to remove the drive.

You slide your new drive into the empty drive bay and, in a lot of cases, you add an expansion card called a *drive controller* to run the new drive. Once you connect the new drive, you have to set up the drive. This can get pretty nerdish, so you may want to bribe a guru to help you out here. If you have to brave the depths of CMOS, FDISK, and FOR-MAT yourself, don't despair—I'll provide the necessary help.

Before you go to the trouble of adding a new hard disk, make the most of what you've got by compressing your files. In addition, if you've been having problems with the hard disk lately, it doesn't mean that the thing is going out. Try using CHKDSK or ScanDisk to ferret out the problem. In addition, you may want to defragment your drive. See Chapter 7 for how-tos.

General Things to Keep in Mind Before Shopping

When shopping for a new hard disk, get the largest one that you can afford. Studies show that you're better off with a hard disk that's three times larger than the one you're using now. Sound ridiculous? Not when you consider how much room most programs consume: anywhere from 15 M to 40 M *each*. If you use Windows, add another 40 M. And of course, if you create anything at all with these programs, you'll use up even more space. I added a 300 M hard drive to my system recently, which I compressed for a total of 615 M. I installed Microsoft Office, Lotus 1-2-3, and a few other things, and I now have only 120 M left. You know your needs better than anyone else, so judge for yourself.

Check This Out...

Square Pegs and Squarer Holes

An important factor to consider when buying a hard disk is to get one that fits. Older computers have larger 5 1/4-inch drive bays, while modern PCs have smaller 3 1/2-inch drive bays. Don't despair; you can buy a mounting bracket to fit a smaller 3 1/2-inch hard disk drive into a fatter 5 1/4-inch bay if needed. The small drive simply screws into the larger mounting bracket, and the bracket mounts at the points where you bolt in a fatter drive.

Too Large?

If your BIOS is too old, it might not be able to handle the larger hard disks sold today. This means you might have to upgrade your BIOS as well. How to tell if this is needed? Well, don't worry. When you buy one of these large babies, the setup program for the drive will not only format the thing for you, but it will also determine whether or not you need a BIOS upgrade. It doesn't actually upgrade the BIOS, but it does load a device driver that helps the BIOS to deal with the large hard disk.

When comparing hard drives, check their capacity (size) and speed (access time). Obviously, you want the largest hard disk you can afford. Also, try to get one with a low access time if you can. The access time tells you how long it takes the hard disk to grab the data you need; the lower the number, the faster the hard disk. Access times range from 10 to 18 microseconds (ms).

Another feature you might want to look for is a cache. A cache (pronounced *cash*) stores the frequently requested data close at hand, so the hard drive can get to it more quickly. Not a lot of hard disks include a cache (sometimes called a buffer), but it's a worthwhile feature to look for.

When you finally buy your drive, make sure that you buy the cables you need to connect it as well. You may think that the cables come with the drive, but in most cases, they're an extra item. If you're replacing your old drive with the same kind of drive, you can probably skip the cables and just reuse your old ones.

Also, make sure that your new drive has the brackets you need to slide the drive into the drive bay. Keep in mind that you should get a drive that fits an empty bay, or get a converter or mounting bracket to make it fit. A mounting bracket is another item that not all manufacturers include with their hard drive kits as standard equipment. If you need one, make sure that the kit has one or that you can get a hold of one; don't worry—they're cheap.

In addition, if you're switching drive types, you need a new controller card. Don't forget to pick one up, or you'll have to make two trips to the computer store. By the way, most newer PCs use an IDE controller.

Take Control!

Actually, the IDE controller doesn't control anything—the controls for an IDE drive are built into the drive itself. The controller allows the drive to override the regular ST-506 controller that the motherboard expects to be there—so you still need to get one if you switch from some other drive type to IDE.

If you're adding a hard drive where none has gone before, you'll most certainly need to upgrade the power supply. Keep this in mind before you start forking out big cash to upgrade something that's basically an antique. (Want a more accurate estimate of your power supply needs? See Chapter 18.)

You can also add an external hard drive, which is nice if you don't have any drive bays open, or you don't feel like messing around inside the PC. They cost a bit more, but it may be worth it. An external hard disk connects through a parallel port, so if you have a printer using your parallel port, you may need to add an I/O card which gives you an extra parallel and serial port. Another option, if you're out of drive bays but you do have space in your machine, is an internal mounting bracket attachment. It literally hangs onto something in your PC case and supports a 3 1/2-inch drive mechanism. All PCs are fairly different from one another, so this option may not work in your PC, but hey, it's worth a try.

In addition, "hard cards," which are hard drives on a card that fits into an expansion slot, are also available. Again, you pay a premium for not having to mess with a drive bay.

Very Important: What Kind of Hard Drive Do You Have?

Before you go shopping for a new hard disk, you need to figure out what kind of hard drive your PC currently has (even if you plan on replacing it). Start by looking at your PC's manual. The next place to look is on the drive itself, on a sticker that has the manufacturer's name, the drive's specifications, and its date of manufacture. This sticker may be located on the top of the drive, or on the rear next to the data connectors. You might even call your PC's manufacturer if the sticker isn't there or if what it says doesn't make sense. In any event, it'll help the salesperson identify the type of hard disk you have.

Why is this so important? Well, the hard disk connects to a *drive controller*, and it's the controller's job to grab (read) data from the drive when the PC needs it. Likewise, the controller saves (writes) data to the drive when asked nicely. So your new hard disk will have to talk to this controller, because it's the controller's job to act as official interpreter between the PC and the hard disk. If you buy an incompatible drive, you'll have to spend some extra bucks on a new controller as well. If you're adding a drive and keeping your old one too, you must buy a drive that's compatible with your old drive because you can only have one drive controller, and it has to be able to talk to both drives.

There are basically four types of drive controllers:

ST-506 This is the oldest type of drive controller, introduced in 1980 by Seagate Technology. ST-506 controllers are used only in very old PCs, such as the original

XT. Basically, this is a turtle compared with the fast controllers used today. Strangely enough, all PCs have this baby on the motherboard, either as a separate chip or as part of the system BIOS, although it's not used for anything but to fool DOS long enough to switch to a real drive controller such as IDE or SCSI. The AT versions of this controller are called WD1002 and WD1003; but the standard here is the same, and so is the connecting cable.

ESDI Short for Enhanced Small Device Interface, Maxtor introduced this type of controller in 1983. ESDI was supposed to replace the ST-506 standard, and to some extent it did, but it's pretty much an antique today.

IDE Short for Integrated Drive Electronics, because the controller is built into the drive itself. By far, this is the most popular drive controller sold today. IDE is sometimes referred to as the AT Attachment interface. A new version of IDE, called EIDE (for Extended IDE) is featured in most PCs today. EIDE allows you to add larger hard disks, and more of them.

SCSI Short for Small Computer Systems Interface, a SCSI controller can control several types of SCSI devices at once, including a hard disk, a CD-ROM drive, and a tape drive. Although it's pretty fast, SCSI drives are much more expensive than IDE. Also, if you want to chain several SCSI devices (such as a hard disk, CD-ROM drive, and so on) to your new SCSI controller, you may run into problems, because lots of SCSI devices are incompatible with each other. If you stick with just SCSI hard disks, you should be fine.

If you want to replace your hard disk, the easiest thing to do is to get the same kind. For example, if you have an ST-506 drive and you don't intend to (or you can't) replace the controller, then replace the drive with another ST-506 drive. (Such a drive isn't generally called "ST-506" because drives that work with the old controller aren't designed specifically for that controller. Instead, they're identified by their encoding schemes: FM, MFM, or RLL. You can learn more about those after you've been given the proper medication.) The only problem is, you may not be able to find an ST-506-compatible drive. Also, if you do locate one, its capacity is going to be so small (around 40 M) that you'll wish you'd never found it.

A better solution for upgrading a ST-506 system is to go with a new standard such as IDE—but plan on getting the controller that goes with the drive. For example, to chuck your ST-506 drive and switch to IDE, you'll need an IDE controller. It's a 16-bit controller, so you'll need a 16-bit expansion port free to be able to install the adaptor card (sometimes called "controller card" because salespeople just don't know the difference sometimes). Thankfully, with IDE at least, the adaptor/controller is really cheap (around $25).

No matter what, if you buy a new controller card, make sure that you buy one that fits the type of expansion bus your system uses. For example, an old XT type PC will need an 8-bit controller card, which is kinda hard to find. Most other systems will use a 16-bit controller, except for old Micro Channel and PCI.

Techno Talk
blah blah
blah bla
oh bl
b

Make Sure You Connect Your Floppy Drives

If you replace your old hard disk controller with a new one, check to see if your floppy drives are also connected to your old one. If so, you need to either get a controller that allows you to connect your floppy drives to it, or buy a separate controller just for your floppy drives. Keeping your old controller probably isn't an option, because it can interfere with your new controller just by being there.

If Your Original Drive Is an ST-506

Unless you're ready to change your controller type, you can only replace an ST-506 drive with another ST-506 drive, which is difficult to find. Also, some ST-506 controllers are designed to work only with drives of a specific size, and no larger. For example, old XT controllers work only with 10 M drives. So sometimes even if you find an ST-506 drive, it may not work with your ST-506 controller.

If you'd prefer to keep your sanity, I recommend chucking the original ST-506 hard disk and replacing it with better technology, such as IDE. Really. Staying with the ST-506 standard is a waste of time. IDE is cheap, fast, and popular. You won't run into a problem getting help for the drive when you need it. Unfortunately, switching standards means that you have to buy an IDE controller so you have the right connectors for your IDE drive, but at least they don't cost much.

If you decide on IDE, you need to make sure that your new drive will work in your system. If you have an old XT, you need to get an IDE drive rated for use in an XT system. Regular IDE drives won't work in an XT, although they will work in just about anything else. Using an IDE drive in an XT isn't much of a bargain, because you have to slow the darn thing down to a crawl in order for it to work. Also, XT-rated IDE drives cost about the same as other IDE drives that hold twice as much data. In my opinion, if you have an old XT and the drive's kaput, fling it into the sewer and start over. It will cost you fewer headaches and less money.

If you decide you like SCSI, you can go that way too, but the drive will cost you more. Also, you have to add in the cost of a SCSI controller, which is much more expensive than an IDE controller. However, a new SCSI drive can be a lot faster than an IDE drive. Also, if you haven't already added a CD-ROM drive or a tape drive to your PC, you can buy SCSI versions and gain some speed. It's important to note that SCSI is not a hard drive controller per se, just a device controller that happens to work with hard drives.

Two SCSIs or Not Two SCSIs?

If you add a SCSI controller to your PC, be careful if you already have a CD-ROM drive running off the SCSI controller in your sound card. Your PC can only have one SCSI controller, so disable the one on the sound card (which probably involves removing a jumper) and connect the CD-ROM drive to the SCSI controller that's running your hard disk. Don't think that this will somehow ruin your sound card; the only reason that some sound cards include a SCSI port is to make it easy for you to connect a SCSI CD-ROM drive to your PC. See Chapters 19 and 20 for more.

If Your Original Drive Is an ESDI

Basically, everything about ST-506 controllers is true here, too. With an ESDI controller, you can run more than one drive, and the second drive is a bit easier to install. Although size is not an issue, speed is. So if you want to add another ESDI drive to your system, make sure you get one that's not *too fast* for your existing controller. ESDI drives can be much faster than IDE drives, yet you pay quite a bit more. Also, present day IDE drives have a higher storage capacity; you probably won't find many ESDI drives over a quarter-gigabyte.

Like ST-506 drives, ESDI drives are hard to find (think: dinosaur), and again, you're better off upgrading to a newer technology such as IDE or SCSI.

If Your Original Drive Is an IDE

If you're replacing your drive, get another IDE (AT Interface) drive. They're inexpensive and easy to find. By the way, some newer IDE controllers (EIDE) enable you to plug up to four IDE drives into them.

If you're adding a second drive, again, go with IDE. Keep in mind that an XT-type PC can only handle one IDE drive. A 386 PC can handle two. Newer PCs with EIDE can handle up to four, and those hard disks can be of a larger (over 1 G) size.

If you decide to buy a SCSI drive, you need a separate controller for it, and you have to get rid of your IDE drive because the drives will just get into a fight. (OK, the drives like each other just fine, but the two controllers won't get along too well.)

If Your Original Drive Is a SCSI

Here, if you're adding another drive, you pretty much have to go with SCSI. SCSI devices connect to each other in what's called a *daisy chain*—kind of like holding hands for a game of whip.

Get the Same Brand If you're adding a second drive to your system, try to get the same brand IDE drive as your first drive. Many IDE drives are notorious for not playing well with other IDE drives, unless they're both the same brand. If you're replacing your drive, your IDE adaptor/controller card will work with any other IDE drive.

Unfortunately, you can't assume that your existing SCSI controller will work with both your old and your new SCSI drive. Some are just incompatible. That means you may have to buy an additional SCSI controller for the new drive. If you're replacing your old SCSI drive, you shouldn't run into a problem.

If you want to use your SCSI controller with other drives, such as IDE, make sure that it uses WD1002 emulation, which in English means it supports the ST-506 standard. WD1002 was the first hard drive controller that IBM installed in its 16-bit ATs (ST-506 was the first to be installed in its earlier PCs). But even though the WD stands for Western Digital and the ST for Seagate Technologies, the WD1002 is really a 16-bit version of the ST-506.

Performing Hard Drive Surgery

Before you scrub up, make sure that you've done the usual: backed up your data, updated your emergency diskette, and so on. See Chapter 12 for details. Unpack your goodies and make sure that you have a hard drive, cables, and brackets (if you're adding an additional drive, that is). If you're replacing your drive, you can steal the brackets from the old drive.

Open up your PC and, as usual, get rid of any excess static. Remove the old drive if you're replacing it. To do that, first remove the cables. (Make any notes you want first.) You will find one or two data cables; these are ribbon cables that lead from the drive to the controller card. You'll also find a power cable; it has four separate wires leading from each end. Generally, to remove either cable, you just pull straight up or out. This doesn't take a lot of pressure, but just be sure to pull the cables by the plastic connectors and not by the wires.

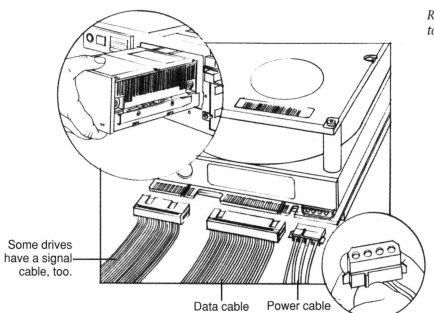

Remove the cables to free your drive.

Some drives have a signal cable, too.

Data cable   Power cable

Once you get the cables off, remove the mounting screws that hold the drive in place. You may find them at the front of the drive, or along the sides. (You may have to remove other drives or cards to get to the screws.) Once you get the screws out, the drive will slide out the front of the PC. If the thing is mounted on its side, push the drive out the back.

If you're replacing your old drive, transfer the brackets to the new one and then slide it into the old bay. If you're adding a second drive, add new brackets to it and slide it into an empty bay. If needed, use your converter mounting bracket to fit a smaller drive into a larger drive bay.

Techno Talk

blah blah blah blah blah bl n bl b

Who's the Boss?

If you're adding a second IDE drive to a system that already has one, then you have to make the second drive the *slave*, which means that it shows up as drive D. (Drive C is the drive that the PC boots from, and it's called the *master* under IDE technology.) To make your new drive a slave, you either have to set a DIP switch or move a small *jumper* (see Chapter 24 for details about jumpers).

185

Once you have the hard drive in, insert the new drive controller card, if needed. To insert a drive controller card, find a slot that's open. Holding the slot cover in place, unscrew the retaining screw. Hold the card at the top with both hands and gently position the edge connectors. Rock the card until it slips into place. Add the connecting ribbon cables for your hard disk or floppy drives.

But There's More...

Getting your new controller card to work takes more than just plugging it in. You'll have to fiddle with nasty things like IRQs and DMAs, whatever they are. Check out Chapter 24, "Fiddling with Ports, IRQs, Addresses, and Such," for help in getting out of this mess.

If you're replacing your old drive controller, remove the cables from it and take the card out. To remove a drive controller card, unscrew the retaining screw, grip the card at the top with both hands, and pull straight up.

Now, attach the data (ribbon) cables to your new drive. Remember that the red wire or stripe along the side of the cable aligns with pin 1 on the connector. Pin 1 is clearly marked with a "1." If you're adding a second ST-506 or ESDI drive to your system, the data cable is connected to the J5 slot-thing on the controller (drive C is connected to the J4 slot). With a data cable that connects two drives, drive D uses the connector that hangs in the middle.

Da Terminata

If you're connecting a SCSI drive, there's a bit more to it. You can link SCSI devices together, so you need to use something called a terminating resistor to indicate which device is the last in the "chain." If the drive is not the only SCSI device in your PC, then you have to remove its own termination resistors or switches so that the SCSI controller will know that it has to continue on from the hard disk to look for more SCSI devices. Yech.

Usually all you have to do is identify these terminator critters and pull them off to disable termination of the daisy chain. (Of course, if your hard disk is the one and only SCSI device in your system, leave the termination thingies on.)

As you prepare to install your new hard disk, keep in mind that each SCSI device has to be given a number. Usually drive C is called device number 0, and drive D is device number 1, but check your manuals to be sure. Also, the manual will tell you how to actually set the device number. Some manufacturers give you a special SCSI device control program; others make it more difficult by forcing you to set the parameters manually on one line of your CONFIG.SYS file. Adaptec-brand controllers use a program in ROM (much like the one in your BIOS) that allows you to set the controller's internal parameters just after you boot your computer.

Now that you've prepared your drive, connect the power cable(s). Remember that these are cables with four separate wires. Generally, the white plug is shaped to fit only one direction; but in any event, the colored wires from the male end should plug into the same-colored wires on the female end.

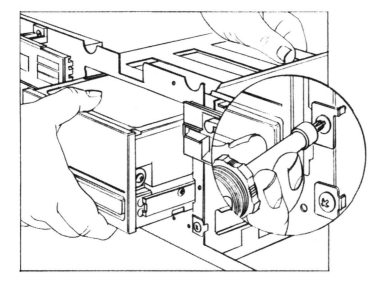

Fasten the drive in place.

Fasten the drive in place with its screws. Then, restore your PC to its former beauty and plug it in. Don't expect much when you start up the PC—you have to set up the hard disk before you can use it. This is the time when you may want to stop and bake those cookies so you can bribe some guru into helping you. If you don't know a guru, you can read the next section.

Uh, Just a Few More Steps Before You Go

Before you can use your new hard drive, you have to get your PC to realize that it's there. You do that by changing the CMOS, which, as you learned in Chapter 4, is the thing that helps your PC remember mundane details such as what day it is and how much memory the PC has. Another detail that CMOS keeps track of is how many hard disks your PC has, and how big they are. So turn on your PC, and as it's booting, do whatever dance you usually do to get CMOS to show its face:

➤ Reboot your computer and press **Ctrl+Alt+Escape**. You can also try **Ctrl+Alt+Enter** or **Ctrl+Alt+S**.

➤ Reboot your computer and watch the screen for a message telling you what key to press for Setup. Then press it. (It may tell you to press **F1** or **F2** or even **Delete**.)

➤ Reboot your computer with its original manufacturer's setup diskette in drive A. This is usually what you need to do for an AT-type 286 PC, because it doesn't provide a friendly way to access CMOS.

Check This Out...

IDE Drive? No Worries (Maybe)!

If your new IDE drive has the same brand and internal parameters as the drive it replaced, then you might not have to change CMOS to get it to work, because your BIOS probably won't notice the difference. Of course, if you add a second IDE drive, even if it's the same brand and parameters as the first, all bets are off—which means that you better dig out your manual and start messing with CMOS.

To tell CMOS about your new drive, you have to know all sorts of creepy things such as how many *cylinders*, *heads*, and *sectors* it has, as well as science-fiction sounding things such as write protect and landing zone. If you're lucky, you'll find this information printed on the hard disk itself; if not, your manual is the second-best bet. Even if you don't understand what the terms mean, the hard drive specs listed on the drive or in the manual are listed the same way as the BIOS setup program lists them, so just type in the numbers from the manual or the drive sticker into the form onscreen. Jump to Chapter 24, "Fiddling with Ports, IRQs, Addresses, and Such," for help in dealing with the CMOS monster.

If you're setting up a SCSI drive, you have to run its software to add a driver to the CONFIG.SYS so your PC recognizes the drive. Next, you'll have to run the setup program that came with the SCSI controller in order for the controller to recognize the drive, too. The SCSI controller has to be able to recognize the hardware so that it can "turn it on," and so in turn, you can have DOS high-level format the drive. Before using DOS, however, you may have to low-level format the SCSI drive. As a matter of safety, as long as your BIOS isn't controlling your hard drives anyway, you should set the BIOS up for **No Hard Drive** at all. This way, you won't accidentally use the BIOS to low-level format SCSI drives. Your BIOS thinks you're using something on the order of an ST-506 and doesn't have a clue about SCSI. Instead, to low-level format a SCSI drive, use the special program diskette supplied by the manufacturer, or use utility software that's rated for SCSI drives.

EZ-Drive

Some drives include a software program called EZ-Drive, which makes setting up the drive a snap. If you can get your hands on a copy, it's well worth the effort, and hey, you'll get to skip the CMOS junk. Other drives include an Auto Configure option in their setup programs that does the same job.

If you bought a large hard disk, it came with a diskette that you need to run about now. Stick the thing in drive A and type **SETUP** at the A:\> prompt. The setup program takes care of the FDISK thing coming up, and FORMAT. It also checks your BIOS to see if you need to use a device driver so that your computer will recognize the high capacity drive. So run the setup program and skip gleefully over the next few paragraphs.

Once you've got the CMOS business over with, your next step is to *partition* your drive. Now, you don't officially have a hard drive yet, so you'll need to boot your system with your emergency diskette in drive A. Although you can use this opportunity to divide a large disk into several smaller ones, you don't have to do this. You can, and perhaps should, have as few as one partition on your hard drive; but having more than one allows you to address one partition as "logical drive" C: and another partition as "logical drive" D:. If you really enjoy this type of confusion, be my guest and sign up for more than one partition.

To partition your hard drive, type **FDISK** at the A> prompt and press **Enter**. If you replaced your old drive, your new drive is the primary DOS partition. So choose **Create DOS partition or Logical DOS Drive** and then choose **Primary DOS Partition**. You can only have one primary DOS partition, by the way; that's the whole meaning behind "primary." Press **Y** to partition the drive.

If you're adding a second drive, you need to partition drive D. Choose **Change current fixed disk drive** and then select D. Choose **Create DOS Partition or Logical DOS Drive**. Choose **Secondary DOS Partition** and press **Y** to partition it.

After you finish with FDISK, your PC restarts. If you replaced your only hard disk, you need to insert your emergency diskette. If you added a second hard disk, just smile and do nothing.

After you partition the new drive, you have to high-level format it. If you replaced your old hard drive, type **FORMAT C: /S** at the DOS prompt to format it and press **Enter**. The "/S" part will make it a "system" disk, so that it can run DOS and boot itself without you having to put a DOS diskette in drive A.

When the thing asks you for a volume label, you can type something clever, such as, **MY DRIVE C.** If you added a second drive instead, type **FORMAT D:** and press **Enter** to format it. You don't need the "/S" part here.

Again, when it asks you for a volume label, you can type whatever you want, up to 11 whole characters. Anyway, once you've formatted your new drive, everything should be okay. So remove any diskettes from their drives and restart your PC to test it out.

What Could Go Wrong

If your new drive won't wake up, open up the PC again and check for obvious things like loose cables and such. Also check to make sure that you didn't put the data (ribbon) cables on backwards. Remember, the red wire or stripe should match up with pin 1 on the data cable connector.

Check to make sure that you partitioned and formatted the thing okay. Type **FDISK** at the prompt, then read the partition table to see if the partitions are really showing up the way you intended. You should have one and only one primary DOS partition.

If you're dealing with two IDE drives, they may not want to play together. You can try switching the slave and master drives with each other. If that doesn't work, you may have to take the new drive back and get a drive made by the same people who made the first one.

The Least You Need to Know

There's a lot to remember when shopping for a new hard disk. Here are some pointers:

➤ First, try compressing your current hard disk to see if you can avoid this whole business.

➤ Then make sure you have an empty drive bay in which you can put a new hard disk. If you're replacing a bad disk, this obviously isn't a problem.

➤ If you don't have any open bays, you can shop for a hard card or an external hard disk instead, or perhaps an attachment mounting bracket.

➤ For the easiest type of addition or replacement, shop for the same kind of hard disk you had before. However, if you're replacing an older ST-506 or ESDI drive, you may want to consider switching to IDE.

➤ Get the largest, fastest hard disk you can afford.

➤ Make sure that your new hard disk will fit into the open drive bay.

➤ If you switch standards, get a new controller card. Keep in mind that you may also need to replace the floppy drive controller if it used the old hard disk controller.

➤ Be sure to purchase cables and rack mounts if needed.

Chapter 15

Make Mine More Memory!

In This Chapter

➤ Figuring out how much RAM you'll need

➤ Buying the right kind of memory chips

➤ Plopping in more money

Random access memory, or RAM, is one of your PC's most precious commodities—it's also one of the most boring. That's because unlike your cool color printer, fax modem, or sound-like-thunder speakers, RAM just doesn't cause your friends to oooh and ahhh in admiration.

Yeah, memory's pretty boring—that is, until you run out of it. You see, before you can work with any kind of data on your PC, the PC must first place the data in RAM. In addition, the PC must copy into RAM any program you want to run before it can read and then carry out any of that program's instructions. So if your PC doesn't have a lot of RAM, and you try to run a memory-hogging program like a word processor to try to edit your 35-page corporate review, you're likely to get an Out of memory message. In English, this means you either have to get something out of RAM (close a document, stop a program, or something), or you have to add more memory to your PC.

If you use Windows, it can shuffle things in and out of memory when you run out of RAM on your motherboard, but even Windows has limits. You see, when you run out of RAM, Windows transfers stuff out of RAM and into *virtual memory*—a holding area on your hard drive. This whole process depends on you having spare room on your hard disk, which puts a crimp on your ability to create and save lots of documents. All this shuffling business can get on your nerves after a while, too, such as when you make one tiny change to a document and then wait ten minutes for the computer to process it.

How Programs Try to Make Themselves Tiny

Okay, technically, an entire program is rarely loaded into RAM, because there just wouldn't be enough room. Most large programs today (such as spreadsheets and word processors) are programmed in smaller units, so that only the units you need to use are actually loaded into RAM at any given time. For example, the Spell Checker in most word processors is not loaded until you activate it. In this way, a program tries to be as small as possible, so that you still have some RAM left over for creating things with the program, such as a letter or two.

RAM, by the way, will cost you about $40 to $50 per megabyte.

So How Much Memory Do I Need?

To run big programs and not have to wait a long time to do it, you need to have lots of memory. How much is enough? Well, some nerds will tell you there's no such thing as "enough" when you're talking about a computer—but I think a good minimum is 4 M (that is, if you don't mind taking frequent siestas), while 8 M is even better. Me, I run with 16 M.

If you prefer a more scientific method, check out the minimum requirement of the programs you want to run—you're not adding them together, you're just looking for the program that needs the greatest amount of memory. Now, take that number and double it.

First, How Much Do You Have?

To figure out how much memory you already have, watch the screen the next time you start your PC. As your computer gets its stuff together so it can face another workday, the POST (Power-On Self-Test) counts down the amount of memory you've got. Don't expect this information to be too enlightening, though. The number you'll see is shown in *kilobytes*, not megabytes, like most people think. To get the amount of megabytes your PC has, divide the number you see by 1024, which is the number of kilobytes in one megabyte.

So for example, when I start my PC, I see the total add up to this number:

16384

If I divide this by 1024, I get 16 M. If your PC counts up memory too fast for you to read it, you can use the MEM command to find out what you have instead. Just type **MEM** at the DOS prompt and press **Enter**. You'll see a listing of your computer's memory. You're interested in the Total memory amount, listed at the bottom of the Total column.

If I Want to Upgrade Memory, What Am I Getting Myself Into?

To upgrade your PC's memory, you have to first determine how much RAM your PC can take. This maximum is based on a number of factors, such as the CPU type, the amount of space on the motherboard, and so on. If you have a 286 PC, then your CPU can only handle a maximum of 16 M of RAM—at least in theory, because your motherboard probably won't support that much. If yours is a 386SX, then your CPU is also limited to a maximum of 16 M of RAM, but with the advent of SIMMs you may just be able to fit 16 M on the motherboard. If you have a 386DX, any type of 486, or Pentium, then there's no problem, because your PC can handle up to 4 G (gigabytes) of RAM, and that's way more than you can afford to put in the thing, anyway.

Don't Sink Too Much into That 286

Before you add a lot of memory to a 286 PC, you may want to consider upgrading the CPU, the entire motherboard, or even buying a new computer—all are better investments than adding more RAM to such a slow PC.

Once you find out that your CPU is up to the job, your next problem is where to put the RAM. Most memory chips go on the motherboard, so you have to open up the PC and see if you have any empty slots open (don't bother with that now, you'll get your sleeves dirty in the next section).

If there's no room on the motherboard, you may be able to add something called a *memory expansion card*, which is a card you stick memory chips on and press into an expansion slot. So to use one of these babies, you've got to have an open expansion slot. Some newer PCs don't enable you to add memory in this way, or if they do, they make you fill the slots on the motherboard first.

Some memory expansion cards come with a "backfill" feature, which means you don't actually have to put chips into the empty slots on the motherboard—the expansion card just fools the PC into thinking they're there. Some PC manufacturers like AST, NEC, Compaq, Hewlett Packard, Zenith, and IBM may make you buy their particular brand of memory cards in order to expand beyond what's on the motherboard. These name-brand memory chips can usually be quite expensive, but they offer RAM that's faster than what you might add otherwise.

Check This Out...

Got a Tandy?
If you have an old Tandy 1000 computer, you need to go to a Tandy or Radio Shack store to get your expansion cards, because memory on the Tandys run on an exclusive circuit that you can upgrade only with Tandy-brand equipment.

In any case, if you buy a memory expansion card, you can buy it either with the RAM chips already mounted, or without the RAM chips and add them yourself. Obviously, you'll want to avoid putting the dumb little guys on yourself, especially if the price for the prepackaged deal seems fair enough. Using a memory expansion board is really a last resort, because it's much slower than RAM on the motherboard.

RAM chips, by the way, come in a couple of popular flavors: old style DIPPs, and newer SIMMs. There are two varieties of SIMMs: 30-pin and 72-pin. The 30-pin SIMMs are smaller; you can find these SIMMs in most PCs, except for the newer Pentiums, which favor the 72-pin variety. By the way, a 30-pin SIMM is mounted on a green circuit board, while a 72-pin SIMM is on a white circuit board, just to make it easier for you to correctly identify them. Some PCs use SIPPs, which are kind of a cross between a DIP-style chip and a SIMM-style chip, but SIPPs aren't terribly popular today.

RAM chips come in two basic varieties.

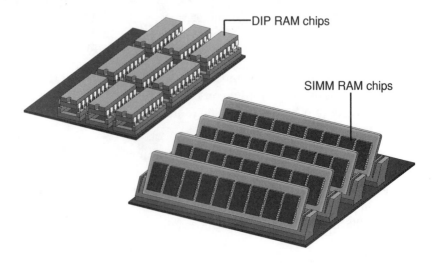

DIP RAM chips

SIMM RAM chips

Once you find out how much memory you can add, and where you can add it, you have to go out and buy the stuff. Buying RAM is almost like playing the stock market, so shop around and decide when and where is the best place to buy. Expect to pay around $50 to $70 a megabyte. There are some tips on buying the right kind of RAM for your PC coming up later in this chapter.

Get a Device Driver

If you're adding memory above 1 M for the first time, you need to install a device driver that can manage extended memory. Luckily, DOS versions 4.0 and higher, as well as Windows, come with HIMEM.SYS, a device driver that does just that. If you have a lower DOS version than 4.0, you may want to upgrade so you can get the HIMEM.SYS device driver so your PC can use memory above 1 M.

Now That I Want to Add More Memory, Is It Possible?

The first bad news you may run into after deciding to "go for it" and add more RAM is the limitations of your PC. Every motherboard has only so many slots reserved for RAM, and of course, your PC's current memory is already using some of them.

So the first thing you need to do is check out your computer manual to find out how much memory your PC can handle. Subtract what your PC already has, and you get the maximum amount you can add. Unfortunately, you may not be able to add that much— I'll tell you why in a minute.

Next, open up the PC and take a look to see how many empty memory slots you still have left. Your RAM chips are arranged in rows of either nine individual chips called DIPs, or memory modules called SIPPs or SIMMs (depending on how they connect to the motherboard).

Now, here comes the problem. Suppose your manual tells you that your PC can handle up to 16 M of RAM, and you know that you've been getting by all this time with a measly 2 M. Now, when you pop the top, you find that all the memory slots in your PC are taken. What gives?

Well, memory is arranged on your PC's motherboard in *banks*. Depending on your motherboard, a bank is usually one, two, or four *rows* of memory chips—each bank is marked with a number, such as 0, 1, 2, or 3. Each bank functions as a *unit*. This means you can upgrade only in increments *of one bank of memory*. You'll see why this might be a problem in a minute.

No vacancies.

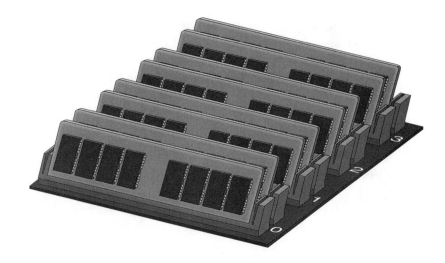

First let's go back to when you opened up your PC and found all your memory slots were full, even though you knew your PC only had 2 M of RAM. It turns out that the motherboard has four banks of memory with two rows each. Each of the eight rows is filled with 256 K memory chips, for a total of only 2 M.

Just keep in mind that each row of memory acts as a unit. So even if you see nine little 256 K chips in a row, they act together to form a single unit of 256 K memory. Sounds strange, but that's how it works. Newer PCs use memory modules called SIMMs with the nine chips soldered onto a single easy to insert circuit board—but it still takes the nine separate chips to make up a single unit of memory.

Look Ma, No Parity!

The nine chips correspond to the nine bits used in parity checking. Some PCs don't bother with parity checking, so they only use eight chips in a row of memory. Even some IBM-type PCs have started to pack the cheaper non-parity checking memory modules, and they've even billed it as a feature, "Now, with *no* parity checking!" Now you may think that removing parity checking is a bit of a stretch just to save a buck or two, but actually, it's quite safe. See, the newer CPUs such as the 486 and Pentium contain advanced memory management that practically removes any chance of a parity error occurring anyway. If a problem does occur, the CPU will catch it long before any parity error checking technique. Just don't try to use the non-parity checking SIMMs in a PC that doesn't have at least a 486 CPU.

Now, going back to the number of banks your PC has, and how that can run you into trouble when you want to upgrade memory. Well, suppose your PC has two banks of memory with four rows each, and that it uses the new memory modules (SIMMs). If your PC is older than a year or so, it probably accepts only the 1 M or 4 M 30-pin SIMMs—so assume that's the case here.

Now, to upgrade memory, you have to fill a bank, and because your PC has four rows in each bank, you have to buy enough memory to fill those four rows. You can't mix and match the SIMMs you use in a single bank, so you'd have to fill your bank with either four 1 M or four 4 M SIMMs. This gives you either 4 M of memory (if you fill a bank with four 1 M SIMMs) or 16 M (if you use the 4 M SIMMs instead.) It also means that you can't add only 1 or 2 M of RAM to this PC—you have to add at least 4 or 16 M, since your PC only accepts 1 or 4 M SIMMs.

If the PC uses the older style individual RAM chips (called DIPPs), then you have more choices because these chips come in more sizes, such as 64 K, 256 K, and 1 M. That means that you can add as little as 256 K (with four rows of 64 K chips) or as much as 4 M (with four rows of 1 M chips) in a bank of memory. Newer PCs such as Pentiums and some 486s use 72-pin SIMMs, which are wider than regular 30-pin SIMMs. They also come in a lot more varieties, including 512 K, 1 M, 2 M, 4 M, 8 M, and 16 M, as you'll learn in a minute.

Laptop Considerations

Just as with any desktop PC, you need to check in your laptop's manual to find the limits to its memory upgrades. For example, you may be limited to 16 M right off the bat. Also, a lot of laptops use old CPUs that really don't benefit a lot from added RAM—in other words, they'll still be as slow as molasses. If you decide that you want to add more memory to your laptop, it may cost you more than you think because most laptops use proprietary memory chips designed for that particular brand.

There aren't a lot of options for adding memory to a laptop. Basically, as long as there's a free slot, and you haven't hit the maximum capacity of the machine, you can add memory. You can't add memory with an expansion card as you can with a desktop PC, mostly because there aren't any expansion slots per se. You connect things to the laptop not through an expansion slot, but through one of its many ports at the back of the PC.

Usually you buy your memory upgrades from the laptop's manufacturer, rather than generic RAM chips. This means that adding RAM to a laptop is more costly than adding the same amount to a PC—anywhere from $10 to $20 more per megabyte.

Try Creating a Virtual Disk

Some of these old dinosaurs do allow you to create a fake hard disk called a "virtual disk" or "RAM disk" out of what RAM they do have. This can at least speed things up a little. The idea behind a RAM disk is that you can copy files to the RAM disk just like any other drive, and the CPU can read those files quicker because they're already in RAM. The RAM disk is created when you boot up, and it's given a letter, just like any other drive, such as E:. You copy data files to this fake drive E and then use those files. You're really using data that's already in memory, so getting to it is faster.

However, because RAM is erased when you power down, a virtual disk can also be a nightmare. If you use one, make sure you copy your data back onto the real life hard disk before shutting down for the day, or all your stuff on the fake drive E will be lost.

Buying the Right RAM

Before you hit the shopping malls, here's some other info you need to know in order to get the right RAM chips for your PC: RAM prices fluctuate more than the price of gas. Shop around and don't hesitate to wait until you think the price is right.

Get the Right Kind

First, you need to know what kind of RAM chips your PC uses, such as DIPPs or SIMMs. In addition, if your PC uses SIMMs, you need to know whether they are 30-pin "low-density," or 72-pin "high-density" SIMMs (which are much wider than a 30-pin SIMMs). Also, SIMMs come in parity checking or non-parity checking styles. If you want to know more, read the sidebar coming up.

Consider Parity Checking

If you're adding SIMMs to your system, there's another detail you need to consider, and that's parity checking. Your system either uses parity checking, or it doesn't. You have to match the right SIMMs (parity checking or non-parity checking) to your system.

Basically, SIMMs come in only a couple of styles, 30-pin or 72-pin. So first you need to get the right style to match the others in your system. The 30-pin SIMMs come in two versions: 9-bit (which are designed for parity checking) and 8-bit (which aren't). The 72-pin SIMMs come with a similar choice: 36-bit (which use parity) and 32-bit (which don't).

Get the Right Speed

Once you know what kind of memory chips or SIMMs your PC uses, you also need to know their *speed*, or "access time," which is measured in nanoseconds (ns). The *smaller* the number, the faster the chip or SIMM. So a 70 ns chip is faster than a 120 ns chip. The speed is marked on the chip itself. In the following picture, the two numbers after the dash tell you that the speed of this chip is 10, which is an abbreviation for 100 ns.

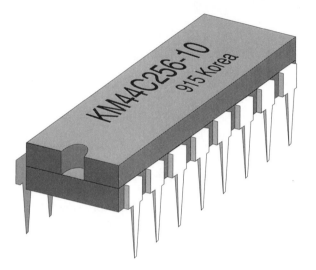

The numbers on the chip tell you its speed and capacity.

Here are some other abbreviations to know:

Number after the dash	Speed in nanoseconds
6 or 60	60 ns
7 or 70 or 70SP	70 ns
8 or 80 or 80SP	80 ns
10	100 ns
12	120 ns
15	150 ns
20	200 ns

You'll most likely find 60, 70, or 80 ns chips on newer 386, 486, and Pentium PCs. On ATs you'll probably find 100 or 120 ns chips, while older PCs use 150 or 200 ns chips instead. In any case, *you must match the speed to the other chips on your PC* (unless you decide to replace your existing RAM chips). In a pinch, you can substitute *faster* chips, but not slower ones.

Not a Catastrophe, Just a Waste

If you accidently add RAM chips that are rated slower than the ones already in the PC, you won't blow up anything, but your PC won't recognize the new RAM chips, so you won't be able to use them.

Get the Right Capacity

After speed, the next thing you need to look at is capacity. In the previous figure, the 256 before the dash tells you that the chip is part of a 256-kilobyte set. Remember that you need eight or nine of these chips to fill a row of memory so you actually get 256 K. *(All the chips in a row of memory must be the same speed and capacity.)* Some PCs make this stuff easier by allowing you to use memory modules, where the eight or nine chips are all soldered together in a single unit of memory. Common capacities for DIP chips include 64 K, 256 K, and 1 M. SIMMs have larger capacities, ranging from 256 K to 16 M.

Faster Chips Aren't a Cure-All

Just because you install faster RAM chips, don't expect your PC to benefit from the speed increase. The speed at which RAM is accessed is set by the PC's internal clock, not the chips. Suppose you replace a set of old 100 ns RAM chips with some new, slick 70 ns units. If you then replace your system's CPU with one that has a faster clock speed, your system may benefit from both the faster CPU and the faster RAM.

Installation: Thanks for the Memory

Get your PC tool kit, do your usual backup, update your emergency diskette, and open your PC (see Chapter 12). Take a look at the motherboard and check out the spot where you can add the new chips. If you've already decided that you have to add RAM through an expansion board, skip this step.

DRAM!

One more bit of memory stuff you should know about, especially if you start shopping for a new PC rather than upgrading. Your PC typically has one main core of memory, made up of chips called DRAM—Dynamic RAM. (This is true whether you insert those chips separately or in a SIMM.) Anyway, DRAM is not exactly the fastest RAM chip manufactured, but it is the most cost-effective for use in large banks of RAM.

To speed up your PC, a lot of manufacturers include a RAM cache (an area in memory that holds the most requested data). This RAM cache is made up of SRAM (static RAM) chips, which beat standard DRAM chips hands down in the speed department. Static RAM, you see, doesn't degrade over time like Dynamic RAM (DRAM), so it doesn't need continual refresh cycles. This makes SRAM more expensive, but certainly fine for use in small RAM caches. By keeping the data you use most often in a cache, your PC can get to it quicker than searching regular memory for it.

Well, a new kind of DRAM chip has entered the market, and it's called EDO (extended data out) DRAM. Although they're not as fast as SRAM chips, they're faster than regular DRAM. Manufacturers are using them in place of standard DRAM chips to speed up regular memory. To keep costs down, these systems typically do not include a SRAM cache. That only slows them down by about 10 percent, even though you save $1500 over a standard DRAM/SRAM cache system.

If your motherboard's full, you may have to yank some chips and replace them with higher capacity chips. A chip puller tool (which looks like large tweezers) is really handy if you find that you have to remove DIP chips. SIMMs don't really require any tool to remove or insert.

Now, before you do anything, make sure that you discharge any static electricity. To remove a DIP chip, start with a small flat edge screwdriver. Gently pry up one of the ends of the chip. Then move to the other end and pry it up a little. Repeat until the chip is fairly loose. You can use the chip puller or your fingers to extract the chip.

To remove a SIMM, first check to see how it's attached. You notice a clip at either end of the SIMM that holds the SIMM in place. To release the SIMM, press down on each clip to release it. The SIMM pops forward a bit. Hold the SIMM at its top edge and lift it out.

Once you remove any old chips that you can't use, you're ready to insert your new chips. Make sure that you are thoroughly grounded before you pick up the chips.

Yank the Banks

In the earlier example, the motherboard was full, even though it had only 2 M of RAM. You can add more RAM via a memory expansion board, but again, some PCs don't enable you to do that. In this case, your only choice is to pull some RAM modules from the lower-numbered banks and replace them with higher capacity modules. Just keep in mind that memory chips work in *banks*, so in this example, you have to pull all the chips in one bank—which, because the PC in question has two banks of four rows each, means that you need to pull four of the eight 256 K SIMMs.

You can replace the four SIMMs with 1 M SIMMs for a total of 5 M. That is, if your motherboard thinks in fives. Most motherboards are marked with the increments they can handle, which is usually something like 2 M, 4 M, 8 M, 16 M, and so on. In this example, you more than likely have to pull *all eight* 256 K SIMMs and replace them with 1 M SIMMs to get a total of 8 M. You can also replace them with 2 M or 4 M SIMMs if your motherboard supports a total of 16 (2 M x 8) or 32 (4 M x 8) megabytes.

Gently pry up the chip you want to remove.

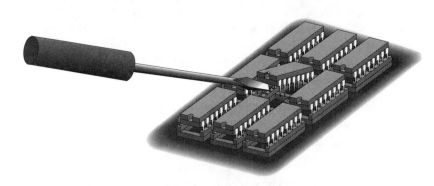

To insert a DIP chip, first make sure that the chip's legs are straight. If needed, turn the chip on its side and press it gently against the side of a table to align the legs perpendicular to the chip itself. Take a minute to use a can of compressed air to clean out any dust around the chip sockets.

Next, look for a notch at one end of the chip. You have to match this notch up with the same notch on the chip socket.

Insert the chip, making sure that you don't accidently bend any of the legs outside of the socket. Press the chip in place. If you're using an insertion tool (another one of those handy gadgets you find in most PC tool kits), place the chip in the tool. Insert the chip into the socket; the tool makes sure that the legs line up correctly with the holes. Press the plunger at the end of the tool's handle, and it applies an even pressure on the chip, securing it into the socket.

To remove a SIMM, release the clips holding it in place.

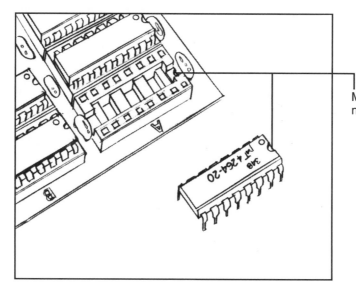

Match up the notch on the chip with the same notch on the socket.

If you're inserting a SIMM, hold it at its top edge. Flip the SIMM so that the notch at one end matches up with the same notch on the SIMM socket. Position the SIMM over the socket and gently insert it at an angle, as shown.

When you insert the SIMM, press it back gently until the tabs pop up to lock it in place. You must insert some SIMMs at a 90-degree angle perpendicular to the socket and rock them backwards into a 10 o'clock position in order to lock them into place.

Once you line up the legs, press the chip into place.

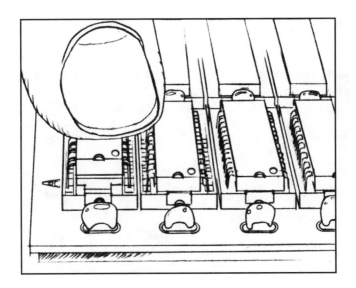

Hold the SIMM at the top edge to insert it.

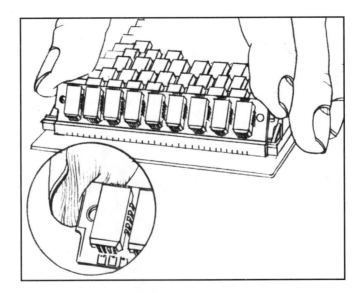

To insert a SIPP, follow the general directions for a DIP chip. First, make sure that you didn't bend any of the SIPP's legs. Next, line up the legs with the holes in the SIPP socket. A SIPP doesn't have a notch to help you line it up right like a DIP chip does, so make sure that the number 1 pin on the SIPP aligns with the number 1 hole in the socket. Use other SIPPs on the motherboard as a guide so you can be sure that you're inserting the SIPP in the correct direction. Press the chip gently into place—if you press too hard, you could wreck the socket, and you'll have to replace your entire motherboard.

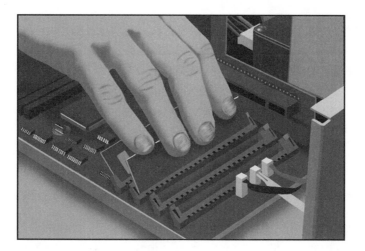

Press the SIMM gently into place.

Finally, check your work to make sure that none of the chip's legs are hanging out. Check your PC manual to see if you have to either flip a DIP switch (which acts kind of like a small light switch), or move a jumper to "turn on" the new memory. You'll probably only have to do this kind of nonsense on old XT PC. If you need help with DIP switches, check out Chapter 24, "Fiddling with Ports, IRQs, Addresses, and Such."

Put your PC back together and turn it on. Your PC will realize that you added some memory, but it'll be confused—you'll know because you'll see an error message. Don't panic—at least not yet. All you need to do is to make sure the amount of memory recorded in CMOS is the correct amount. Newer BIOSes will automatically update this figure; but if it's wrong, you need to do it yourself. If you need help, see Chapter 24 again.

What to Do If You're Upgrading Your Laptop

First, make sure that you protect your data and then turn the laptop off. Getting into the system board of a laptop is not as simple a process as flipping open the hatch. With most laptops, all you have to do is remove a latch by pressing down and sliding it in the correct direction (like removing the latch on a remote control). With others, you have to work a little bit harder; you may even have to unscrew the keyboard from the bottom of the case. Check your manual for complete directions on how to disassemble your laptop.

Once you find the memory sockets, they pretty much work the same way as the ones you find in desktop PCs. Just make sure that you line up the memory modules correctly and push it gently into its socket.

What Could Go Wrong

If your PC doesn't recognize your new memory, you may have forgotten to flip the right DIP switch or to move the right jumper. Check the PC's manual to see what you need to do.

You can also recheck the chips you inserted to make sure that each one is firmly in place. Also look for any pins that might not have made it into the right socket.

If you inserted a chip in the wrong direction, you may have burnt it out. If that's the case, you need to replace the chip.

If all this fails, then it's time to put your PC back like it was. Take out the new memory, put back any old memory chips in their old locations, then power on the system with your emergency diskette in the drive. Remember, your emergency diskette has the AUTOEXEC.BAT and CONFIG.SYS files for your computer back up before you started the upgrade process. If you get a prompt and everything appears in order, the problem was evidently with something you added (or took away). If the problem persists, however, the problem was caused by the upgrade process itself, and it may be time to take the machine to the shop.

The Least You Need to Know

Getting the right kind of memory for your system is probably the hardest thing to do. Here are some pointers to help you along the way:

➤ Check your PC's manual to determine its maximum amount of RAM.

➤ Type **MEM** at the DOS prompt to see how much memory your PC has.

➤ Buy at least enough memory so that your PC has 8 M minimum (maybe 4 M if you're really on a budget). Buy more if you can afford it.

➤ Open up the PC to see where you can put more RAM chips. Adding memory through an expansion card is sometimes an option.

➤ While you've got the PC open, check out what kind of chips your PC uses: DIPs, SIMMs, or maybe even SIPPs.

➤ Also know the speed (in nanoseconds) of the RAM chips and their capacity.

➤ Shop around when buying RAM chips; their prices change daily.

Getting a Clearer Picture

There are two pieces to your PC's video pie: the monitor itself, and the video card. The monitor's in charge of displaying the best picture it can; it sets the upper limit of what you're gonna see. The video card, on the other hand, assembles the image you want to display; it determines the level of detail and the color palette that the monitor can use. To get the best picture, these two parts need to work together.

In other words, if you have a lousy monitor, buying a super great video card isn't going to make you happy. On the other hand, you'll be equally displeased with the combination of a super expensive monitor and a dime-store video card. So match the capabilities of both to get the best results.

Do You Really Need It?

If all you use are text-based DOS programs, you don't really need to worry about the quality of what you're seeing. If you use Windows or OS/2 Warp, with their fancy fonts and pretty pictures, you'll want to invest in a good video system. Also, you don't need to worry about getting a fancy color monitor if you'll be using your computer to crunch numbers rather than to work with graphics.

Uh, There's Something Wrong with My Monitor

Before you decide to throw everything out and invest in a new video system for your PC, here are some things you should check:

➤ If you see a faint after-image of some program on the screen, it could be that you left that image on-screen for too long, without any movement going on. When that happens, the unchanged image starts to burn itself into the screen. If that's happened, there's not a lot you can do now. To prevent burn-in, get yourself a good screen-saver program.

➤ If your once-quiet monitor suddenly starts making a loud humming noise, it may be that the old guy is going out, and you'll have to replace it soon. If the monitor only squeaks while you're in a particular program, could be that the program is trying to make the monitor display stuff which it's not capable of. If you can switch the program to plain VGA mode, chances are your monitor (unless it's a dinosaur) can take it. Check out the upcoming section for the lowdown on video modes.

➤ If your monitor starts displaying funny colors or no color at all, check the cable to ensure you plugged it in all the way. Also, look at the video plug for any bent pins. If you find some, bend them back (gently, gently). If the funky colors appear only when you're using a particular program, check its setup to see if you can change the *palette* (a fancy word for color wardrobe).

Changing the Colors Can Help

When you're using a monochrome (one-color) monitor like the ones you find on a lot of older laptops, selecting a different palette can really help you see what's on-screen.

➤ If you're having trouble reading what's on-screen, another thing you might try is playing around with the contrast and brightness knobs. The contrast knob is marked with a half white, half black circle; the brightness knob is marked with a little sun symbol.

If I Want to Upgrade, What Are My Options?

To understand what you can upgrade to, you need to know a little about video modes:

MDA, CGA, and EGA   MDA, or monochrome display adapter, is an old monochrome standard that only displays text, not graphics. CGA, or color graphics adapter, was the first color video standard; it displays text in 16 glorious colors, or graphics in two to four colors. Old XTs have CGA monitors, which are like glorified TV sets. EGA, enhanced graphics adapter, came later and improved on CGA somewhat; it can display both text and graphics in 16 colors. The original ATs use EGA monitors, making them the first digital color monitors designed specifically for use with a personal computer.

Hercules Graphics Adaptor   The first high-resolution monochrome video standard, HGA, is still in use by a surprisingly large number of systems. In the 1980s, color was expensive, so buyers settled for monochrome—and Hercules was monochrome. If you bought a used computer from a bank auction, there's a two-in-three chance it uses Hercules Mono. Hercules is still a major manufacturer of video cards; but unlike the old days, today's Hercules brand card *is not a Hercules Graphics Adapter card*—it is an SVGA card. If you look hard enough, you can find an HGA replacement card for very little money.

VGA (Video Graphics Array)   VGA made its first appearance in 1987, increasing the number of available colors to 256. VGA is by far the most common video mode in use today. Monochrome monitors have recently been adapted to use VGA; so a new high-resolution mono monitor needs a VGA card (not necessarily SVGA), and VGA cards are cheap.

8514/A   This is the first very-high-resolution graphics array, although relatively limited in color. If you're using an IBM PS/2, and the pixels (the dots on the screen that make up the images) look really small, then you may be using 8514/A graphics.

XGA (eXtended Graphics Array)   IBM's be-all, end-all graphics array that was supposed to put VGA to shame, but it never really got accepted as a standard. Some IBM-brand monitors require an XGA adaptor.

SVGA (Super Video Graphics Array) SVGA takes the more common VGA mode and improves upon it. SVGA isn't a standard per se, but when you buy SVGA, you typically get the capability to display more colors at higher *resolutions*.

Here's what text looks like at 640 by 480 resolution.

Look here and you'll see some fuzziness in the way the letters are displayed.

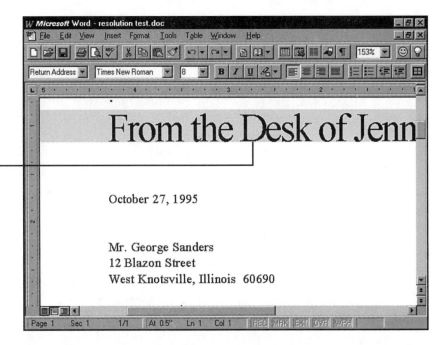

Here's that same text at 1024 by 768 resolution.

At higher resolutions, you don't get the fuzz.

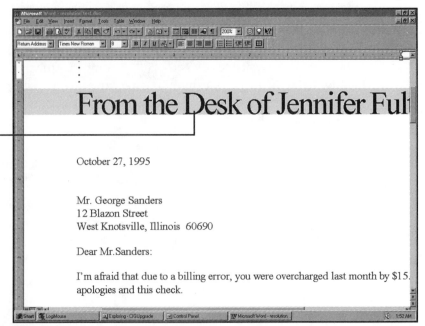

So What's Resolution?

Well, the image you see on-screen is made up of tiny dots called pixels. A screen's resolution is determined by the number of pixels that appear on the screen. Common resolutions include 640 by 480 (that's 640 pixels across by 480 pixels down), 800 by 600, 1024 by 768, and 1280 by 1024. At lower resolutions, there are fewer pixels to fill the screen, so they're bigger and fatter. At higher resolutions, there are more pixels, which are smaller, so they provide finer detail to an image.

To get the best image, you need to match up a good video card with a good monitor. So if you're currently looking at an old EGA or CGA monitor, you'll need to replace both the monitor and your video card because you can't mix and match video standards. For example, you can't just hook up an old EGA card to a new VGA monitor.

If you have a VGA monitor, you can upgrade to an SVGA (accelerator) card, but you won't see any improvement in resolution (the monitor controls the upper limits of that). Also, you may only see a small improvement in speed because the card has to step down to VGA mode in order to work with your monitor; in some situations, you may even experience slower speeds. Your best bet here is to upgrade to an SVGA monitor and a good SVGA graphics card.

Update the Card, Too

Keep in mind that VGA and SVGA monitors produce an analog signal, which of course you can't connect to older MDA, CGA, or EGA video cards (which produce digital signals), even though you might want to try. So updating just your monitor and not the card isn't a likely scenario.

Okay, You Sold Me. So What Should I Look For?

When shopping for a monitor, the salesperson will throw a lot of goofy sounding words at you, trying to confuse you into letting go of your wallet. Here's some information you should take with you for self-defense:

Resolution Okay, I've already gone over this one. Look for the higher resolutions such as 1024 by 768 (good), 1280 by 1024 (better), and even 1600 by 1280 (best). Expect to pay bigger bucks for higher resolutions. A standard VGA monitor supports

Monitor Prices
Expect to pay anywhere from $300 to $2,000 for a monitor. You can probably get a decent one for around $400 to $450.

one resolution—640 x 480. The better (uh, that means more expensive) SVGA monitors support multiple resolutions and are for that reason called "multiscan" monitors. Besides, it's a cool, sci-fi-sounding term.

Size This one's easy; it's the size of the viewing area. Monitors today are usually 14 or 15 inches (measured diagonally), but, for a price, you can get a monitor that's anywhere from 17 to 21 inches.

Dot Pitch Basically, this is the on-screen distance between those little pixels. A good number to look for here is .28 mm (millimeters); the lower this number is, the sharper the image on-screen. Each pixel on a low dot-pitch monitor is less fuzzy around its edges, so color pictures are crisper. This is because there's less fuzz in between the colors.

Refresh Rate Sometimes called the scanning frequency, this tells you how often the electron beams (cathode rays) update the image on-screen. The faster the refresh rate, the less flickering you'll see. 70 Hz is a decent speed for 1024 by 768, while 60 Hz is average for a higher resolution like 1280 by 1024. (At higher resolutions, it's normal for the refresh rate to go down.) Multiscan monitors (monitors that support multiple resolutions) that alter their refresh rates for added clarity at the lower resolutions are called "multisync" monitors (another cool, sci-fi-sounding term).

Match the Refresh Rates

The refresh rate your monitor uses must match at least one of the rates your video card supports. (If you buy a multisync monitor which is capable of supporting multiple refresh rates, making a match between it and a video card is easier.) If you mismatch the two, you can wreck your monitor. On the back of each video card's package is a list of resolutions and corresponding refresh rates which the card supports. Finding the refresh rates for a monitor isn't as easy; you'll need to ask a salesperson or support representative to supply you with literature from the manufacturer. You'll need the monitor's information later when setting up your video card, so it's worth the trouble to get it.

Video Bandwidth This is the maximum frequency at which the monitor is capable of operating. It's the same as the maximum horizontal resolution multiplied by the maximum vertical resolution multiplied by the maximum refresh rate. In short, it's the size of the biggest video signal the monitor supports. The higher, the better; 65 MHz to 75 MHz is about average. (Compare that to 3.58 MHz for the standard North American TV signal.) The video bandwidth of any resolution probably averages out close to this maximum value; as resolution increases, the refresh rate proportionally decreases.

Interlacing   An interlaced monitor paints an image on-screen by first updating all the even-numbered rows (starting with the first, row "0"), then skewing the electron guns by half-a-pixel and updating all the odd-numbered rows in-between. It's like painting an American flag starting with all the red stripes, then filling in all the white stripes. The first multiscan monitors had to support interlacing in order to produce 800×600 and 1024×768 images, because they weren't really capable of scanning a single image at these high resolutions. Interlaced video can result in an annoying flicker that can strain your eyes. Most monitors today are non-interlaced, which means that they paint the image on-screen sequentially.

Surface   This is the second easiest, second least-technical issue on this list. Average monitors, like average television sets, are ever-so-slightly convex (curved toward the viewer). Sony patented and then licensed the patent for picture tubes with a *flat screen*; its contents aren't distorted by the shape of the tube. You pay more for a flat screen, and you may not notice the difference in the store—but just use one for an hour or two and ask your eyes how they feel.

Energy Star or DPMS   Your monitor is the most energy consuming part of your PC, so getting an energy smart monitor (one that carries the Energy Star logo) can save you about $75 a year on your electric bills.

Multiscan, Multisync, Multi-mode   This kind of monitor can switch between several kinds of video modes easily, making it simpler to get your monitor to work with your video card. Technically, a multiscan monitor is one that supports several resolutions. A multisync monitor can adjust its refresh rates for all the various resolutions it supports. A multimode card is capable of "fudging" older video modes such as CGA or Hercules Mono if for some reason you're using a program that requires such a mode.

When shopping for a monitor, by all means, test it! First, go into Windows and look at all the icons. Are the ones at the middle of the screen as crisp looking as those at the edges? Can you read the text in the title bars without a lot of effort, even at 640 by 480 resolution? Look at the edges of the lines on-screen. Do they bend slightly at the edges, or are they sharp and crisp?

Start a word processor such as Write or WordPad. Type a few words in a small font and look at the letters. Are they fuzzy, or sharp and easy to read?

Go into a graphics program such as Paintbrush (which comes with Windows 3.1) or Paint (which comes with Windows 95) and draw a big circle. If it looks like a circle and not a flat tire, the monitor probably works well with graphics. Finally, play with the monitor's controls. Does the image jump as you turn the brightness up and down? If so, that's a sign of a cheap monitor. If your monitor passes all these tests, you'll probably be very happy with it.

Shopping for a Video (Graphics) Card

The main thing to keep in mind when you shop for a new video card is that it must match the capabilities of your monitor. Otherwise, the card may not even work at all. To do that, you should look closely at the resolution capabilities and refresh rates of both the monitor and the video card.

Watch Out If You Have Local Bus Video!

Some PCs with local bus video have the video stuff built into the motherboard. Before you can upgrade, you have to disable the video thing on the motherboard and then add the video card you want to use. To do this, you have to flip a DIP switch or move a jumper. Check out your PC's manual for help on what to do—if you need help setting the DIP switch or jumper, see Chapter 24, "Fiddling with Ports, IRQs, Addresses, and Such."

When you go shopping for a video card (sometimes called a graphics card, by the way), don't let all the techie terms throw you:

What's It Gonna Cost Me? A video card costs anywhere from $60 to $375, depending on the card's capabilities. You can probably find a pretty decent one for around $175.

Accelerator Accelerators used to be separate, but video cards today all "accelerate," which means they have on-board chips that take over the responsibility of handling the video from the CPU. This makes the process of keeping your screen updated a whole lot faster.

VESA or VL-Bus Fits into a VL-bus expansion slot, that is, if your PC has one. A *local bus* slot provides a super fast pathway to the CPU, kind of like driving down one of those "Ride Share" lanes on the highway during rush hour—the video signal avoids the other computer "traffic" and gets to the CPU much faster. VESA local bus used to be the most common, but it has been replaced by PCI bus.

PCI Fits into a PCI expansion slot, which you'll find on Pentium-type PCs. Like VL-bus, PCI provides a similar "super fast highway lane" to shuttle video information to the CPU as quickly as possible. PCI was not designed exclusively for video, so you can use a PCI bus slot for something other than your video card if you want.

Video RAM On-board memory allows the video board to assemble the image before passing it onto the monitor. It also controls the amount of colors the video card can produce. Get a card with at least some on-board RAM—preferably 1 M. If possible, get a card that uses VRAM (video RAM) memory, not DRAM (dynamic RAM), which is slower. VRAM chips are cheap and don't use parity checking. (Remember that term from Chapter 15?)

8-bit, 16-bit, 24-bit, and So On These are the number of bits used in one "word" of information in VRAM. Here's a little formula you can play with on your calculator—at the video card's lowest supported resolution, 2 raised to the number of bits equals the total number of colors the video card can display; anywhere from 256 colors to 16.7 million (2 to the 24th power). Cards that advertise 64-bits and higher don't provide more colors—they simply use the extra bits for faster storage and retrieval of the video image.

Cheaper DRAM
There are some new DRAM chips on the market that approach VRAM performance at a lower cost: synchronous DRAM (SDRAM) and Rambus DRAM (RDRAM). The latest PCs are all being sold with them. Certainly a good way to get fast, fast, fast video at an incredible price.

Check This Out...

One other important factor you need to consider when shopping for the perfect video card is whether or not that card will work with the programs you want to use. If you use Windows or OS/2 Warp, make sure that the card supports that program. If you want to upgrade to Windows 95, make sure that it works with that, too. If you use DOS only, you'll have to make sure that the card supplies a *driver program* to help it talk to the specific programs you run, such as AutoCAD, Microsoft Word, Lotus 1-2-3, and so on.

Connecting a New Monitor (Difficulty Factor: -10)

Connecting a monitor to a PC is not terribly difficult. First, however, you may have to put the monitor together. That is, you may have to attach the base to the monitor.

To attach a swivel base, you start by flipping the monitor over. You may notice some slots into which you can slip the connectors on the base. Do that and flip the completed monitor back over.

To connect your monitor to the PC, make sure that its power switch is off. Plug the monitor's connector into the back of the video card. Now, take the power cord for the monitor and plug that into the wall.

Plug the monitor into the back of the video card.

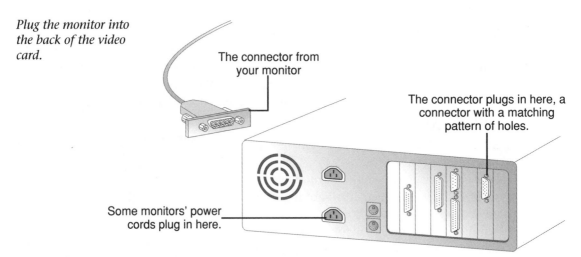

The connector from your monitor

The connector plugs in here, a connector with a matching pattern of holes.

Some monitors' power cords plug in here.

Plug It into the System Unit Instead

Some older style monitors don't plug into the wall, but instead plug into the system unit. So if your monitor's plug doesn't fit into the wall outlet, don't force it. It's probably one of the types that you need to connect through the system unit.

Adding Your New Video Graphics Card

Adding your new video (graphics) card is similar to adding any new card to your PC. Before you start, take the usual precautions: do a backup, update your emergency diskette, and so on. (See Chapter 12 for help.) And before you begin to work, make sure you discharge built-up static by touching something metal, such as a metal desktop or filing cabinet. Ready? Then take the cover off the PC.

First, remove the old video card. To do that, disconnect the monitor from the card. Lay out some paper on your desktop. Unscrew the retaining screw holding the card in place. Once again, make sure to discharge any static before continuing. Grasp the video card at the top and gently pull it straight up. Lay the old video card on the paper for now.

Next, unwrap your new video card. Before you touch it, discharge any built-up static and then remove the video card from its static bag. You can put the old card into this bag to keep it safe, if you want.

If you're putting the card into a different slot than the previous card (for instance, into an unused VL-Bus or PCI slot), then set it down on the paper for now. Restore the slot cover for the old slot and screw in its retaining screw. Remove the retaining screw from the slot you want to use with your new video card and remove the slot cover. There! Now you can insert the new video card.

Uh, almost. If your PC doesn't have a video card per se (its video is handled by a special chip on the motherboard), you have to turn off your old local bus video chip first. Check your manual; this usually requires some switch setting and jumper pulling. If you need help, see Chapter 24, "Fiddling with Ports, IRQs, Addresses, and Such."

Hold the video card at the top with both hands and position its connectors over the expansion slot. Press down slowly until the video card slips into place. Screw the retaining screw back in.

> **Check This Out...**
>
> **Change Your Windows Driver First**
> Before you start taking everything apart, you may want to change the Windows display driver to something friendly, such as its generic VGA driver. This keeps you from seeing junk when you start Windows. Later on, you can switch to the new video driver you install. If you need help, see Chapter 23.

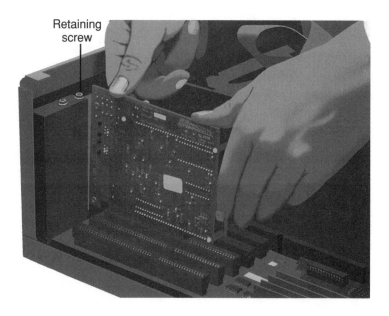

Retaining screw

Push your video card into place.

Connect the monitor to the card and turn the PC on to test your connection. If everything works right, turn the PC back off and put its cover back on. Now you need to install your *driver*; you find this on the diskette that came with the video card. The driver is the program that helps your PC talk to the video card so it can translate its signals properly for the monitor. If you need help installing the driver for DOS or Windows, see Chapters 22 and 23.

What Could Go Wrong

If you're having trouble with the monitor, first check to make sure that you properly connected it to the PC, and that none of the pins on the connector are bent. This is usually the trouble if your monitor suddenly starts showing one color, or no colors at all.

Check to make sure that the card fits properly in its slot. If necessary, take the card out and put it back in again. Check to see if there are any switches or jumpers on the card that you have to set to make it work.

The Least You Need to Know

When choosing a new monitor and video card, remember these things:

➤ Make sure that your monitor and video card will work together. Compare resolutions and refresh rates.

➤ *Resolution* is determined by the number of pixels that appear—the higher the resolution, the more pixels. *Dot-pitch* is the distance between pixels. The closer the pixels are, the better the image.

➤ *Refresh rate* is the rate at which the screen image is refreshed, or updated. The faster that's done, the less flickering you're likely to see.

➤ *Interlacing* is a process where the image is updated by painting the even rows of pixels first, then painting the odd rows.

➤ A *multiscan* or similar monitor can handle several different types of video resolutions, which makes it easier for you to find a video card that will work with it.

➤ Most video cards today are accelerators; they include a chip which takes over the PC's video business so that the CPU doesn't have to bother with it.

➤ *VL-bus* is a special kind of expansion slot that enables the video signal to shoot straight from the video card to the CPU. This makes things appear on-screen faster.

➤ *VRAM* is a special kind of RAM chip that is faster than ordinary DRAM chips. It is used exclusively in the memory of a video card.

Replacing a Floppy Drive

Diskettes come in two basic sizes: 5 1/4-inch and 3 1/2-inch. Older PCs typically contain only one 5 1/4-inch floppy drive which is pretty inconvenient these days; most people are using 3 1/2-inch disks because they hold more data. To be able to install most new programs and to share data with coworkers, you'll probably need to add a 3 1/2-inch drive. (Actually, to be truly cool, you'll have to add a CD-ROM drive too—but that's another chapter.)

Of course, even if your PC has a 3 1/2-inch drive, that doesn't guarantee that your troubles are over. That's because the darn things not only come in different sizes, but also different *capacities*. Low-density drives can only read low capacity "double-density" diskettes, which means that if you're trying to use a 3 1/2-inch low-density drive, it can only read diskettes with a capacity of 720 K. (Low-density 5 1/4-inch diskettes have a capacity of only 360 K.) Low-density drives can't read high-density diskettes, such as 5 1/4-inch 1.2 M diskettes, or 3 1/2-inch 1.44 M diskettes. So if your PC has only low

You Need an Empty Drive Bay To add a new drive to your PC, you have to have an open drive bay. You'll probably notice a slot with a blank cover on the front of your PC—you can place your new drive in this open drive bay.

density drives, you'll want to upgrade to high-density drives soon. (Yes, you read right, "double-density" is the lower of the two.)

If you're not sure whether your drive is a high-density one or not, format a diskette and see how much free space is listed after the formatting is done. If you have a diskette that you know is double-density (it's marked "DD" or "2D" someplace) and you can't format it using just the plain vanilla FORMAT command, chances are you have the high-density floppy drive—which, if you'll remember, is a good thing. Another way you can tell: Take a look at the diskettes your drive normally uses. High-density 3 1/2-inch diskettes are usually marked HD someplace, and they have two tiny holes, one on either side of the disk. A high-density 5 1/4-inch diskette *does not have* a colored ring (a hub ring) around the inside edge of the circle that's located in the middle of the diskette.

Hey, Something's Wrong Here

Some of the problems that occur with diskette drives have more to do with "operator error" than something that's actually broken, so you might be able to fix whatever's wrong without replacing the drive. For example, you might start up your PC one day and see this nonsense:

> Non-system disk or disk error. Replace and strike any key when ready.

Nothing's wrong with your diskette drive, or the hard disk itself. In fact, nothing much is wrong at all; you simply left a diskette in drive A when you booted (started) your system. Take the silly thing out and reboot your PC by pressing **Ctrl+Alt+Delete**. Do not strike a key like the message tells you to—doing that can infect your PC if the diskette that was left in the drive has any viruses.

The PC Can't Read My Diskette!

If you insert a diskette with the hope that your PC can read its data and it can't, check a couple of things first before you chuck the diskette (or the drive). First, remove the diskette and tap it in your palm a few times. This aligns the magnetic material inside. Reinsert the diskette and see if your PC can read it now. Be sure to close the door on a 5 1/4-inch drive—if you didn't before, that may be the reason why your PC can't read the diskette.

Next, you may want to try using the diskette in somebody else's computer. If it works there, that can mean that your drive's having some problems. Try another diskette in your drive. Same trouble? Well, before you call 911, check CMOS to see if the drive is set up properly (see Chapter 24 for help). You can also open up the PC and make sure that the drive's cable hasn't come loose or something else equally as silly.

If the diskette doesn't work in your friend's drive, then something may be wrong with the diskette. Did you format the diskette properly? If you copied data to the diskette, the disk was formatted, but it may not have been formatted correctly.

If you're trying to copy something to the diskette and you can't, the problem may be that the diskette is *write-protected*, which somebody did to keep the data on the disk from being overwritten. Remove the tab from your 5 1/4-inch floppy (it looks like a piece of tape) or flip the tab back down on your 3 1/2-inch floppy. (On a 3 1/2-inch floppy, the write protect tab is located in the upper left-hand corner when the diskette is flipped on its back.) After you do this, you can use the diskette again.

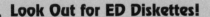

Look Out for ED Diskettes!

There's a new kind of diskette out there that you should be aware of because it looks like a 3 1/2-inch diskette, but it isn't. If your diskette is tattooed with the letters "ED," then it's an extended-capacity diskette. Mr. ED can hold a lot more data (4 M) than his similarly sized friend, but he only works in an extended-density drive. Don't worry about running into many of these guys soon—they're fairly expensive, so most people don't use them.

If the drive still can't read the diskette, check its capacity. Are you trying to read a high-density diskette in a low-density drive? If so, it won't work. If you're sure that the diskette is the right capacity for your drive, and the diskette came from a coworker, then it may be that his drive, or your drive, is out of alignment. If the problem keeps cropping up with other diskettes, you should check out the guilty drive—just keep in mind that repairing the drive may cost more than replacing it.

A Mac Disk Won't Work

If you borrowed a friend's Macintosh diskette, it probably won't work in your PC, unless it came from a Power PC. That's because most Mac diskettes are formatted funny, at least from a PC's point of view. (Unfortunately, this will sound pretty strange when you discover that your friend's Mac can probably read your PC's diskettes, but I can't help that.)

If you get an error message while trying to use your diskette (like Sector not found), you should try to copy whatever you can off the diskette. If the drive won't let you copy anything but you need to save an important file, you'll have to use a disk recovery utility like the ones you'll find in Norton Utilities, PC Tools, or Mace Utilities. Uh, good luck.

I Can't Format This Diskette!

If you try to format a diskette and you get some bogus message about "invalid media" or something, you probably tried to format a diskette to the wrong capacity. For example, if you insert a low-density diskette into a high-density drive and type this:

FORMAT A:

You get an error message because the drive tries to format it as if it is a high-density diskette. If it is of the 3 1/2-inch variety, then try something like this:

FORMAT A: /F:720

If it's a 5 1/4-inch diskette, try this instead:

FORMAT A: /F:360

Which Drive Is Which?

If you can't format your diskette because you're having trouble figuring out which drive is A and which is B, type **DIR A:** and look to see which drive light comes on. The drive that lights up is A. If you get an error message telling you: Not ready reading drive A. Abort, Retry, Fail?, press A for Abort.

Shopping for a New Drive

Before you go shopping for your drive, take a scout team and assess the situation: does your PC have an open drive bay? If not, you can replace your existing 5 1/4-inch drive with a combo (dual) drive that crams both a 5 1/4-inch drive and a 3 1/2-inch drive in the space that one drive normally takes up. Or, you can add an external floppy drive that sits on your desk and attaches to your PC through a parallel port (the same kind of connector that you use to attach a printer—of course, this option only works if you have two parallel ports, or if you don't have a printer).

The Cost

A new high-density 3 1/2-inch floppy drive runs about $45, while a high-density 5 1/4-inch drive costs about $55. A combo (dual) drive runs about $90. External floppy drives cost around $180.

If you're running out of drive bays and you're thinking about adding a tape backup at some point, you may want to consider the new 3 1/2-inch diskette drive/tape drive combos that are new on the market. They retail at around $200. Both diskette and tape drive parts use the same floppy drive controller, so for a tape drive, they're relatively easy to install.

There are two other options when considering a floppy diskette upgrade:

➤ Iomega Zip™ and SyQuest EZ™ drives, which use relatively inexpensive magnetic disk cartridges about the size of a 3 1/2-inch floppy diskette to record around 100 M worth of data. These are actually more like single-platter hard disks, so they're actually less volatile than tape cartridges.

➤ Magneto-optical "MO" drives, which can store anywhere from 20 M to 1.3 G on a shiny optical disk enclosed in a cartridge. MO technology stores data using both a magnetic field and a laser working in partnership, but MO reads that same data optically like a CD-ROM, so your backup data is very non-volatile (less likely to degrade over time). The least expensive MO mechanism is called "floptical," because the disc cartridge is about as small as a 3 1/2-inch diskette, though it holds about 21 M of data.

No Assembly Required (or Wanted) When shopping for an external floppy drive, make sure that you buy one that is already assembled, with a built-in power supply. Look for a connecting cable, too. Also, it should come with a diskette that contains software for updating your BIOS if needed.

What Size Are Your Drive Bays?

Next, you should find out what size the drive bays are. Most today are half-height, which means that they are half the height of the older bays like the ones you find in an XT or some AT-type PCs. Half-height bays are about 1 1/2 inches tall, while a full-height bay is 3 inches. If you have a full-height drive, you'll need to get a cover plate and adapter kit to help you adapt today's half-height drives to fit it. The good news is that these cover plates are not terribly expensive.

How Are Your Drives Mounted?

The next question you need to answer is this: how are the drives mounted inside your PC—do they ride rails, or are they held in place by some screws along the side? If your drives use rails, then you'll need to make sure that the drive you purchase has its rails included in the box. Otherwise, you'll need to purchase them separately. (If you're replacing a drive, you can reuse its rails to mount your new drive—no need to get new rails.)

How are the drives attached to the PC?

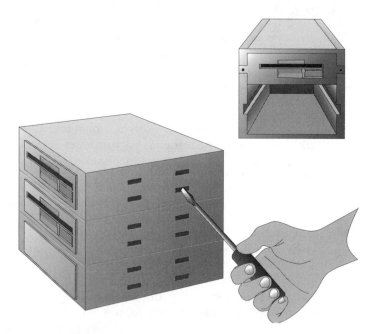

Will Your Floppy Controller Cable Accommodate Your New Drive?

Also, while you have the PC open, you need to check to see if your existing floppy controller has an additional connector for a second floppy drive (most do). Look at your current floppy drive; there you find a fat ribbon cable leading from it to the floppy controller that is located either on the motherboard or on an expansion card. If you see a connector located in the middle of this cable leading nowhere, then you have the connector you need for your new floppy drive. Otherwise you need to get a Y-cable that splits the single connection into two connectors. Also, keep in mind that your new floppy may have either a pin connector or an edge connector. The cable in your PC needs to support the type of connector on your floppy drive, otherwise you need to get a converter (most drives include such a convertor in case you need it, but ask if you're not sure).

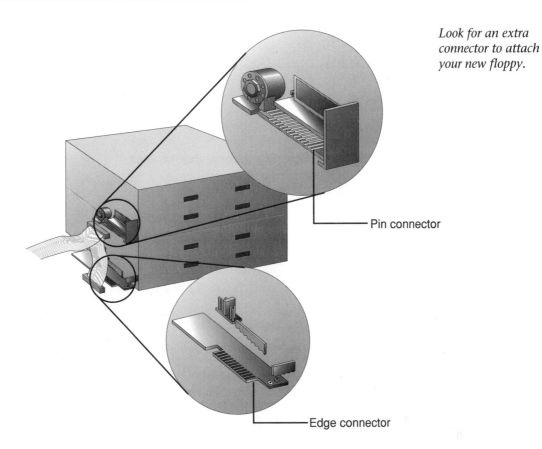

Look for an extra connector to attach your new floppy.

Pin connector

Edge connector

Is There an Open Power Connector?

In addition, look at the power supply and locate an open power connector. Running from the power supply are several connectors, each with four tiny wires and a white plastic tab at the end. Look for an open one to connect to your new floppy. If you don't find an open power connector, you have to get a Y-cable to split the power connection to the existing floppy drive into two so that you have an open connection.

PS/2 and Compaq Drives

If you own a PS/2 or a Compaq PC, chances are that it requires you to buy that brand of floppy disk drive, and *no other*. These PS/2 and Compaq drives will probably cost you a bit more than generic drives—but they're the only ones that will work in your system.

Check Your DOS and BIOS

Finally, before you run out and buy a high-density 3 1/2-inch drive for your PC, you need to see if your PC is ready for it. First of all, check your DOS version by typing **VER** at the DOS prompt and pressing **Enter**.

As long as your DOS version is DOS 3.3 or higher, you'll have no problem running the new drive. If your DOS version is lower than 3.3, you'll have to upgrade, because your DOS is so old, it just won't be able to understand the technology behind 3 1/2-inch high-density drives. If you want to use the new extended-density ED 3 1/2-inch drives instead, you're going to need DOS 5.0 or higher.

If your PC is really a dinosaur, you might also have to upgrade its BIOS too. The BIOS is a set of chips on the motherboard that handles all the boring input and output tasks. Reading data from a floppy disk falls under its job description. If the BIOS is old, again, it may not know how to deal with the newer 3 1/2-inch drives. One way to get around this problem is to buy a new drive controller with a chip that can handle the drive for the BIOS—however, some very old PCs won't accept help in this manner. Another way is to find a software program called a *driver* that does the same job. Or you can simply update the BIOS itself. To tell whether or not you'll need this kind of upgrade, start with your PC's manual. If it refuses to shed any light, then try the CMOS. What options does it include under floppy drives? If you find out that you have to upgrade the BIOS to support your new drive, see Chapter 13 for help in dealing with the BIOS guy.

Check This Out...

You May Be Out of Luck Adding a high-density 5 1/4-inch drive to an older PS/2 may prove impossible: its BIOS does not support it, and finding a replacement BIOS is difficult if not impossible.

Shopping for a Drive for Your Laptop

Laptops offer their own set of headaches when it comes to upgrading, because they are so tiny and often don't have the room. In the case of a floppy drive, you'll probably be connecting any additional floppy drive you want to add through some kind of special port on the back. For example, if you want to add 5 1/4-inch capability to your laptop, you need to buy an external floppy drive and connect it through a cable to the back of the laptop. (Which of course, you'll have to disconnect when you need to pack up the laptop and take it with you.)

Rather than adding onto a laptop, you may want to consider adding a drive to your desktop unit that's compatible with the one in your laptop unit. For one, it's cheaper, and two, you probably use your desktop PC more often. For example, if your new laptop uses a 3 1/2-inch high-density drive, rather than add an external 5 1/4-inch drive to the laptop to make it compatible to your desktop PC, add a 3 1/2-inch drive to the desktop instead.

Drivers: Dream or Nightmare?

Using a driver to update your BIOS may sound like a dream—after all, you don't have to mess with CMOS or the BIOS chips themselves. Using a driver creates certain problems though. For example, your computer has to load the driver into memory first, before it can activate the drive. So you can't use a driver for drive A, because then you can't boot from A in an emergency. The drive doesn't "exist" until the driver is loaded, and that doesn't happen until you boot the computer.

Also, a lot of backup and utility programs take over total control of floppy drives when you activate them, and they ignore any driver programs in memory. This makes them incompatible with your driver-run floppy disk drive. As a final irritant, driver programs usually assign some bizarre letter to the floppy drive, such as E: instead of what you expect, such as B:, which makes working with them a headache.

However, sometimes a driver is the only thing that will get your new floppy to work in your system. Because of this, most floppy drives come with a software driver that you can install if needed.

Putting Your New Floppy in Drive

Once you bring your new floppy drive home, it's time to connect it. To install an external floppy drive, you usually connect its cable to an open parallel port. Then connect the power cable, turn it on, and you're set (except for running the setup software, that is).

To install an internal drive, prepare your system in the usual way, following Chapter 12's instructions: run a backup, update the emergency diskette, and so on. Then turn the power off, open up the PC, and discharge any static electricity you've built up.

First, if you're replacing a drive, remove the old drive by disconnecting its data cable and then its power cable. The data cable is a wide, flat ribbon cable, while the power cable is made up of four separate wires with a small white connector on the end.

Next, remove the four screws along the sides of the drive that hold the drive in place. Slide the drive out the front of the PC. Remove the two rails on the drive (if any) and attach them to the replacement drive.

If you're not replacing a drive but simply adding a new one, then you still need to do some preparation. First, remove the faceplate that covers the empty drive bay. You can usually do this by gently prying it off with a flathead screwdriver. Keep the faceplate; it makes a great bookmark, or it may actually come in handy later if you ever remove the drive. If the bay uses rails to connect the drive, attach a set of rails to either side of your new floppy. You may find a pair of rails in the open drive (some manufacturers have

229

thought ahead here), or you may have to purchase a set yourself. Other drives don't use rails at all; instead, you simply screw the drives directly in place. In that case, ignore this rail business.

Remove the cables from your old floppy drive.

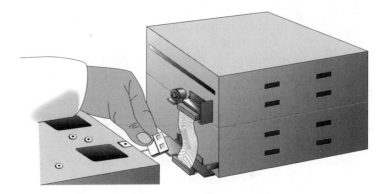

If your new drive is of the 3 1/2-inch variety, you need to mount it into an adapter so that it fits into your regular 5 1/4-inch drive bay. (Of course, if your PC has a 3 1/2-inch bay, you can dispense with this nonsense.)

Attach the drive adapter to your 3 1/2-inch drive.

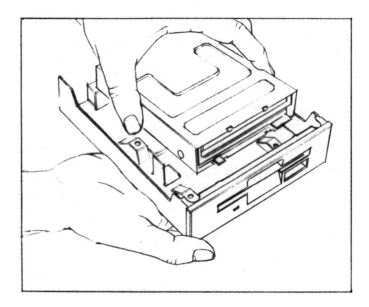

Next, you have to deal with the cable adapter that converts the drive's pin connector to an edge connector, so it works with the rest of your system. This usually entails simply connecting the cable on the drive adapter to the pin connector on the 3 1/2-inch drive.

Sometimes it gets a little harder, and you have to plug a converter board into the back of the drive. In any case, once you connect the converter, screw the drive into the adapter. You get the best success if you screw in each of the screws just a little and then adjust the drive so that you can easily insert and eject a diskette out the front. Once the drive is set properly, tighten each of the screws. Attach drive rails (if needed) to the drive adapter assembly.

Now, if your new drive is drive B, then remove the terminating resistor. It's not too hard to find; it's usually marked TR or T-RES. Look for either a lone chip, a jumper, or a set of DIP switches. If the drive is a 3 1/2-inch drive, forget the terminating thing because it doesn't come off. You only have to remove the TR from a 5 1/4-inch drive that's acting as drive A. In other words, only remove the TR if the drive is *not* located at the physical end of the cable, which is drive B's usual position.

Okay, now that that's over, slide the drive about halfway into its bay and connect the power cable and the data (ribbon) cable. One end of the data cable has a twist in the ribbon itself; this connector identifies drive A. The other non-twisted cable connects to drive B. If you're adding a dual drive (combo drive), connect it as drive A. Make sure that you don't connect the ribbon cable backwards—align the striped edge with the number 1 pin on the connector. (If you look at the numbers on the connector, you see that there are lower numbers at one end.)

If you don't have an open power connection, disconnect the power connector from the existing floppy drive and connect a Y-cable to it so that you now have two connectors. Reconnect the power to the existing drive and then use the remaining open connector on the new drive. Again, make sure that when you connect any data cable, you align the striped edge of the ribbon with pin number 1 on the connector.

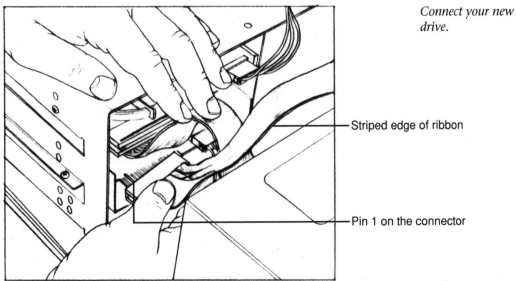

Connect your new drive.

Striped edge of ribbon

Pin 1 on the connector

Once the drive is in place, slide it the rest of the way into the bay and screw it in. Most drives have four screws (two on each side). If the drive is not mounted on rails, this can get a bit tricky; just line up the holes on the drive with the holes on the side of the bay and screw each of the four screws just a little. This gives you a little "play" so you can line up everything okay. Once you correctly line up the drive, screw everything in the rest of the way.

Screw your drive into place.

Now that it's connected, test your drive. Turn the power back on and see if it can read a diskette. If you added a new drive, you probably have to flip a switch, move a jumper, or mess with CMOS so that the PC acknowledges it first—see Chapter 24 if you need details. Once everything's okay, turn the power back off and close up your PC.

What Could Go Wrong

If your new drive doesn't work, don't panic. First, check the connections and make sure they're tight. Also, check to make sure you didn't flip the ribbon data cable and connect it backwards—the striped edge of the ribbon aligns with pin 1 on the connector.

If drive A and B are reversed, you need to swap the data (ribbon) connectors of the two drives to straighten things out. Remember that the data cable with a twist in the ribbon connects to drive A. For example, if you want your new 3 1/2-inch drive to be drive A, then place the connector with a twisted cable on drive A, and use the other connector on the data cable to connect drive B.

If neither drive is working now, you may have accidently set them up with the same letter. Usually this nonsense is taken care of by the twist in the ribbon cable; the drive closest to the twist in the cable is assumed to be drive A. This twist reverses the DS (drive select) setting on the drive. Normally, each drive comes from the factory set up as drive B. When you plug the cable with the twist in it into your first drive, it changes to become drive A.

When you work with a PC that is designed to only have one floppy drive, and you add a cable to create a second connection, neither cable has a twist in it. So both drives become drive B. To fix this problem, make sure that drive A has its DS jumper or switch set to the lowest setting, which is usually 0 or 1. Set drive B to the second DS setting, which is usually 1 or 2.

If you installed a dual or combo drive (one of those thingies with both a 5 1/4-inch and a 3 1/2-inch drive in it), you need to do some fiddling to tell the PC which one's A and which one's B. Look in the manual for help on this one, but it'll probably tell you to move a jumper on the drive somewhere.

If you notice that the drive keeps showing a directory listing of an old diskette, and not the current one, you may have changed the disk change (pin 34) setting incorrectly. Again, you need to enable this setting for all drives except a low-density 5 1/4-inch drive (it has a jumper on it). Also, this could be a sign of a data cable gone bad. Get a replacement and try again.

If you notice that your higher density drive doesn't realize when you insert a low-density ("double-density") diskette into it, or it has trouble reading and writing to low-density diskettes, the media sensor setting is messed up. Make sure that the setting is *enabled* (on).

If your PC's really old, you may have to update its BIOS so that it will recognize the new drive. If you have a software upgrade, run its setup program to update the BIOS. If you bought some new BIOS chips, install them with the help you find in Chapter 13. If you bought a new controller card, you need to install it and connect the new drive.

The Least You Need to Know

When you go out shopping for a new floppy diskette drive, here's what to look for:

➤ Before you go shopping, check to see if you have an open drive bay. If you don't, consider replacing your current floppy with a combo drive, or adding an external floppy diskette drive.

➤ If you have older full-height drive bays, you need a cover plate and adapter to fit the new half-height drives into it.

➤ If your drives ride the rails, be sure to get a pair of rails when adding a new drive.

➤ Check to see if you have an open connector on the floppy drive data (ribbon) cable. If not, get a Y-cable so you can split the existing cable and get an extra connector.

➤ Check also to see if there's an open power connector. If not, again, you should get a Y-cable.

➤ If you're adding a high-density 3 1/2-inch drive, check to see if your DOS version is at least DOS 3.3.

➤ Check your PC's manual to see if the BIOS accepts newer 3 1/2-inch drives.

➤ Keep in mind that some PCs, such as Compaqs or PS/2s, require that you buy their specific drives, and not a generic one such as Teac.

➤ Adding a floppy drive to a laptop is pretty difficult. Avoid doing this if possible.

Chapter 18

Powering Up the Power Supply

In This Chapter

➤ Is it time to replace the power supply?

➤ How to anticipate power supply needs

➤ Installing a new power supply

➤ Other power toys

Believe it or not, your PC does not work on regular household AC current. In fact, the 120 volts that AC current puts out would quickly fry all your wimpy (I'm sorry, I mean delicate) computer parts.

So your computer's power supply takes the AC current from the wall outlet and transforms it into low voltage (5 volt) DC current. The stuff in your computer then sucks what it needs from the power supply. Occasionally, the power supply peters out, or, in your upgrading frenzy, you may overtax it. This chapter will tell you what to do in either case.

How to Tell When You Need to Replace Your Power Supply

Old XTs had a small 135-watt power supply. Older PCs had even less power, more like 63-watts. However, most PCs today have a power supply that puts out 200 watts. To keep all the PC parts happy, match your computer's needs to the power supply:

PC Part	What It Needs to Stay Happy	Your Totals
3 1/2-inch hard drive	5 to 15 watts	_____
5 1/4-inch hard drive	15 to 30 watts	_____
3 1/2-inch floppy drive	5 watts	_____
5 1/4-inch floppy drive	10 to 15 watts	_____
CD-ROM drive	20 to 25 watts	_____
1 M of memory	5 watts	_____
Average expansion card	5 to 15 watts	_____
Monitor (if powered by the PC)	35 watts and up	_____
Motherboard	20 to 75 watts	_____
286 CPU	20 to 40 watts	_____
386 CPU	25 watts	_____
486 CPU	35 watts	_____
Pentium CPU	35 to 40 watts	_____

Use this table to add up the total number of watts you're currently using. Then, whenever you want to add some new gizmo to your PC, add in the number of watts it needs to determine if you also need to upgrade the power supply. Of course, you can fudge a little, since a lot of devices don't actually suck any power until you use them—this includes things like the floppy drives and CD-ROM drives. A general formula for calculating wattage is voltage times amps.

If you try to start your PC and nothing happens, it may be a power supply problem, but it's hard to tell. One thing to listen for is the fan—if the power supply is working, the fan is on. If you're not sure if you hear the fan or not, hold your hand at the back of the PC to see if you feel any air coming out.

Before you jump to any conclusions though, test the wall outlet to see if it works. If it passes the test, unplug your PC from its surge suppressor and plug it directly into the wall to see if it works. If it does, the problem's with the surge suppressor. Reset the surge suppressor and try it again.

If your power supply peters out, it may be that it got zapped by a lightning strike. If you don't use a surge suppressor, this can happen. After you replace the power supply, make sure you get a good surge suppressor to protect your PC from damage in the future.

If your PC can't remember what day it is when you power up or if the CMOS settings keep turning up missing, it probably has nothing to do with your power supply—instead, the CMOS battery is going out. Remember that the battery is what helps the PC remember what stuff you've installed and what day it is, even after you turn the power off. The power supply keeps things charged once you turn on the PC. If you decide that the battery is the problem and you need to replace it, see Chapter 13 for help in that department.

Check This Out...

Don't Get Zapped!
When your power supply no longer works, you replace it. Under no circumstances should you try to fix it, because this can very well electrify you—even if the PC's unplugged.

If you change the battery and the PC keeps forgetting the date or the CMOS settings, you may have a weak power supply—so weak that it can't keep the battery charged.

If your PC's parts keep burning themselves out, the problem isn't that your power supply is putting out too little power, but *too much*. In any case, it's time to replace the power supply.

Going Shopping for a New Power Supply

Most of the PCs in stores today come with a 200-watt power supply, which is usually adequate for most people's needs. However, that's no guarantee that if you buy cheap, you won't get stuck with less. In any case, if you add a lot of stuff to your PC, you may want to upgrade the power supply to 250 or even 300 watts.

The next factor in your selection is the number of power connectors (power plugs). Most power supplies come with four, which is adequate, but more is better. You also need to make sure that the two motherboard connectors coming off the power supply will work in your system: some motherboards require rectangular connectors, while others use square ones. Your best bet is to simply open up your PC and take a closer look.

Additional features to look for include extra fans (for cooling the PC—a good idea if you plan on cramming a lot of expansion cards and other components into the case), and a noise reduction system, which at least makes a valiant attempt at keeping the PC relatively quiet.

Check This Out...

"Watt" It Will Cost
A 200 watt power supply costs about $35 to $45, while 230 or 250 watts run from $50 to $60.

Power supplies come in various sizes, so you may want to remove your old one and take it with you to the computer store, or at least take its measurements. Height is usually a critical factor in whether or not a power supply will fit in your PC's case.

If you run into problems finding a compatible power supply, you may need to purchase one from your PC's manufacturer.

Other Neat Power Toys

If you don't want to lose another power supply (or the PC itself), you need to invest in a good surge suppressor. When shopping for one, remember that you get what you pay for. In other words, if you spend only 10 bucks, you get only $10 worth of protection—which isn't bad, but it's not all that good either. Cheap surge suppressors offer only marginal protection against surges. More expensive surge suppressors meet much higher standards and are specifically rated for use with computers.

When comparing surge suppressors, look at several factors, including surge suppression capacity (measured in joules or watts/second)—obviously, the higher the capacity for protection, the better. Another feature to look for is EMI/RFI filtering, which reduces the impact of nearby electromagnetic fields or radio waves (uh, "line noise") on incoming current. Also, look for a surge suppressor which provides modem or fax protection. Overall, a UL 1449 rating is an excellent indicator of a good surge suppressor. Expect to pay around $50 to $80 for one.

A surge suppressor can't protect you against all power problems. For example, if your PC suddenly loses power due to a storm (or little Billy's fascination with wall outlets), then you lose whatever work you haven't yet saved.

If you can't afford to accidently lose some work just because nature decides to play a trick on you, then you need to set up your program to automatically save your work for you at timed intervals, such as every ten minutes. If you still can't sleep at night even with such protection, you may want to think about adding a UPS (uninterruptible power supply). When the power goes off, a UPS kicks in and provides enough juice to your PC so that you can save your work, log off, and grab a snack while you wait for the power to come back on. As an added bonus, a UPS also acts as a surge protector. The more expensive ones power down your system safely, even when you're not around.

A UPS will cost you around $90 to $300 for anywhere from 200 to 650 watts. The wattage here needs to match your system's requirements. However, if you buy a UPS with higher wattage, you'll be able to keep the PC powered up a bit longer—for up to 25 minutes in some cases. More complete UPS systems with better surge protection and automatic shutdown systems run about $200 to $700 for 200 to 670 watts.

If you ever need to add a device to your PC and you're out of power connectors (power plugs), you can purchase a Y-cable to split one of the connectors into two connectors instead. Plug one end of the Y-cable into the power plug, and, at the other end, there are two connectors—one for the device from which you originally stole the power plug, and a second one for your new device.

Your PC's Biggest Fan

If you've added several toys to your PC lately, you may want to think about adding a fan card. Yes, it's just what it sounds like—a fan mounted on an expansion card—and it's inserted just like any other expansion card. Your power supply comes with a fan, but it may not be able to keep things relatively cool, especially if you've crammed the inside of your PC with lots of stuff. A fan card adds extra circulation to problem areas, especially the motherboard in cases where a huge CD-ROM drive separates it from the power supply fan.

Installing a Power Supply

Once again I feel compelled to remind you that if you try to open the power supply itself (even if you've unplugged it) the electricity that's built up inside can knock your socks off (and possibly kill you). However, there's no cause for alarm here—power supplies are perfectly safe *as long as you don't try to open them.*

Start off by taking the usual precautions such as backing up your system (details in Chapter 12). Turn off the PC and unplug everything.

Before you start ripping things apart, take a piece of masking tape to mark each plug so you can remember the device to which the thing connects. Then remove each power plug from the power supply. The two big ones connect to the motherboard. The power plugs have four wires each, with a small white plastic connector at the end. To remove a plug, you rock it back and forth a bit so you can pull it loose. Just don't pull on its wires to remove a plug; instead, hold it by the white part.

Next, disconnect the on/off switch (some power supplies have built-in power switches, in which case, skip this step, pass go, and collect $200). Once you disconnect the on/off switch, unscrew the power supply—you find the screws in the back, along the edges. Just be careful to unscrew the power supply, and not the fan inside—if you keep to the outer edges and stay away from the fan area, you're okay. Also, make sure you put the screws in a safe place so you can locate them again later.

Clear a spot on your desk, lift the power supply out, and put it on the space you cleared on your desk. If your PC is a desktop unit, there are probably a couple of retainer tabs at the base of the case holding the power supply in place from the bottom. To release the power supply from these tabs, you need to lift the supply up just a bit and push the supply toward the front of the case. Once you free the power supply, use a can of compressed dust remover to clean up the inside of your PC a bit.

Unplug the devices connected to the power supply.

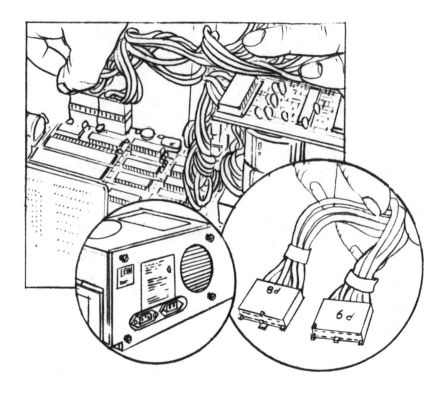

Push the power supply forward to release its retaining tabs.

Power supply—

Retaining tabs—

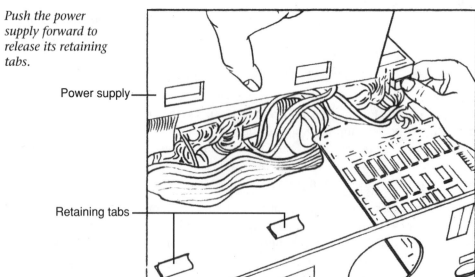

Before you insert your new power supply, make sure that it's set for the proper voltage (that's 120v for Americans, and 220v for Europeans and other metric-ites.) You'll find a switch for this purpose along the back.

Now, look at the bottom of the power supply and note the position of the two holes. These two holes need to match up with those retaining clips at the bottom of your desktop case. Pop the new power supply into place and then slide it toward the back of the case in order to engage the retaining tabs. Once the power supply is in place, screw it in. Start each of the screws just a little, align the supply, and then screw each one in fully.

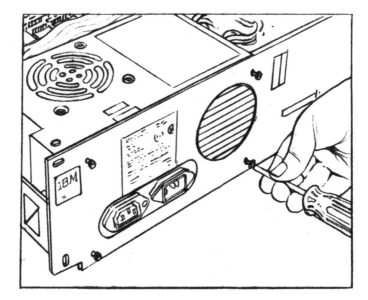

Screw the new power supply in place.

Finally, reattach each of the power plugs to their original devices. Each device gets a power plug, but not any one in particular—in other words, there isn't a specific plug for the floppy drives, the hard disk, and so on. Of course, the two big power connectors are reserved for the motherboard, thank you very much. These twins are usually marked P8 and P9. The power plugs can fit only one way because they are tapered, so don't force a plug—you may have it backwards. By the way, as you connect the motherboard plugs, make sure that the dark wires on each connector cable lie next to each other.

Reconnect the power cord and turn the PC on to see if anything happens. If everything's okay, turn the power back off and put everything back together.

The Least You Need to Know

Obviously, your PC is nothing more than a boat anchor if it doesn't have a working power supply. Here's what you need to know:

➤ *Never, ever, ever* try to open up the power supply to try to fix it. Even with the PC unplugged, opening up the power supply can kill you.

➤ The power supply converts the high voltage electricity coming from the wall outlet into lower voltage electricity that won't burn up your delicate PC parts.

➤ Your PC also has a battery, which doesn't power the PC, but instead helps it remember important stuff like what day it is, even when the power is turned off.

➤ When adding new toys to your PC, add up the total power drain to see if your existing power supply can take it. You may need to upgrade the power supply too.

➤ If you're not sure whether or not the power supply is working, listen (or feel) for the fan. When the power supply is on, the fan is working.

➤ When shopping for a new power supply, take your old one with you. It's the easiest way to make sure that the new one will work with your PC.

➤ To protect your PC, you need to invest in a good surge suppressor, which costs between $25 and $100. To protect against data loss due to a temporary loss of power, invest in a good UPS (uninterruptible power supply).

➤ If you need to plug in a device and you don't have an open power plug on your power supply, you need to get a Y-cable to split one of the connections into two.

Part 4
Upgrades That Will Make Your Neighbor Jealous

Some upgrades take your PC from the dark ages and put it into the here and now. I mean, face it, what PC today doesn't include a CD-ROM, modem, and cool sound card and speakers?

So what if your neighbor Bill has a DSS satellite, a cellular phone, and a pager? His PC has only 2 M, an ancient 5 1/4-inch diskette drive, and an old EGA monitor. And because his other toys have put him into so much debt, it's unlikely that'll change anytime soon.

So the kingdom, for now, is yours.

Chapter 19

Adding a CD-ROM Drive

In This Chapter

➤ Narrowing down your choices when shopping for a CD-ROM drive

➤ The difference between IDE and SCSI drives

➤ Installing your new CD-ROM drive correctly

In today's market, a CD-ROM drive is quickly becoming a necessity. Sure, you can install most programs today with a 3 1/2-inch diskette drive and about 20 or so disks, but soon, you might not be able to because it costs manufacturers a lot less to put their programs on a single CD-ROM. Some programs even include extras you don't get in the diskette version; it's worth your while to add a CD-ROM drive for that reason alone. And when you're not installing software, you can use your CD-ROM drive to entertain you with music while you work.

If I Add a CD-ROM Drive, I No Longer Need a Diskette Drive, Right?

Well, no. Your CD-ROM drive can only read CD-ROM discs—it can't write to them. The "RO" part of "CD-ROM" by the way, stands for "read-only."

So What'll It Cost Me?

A 4x (quad-speed) CD-ROM drive will run around $200 to $400. Faster 6x (six-speed) CD-ROM drives cost between $300 and $500. Multimedia kits with 4x CD-ROM drives and 16-bit sound cards run around $300 to $500. More about CD-ROM types in a moment.

Studying Your Options

There are a lot of options to think about when buying a CD-ROM. First, you have to decide if you want an internal one that fits into an empty drive bay, or an external one that sits next to the PC. In addition, Sony offers a portable CD-ROM drive that looks like a personal CD player, but acts like an external CD-ROM drive—so your choices are wide open.

If the Size of Your Wallet Is the Most Important Factor

If cost is the most important factor for you when purchasing a CD-ROM drive, then consider getting a multimedia package, which includes a sound card, speakers, and a CD-ROM drive at one low price. But beware if you decide to get a sound card with a connector for a SCSI CD-ROM: if you want to upgrade your sound card later on, you'll be limited to a sound card that can run your particular SCSI CD-ROM drive. If you can't find such an animal, then you'll need to purchase a separate SCSI adapter card to run the CD-ROM drive.

If you buy a multimedia package that includes a sound card with a connector to an ATAPI IDE CD-ROM, you won't have a problem if you upgrade the sound card later on. First of all, your IDE CD-ROM will be compatible with any sound card you get that has an IDE connector. And if you decide to purchase a sound card with a SCSI connector instead, you can always plug the CD-ROM into your IDE hard drive controller (that is, if your PC has one).

To be able to use an internal CD-ROM drive in your PC, you need to make sure you have an open drive bay to use. Also, you may need to purchase drive rails that connect to the drive and enable it to slide into your drive bay. CD-ROM drives sold today are designed to fit into standard half-height drive bays, but if you have an older PC with a full-height bay, you'll need drive rails to hold the CD-ROM drive in place. If you don't have an open drive bay, you can buy a combo floppy drive (which combines a 5 1/4-inch and a 3 1/2-inch floppy drive into one unit) or a combo floppy and CD-ROM drive (which combines a 3 1/2-inch floppy drive with a CD-ROM drive in one unit). Combo drives save you a drive bay, and they also save you a bit of money, too.

An external drive doesn't require an open drive bay, but it will cost you a bit more, so there's your wallet to consider. But an external drive is a lot easier to install, and you can also share it with your coworkers.

Next, decide what speed you can afford to buy: 2x, 4x, or 6x. A 2x (double-speed) drive is twice as fast

as the original CD-ROM drives are. A 4x (quad-speed) drive is four times faster, and a 6x (six-speed) drive is six times faster. Of course, they cost more too. And yes, 8x is just now becoming available, so if your need is for speed, then you might consider getting one (and spending more). Another way to increase drive speed is to include a cache, which allows it to access frequently used data quicker. Most drives come with a 128 or 256 K cache.

Techno Talk

blah blah blah bla bla bl

Words, Words, Words

When you go shopping for a CD-ROM drive, salespeople will throw a lot of terms at you, such as *data transfer rate*, *access time*, and *seek time*. Well, the data transfer rate is the rate at which the PC can receive data from the CD-ROM, usually measured in kilobytes per second. A 4x drive delivers about 600 KBps, while a 6x drive hovers around 900 KBps. The seek time of a CD-ROM drive is a measure of how long it takes (on the average) for the PC to find stuff on a disc—not to read it, just to find it. Access time is how long it takes for the drive to respond to the PC's request for data by finding that data and sending it on to the PC. Look for around 200 to 150 ms (the lower, the better).

Another option to look at is whether or not the drive plays audio CDs. Most do anymore, so this isn't really a big feature—but the drive needs to come with some kind of software that enables you to control and play audio compact discs. Windows 95, by the way, includes just such an item, called CD Player, accessible through the Programs/Accessories/Multimedia menu. You may also be interested in asking whether or not the drive supports Kodak Photo CDs. For example, you can have your travel photos and such put on a Photo CD, so you can view them on-screen, use them as a background in Windows, or import them into a word processing document. A Photo CD is not just for fun and games; it's a pretty nice feature for a real estate agent who wants to use it to store home photos, or for someone who works with lots of graphics.

Should I Look for Plug and Play?

If you're using Windows 95, you may want to make sure that your CD-ROM drive is Plug and Play-compatible, which guarantees that Windows 95 can work with it. Plug and Play (PnP) is a system that enables operating systems like Windows 95 to automatically recognize a new device as soon as you plug it in and, at least for the most part, "install" that device's supporting software. Don't let PnP be the deciding factor, however; lots of CD-ROM drives work perfectly well with Windows 95 even though they are not listed as Plug and Play.

Also, keep in mind that Plug and Play requires three elements to work: an operating system such as Windows 95, a Plug and Play device, and a BIOS which supports PnP. If your PC was manufactured prior to 1994, chances are it does not have a PnP BIOS. Of course, you can always upgrade the BIOS, too (see Chapter 13 for the details).

When choosing your new CD-ROM drive, consider whether or not it includes a *caddy* for loading. The cheaper ones don't, making them a bit less sturdy, but perfectly fine. The main consideration here is if you plan on mounting the drive vertically, rather than horizontally. In that case, a caddy is needed to support the disc so that it can be read consistently. So if you plan on mounting the drive vertically, spend the bucks to get a caddy-loaded CD-ROM drive. A caddy is also helpful in faster 6x or 8x drives, which benefit from the extra stability.

CD-ROM drives that use a loading tray are sturdy.

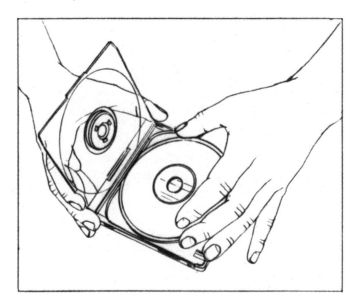

If you want to give multimedia presentations that use lots of CDs, you may want to consider a drive with a CD-ROM changer. A changer holds several discs at one time and switches between them as programmed, without making you switch discs yourself all the time. Of course, this feature makes the CD-ROM drive cost quite a lot more.

The Business of Which Interface to Choose

A pretty important feature to consider is the type of interface the CD-ROM drive uses to communicate with your PC. CD-ROMs sold today follow one of two interface schemes: either SCSI or IDE (sometimes called ATAPI IDE, PCI IDE, or EIDE). So how do you choose?

Well, if you choose SCSI, you'll need to make sure that the CD-ROM drive comes with a SCSI adapter to connect your CD-ROM drive to your PC. Sometimes you can kill two birds with one stone by getting a sound card that supports SCSI and then connecting your SCSI CD-ROM drive into it. If you plan on using your CD-ROM with an existing SCSI controller, make sure that the two are compatible. Many aren't. Just keep in mind that of the two, a SCSI adapter is gonna cost you more than an IDE adapter.

Now, before you run out and choose an IDE CD-ROM drive, there are some other factors to consider, some of which may send you running back for SCSI. IDE drives are actually EIDE drives, which means that they are an enhanced version of typical IDE (Integrated Drive Electronics). IDE, you may recall, is the most common type of hard disk available, so chances are pretty high that you've got one of them in your PC right now. IDE can support up to two devices, so if you only have one hard disk, you can plug your EIDE CD-ROM drive into the open connector, and you won't even have to worry about buying any kind of extra card.

The problem with this is that IDE limits you terribly. EIDE was designed as a faster alternative, and by plugging your EIDE drive into an IDE connector, you're effectively putting a five ton weight on it. In other words, don't expect your new drive to be fast. You're much better off spending around $50 to $75 more and getting a new EIDE adapter to go along with your new drive. The new adapter will allow you to take advantage of the speed of your new CD-ROM, while also allowing you to plug up to four total devices into it. You see, besides speed, EIDE also improved on the old IDE limit of only two devices.

Check This Out...

One More Alternative
Instead of buying an EIDE adapter, you can purchase an IDE sound card and plug your CD-ROM drive into it. You might also want to purchase the two together in a multimedia kit to save even more bucks. But again, if you connect your CD-ROM to a sound card, you're tied to it. Upgrading your sound card later on may be a pain, because you'll have to find one that supports your CD-ROM drive.

249

If your PC already has two IDE hard disks, well, then you'll have to get the EIDE adapter card whether you like it or not.

Anyway, once you get the adapter, you'll have to disable your old IDE hard disk controller and reconnect your IDE hard disk(s) to this new adapter card. That's because your PC can't handle two hard disk controllers (the EIDE card and your old IDE controller) at the same time. This assumes that you can disable the IDE controller; on some older PCs, there's no way to do it. So for some, this whole IDE business may be more trouble than it's worth, and you're better off with SCSI. On the other hand, IDE CD-ROM drives are usually less expensive than their SCSI counterparts, so it's worth a minute or two of investigation before you decide.

Also, if you have a newer PC that features a PCI IDE local bus, then a matching IDE CD-ROM drive (sometimes called EIDE) may be a better choice for you than SCSI, because it can hook into your local bus and run fast, fast, fast.

Aaaiiii! More Letters!

IDE, you may recall, is a standard for controlling hard disk drives. Well, it's been adapted into a local bus scheme that enables it to "drive" just about any device you plug into it at a faster rate than a VL-bus (VESA local bus). As a local bus, PCI IDE costs more, so you won't find it on your PC unless you've got a 486 DX4 or a Pentium. If you have an older 486, you'll probably find a VL-bus instead.

Now That You've Bought One, Here's How to Install It

The way you install a CD-ROM drive depends, of course, on whether that drive is an internal or external one. Also, if you're replacing a busted drive, you'll have to remove it first. To remove a CD-ROM drive, make sure you prepare your system following the instructions in Chapter 12. Then, turn the power off, open up the PC, and discharge that darn static electricity.

Now, to remove the old drive, start by disconnecting its data cable first (that's the wide, flat ribbon cable). Next, remove the audio cable if there is one; it's the small cable on the left. Finally, remove the power cable; it's got four separate wires with a small white connector on the end. It might be kinda hard to remove, but just wiggle it back and forth a little, and it should come out fine. Just don't pull the power cable by its wires; pull it by the white connector instead. Next, unscrew the drive and slide it out the front of the PC. If the old drive uses drive rails, remove them and screw them into the new drive.

Well, now that you've got that out of the way, there's one more thing to do before you can install the new drive.

Installing the CD-ROM's Controller Card

Whether or not your drive is an IDE or a SCSI CD-ROM drive, it must connect to some type of *controller*. This will be either an EIDE adapter, a SCSI card, or a sound card, depending on the drive that you chose.

Follow the usual presurgical procedures: make a current backup, update your emergency diskette, and get rid of any static electricity. Then open your PC.

Before you insert the card, make sure that it's set up properly. For a SCSI card, this may mean setting a jumper or two to set the IRQ, DMA address, and SCSI ID. Usually, you should not change anything at all, but instead, simply jot down the default settings and compare them to similar settings for your other devices. If you find an IRQ conflict, for example, then you need to change the IRQ setting in the SCSI card. I can't help you much on this one; you've got to figure out what IRQs other devices are currently using and then select a unique one for this drive. Don't let this IRQ you too much; see Chapter 24 for more help.

If you're installing a sound card, well, skip to the next chapter for details.

I Don't Have an EIDE Card, but I Have an EIDE Drive!

Uh, before you get too confused, you might not have an EIDE card unless you elected to buy one. You see, if your system only has one IDE hard disk, you can attach your CD-ROM drive to the extra connector, and you're done.

If you did buy the EIDE card, then you have to disable your original IDE controller. Open up your PC and grab the data cable for your hard disk—it's not hard to spot; it's the flat, wide ribbon cable attached to the hard disk. Follow it back to wherever it leads—either to a multifunction expansion card, or to the motherboard itself. Somewhere near this location is (hopefully) a jumper that you can pull to disable the IDE connector. You definitely need to check the manual for help with this one—you don't want to pull the wrong jumper and end up disabling something else.

If you can't find a way to disable the IDE controller, then you're out of luck. Better pack everything back up and trade it in on a SCSI CD-ROM drive.

If you're installing an EIDE card, make sure that the switches are set correctly. Usually you can leave the first set of switches as is; but the second set of switches controls the second connector, so you may want to mess with them. You see, even if you're connecting just one hard disk and one CD-ROM drive to the EIDE card, you'll probably want to use both connectors, because the slowest of the two devices on a cable determines the speed of both devices. There's no sense slowing down your hard disk just because the CD-ROM drive can't keep up, so put them on separate connectors. If you're using two hard disks and a CD-ROM drive, put both hard disks on the first connector, and the CD-ROM drive on the second.

Anyway, to turn on the card's second connector, the last set of switches must be set to "on."

To install the card, unscrew the retaining screw for the slot you want to use and remove the slot cover. Hold the card at the top with both hands and position the edge connectors on the bottom of the card over their slots. Gently press the card into place with just the right amount of downward pressure. (Don't force the card into its slot.)

Gently press the expansion card into its slot.

Retaining screw —

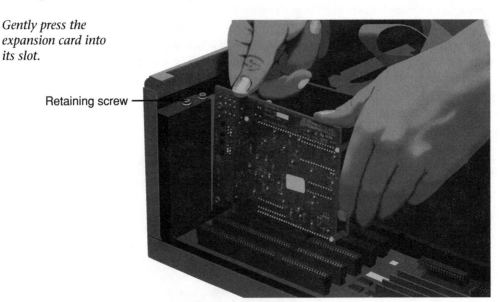

Installing an Internal CD-ROM Drive

Now, you're finally ready to install the drive. Again, before you touch any part of your PC, make sure you've banished the static guy by grounding yourself first. With the cover off, remove the faceplate for the drive bay you've chosen. It's sometimes part of the cover, and other times, it's part of the case itself. You can usually stick a flathead screwdriver just under the rim of the faceplate to pry the thing off.

If You're Installing a SCSI CD-ROM

If your new drive's a SCSI, you've got to set its switches. These things control the SCSI address for each device in the SCSI chain (number 0, 1, 2, and so on). Just set the drive to a number that doesn't match that of any other SCSI devices in your PC. By the way, the adapter has an ID too; it's usually set to ID 7, so choose something else for your drive, such as 6.

Also, you've got to remove the terminator on this SCSI drive if it's not the last one in the chain. You see, each SCSI device in your PC connects to the same SCSI controller card. One end of the SCSI chain is at the controller, and the other end terminates with the last device. Between the controller and this last device (whatever it is) there may be up to six other devices.

Now, SCSI devices come with something called a *terminating resistor*. Nothing fancy; just a little plug-thing—but it's there to stop (terminate) the SCSI signal at the end of the chain. If your CD-ROM drive is one of these middle guys, you've got to remove its terminating resistor in order for the SCSI signal to continue to other devices further away from the controller. You're looking for a jumper or a chip called T-RES, or just TR. Once you find it, just pull the T-RES plug off of the drive. Of course, if your CD-ROM drive is the last guy you plugged into the cable leading from the controller, then leave the terminating resistor *on*.

If You're Installing an EIDE CD-ROM

If your new drive's an IDE drive, then you may need to change some settings before you insert it. You need to set a jumper on the drive to designate whether this one's a master or a slave. The master in this case is the first IDE drive, while the slave is drive number two. If you plan on putting your hard disks on one connector cable and the CD-ROM drive on another, then your CD-ROM drive can remain set as "master" even if one hard disk on the other connector is also a "master," because the CD-ROM drive is the only device on that cable. If you connect the hard disk and the CD-ROM drive to the same cable, then set the CD-ROM drive to "slave." Check the manual for details, but this usually involves moving one simple jumper.

Now Back to Our Regularly Scheduled Program

Once you've got it all set up, slide your spankin' new CD-ROM drive into the open bay. Don't bother to screw it in yet; you've got to plug the thing in first.

There are three cables you've got to plug in. Start with the power cable (the one with the white connector). You probably have a free power cable running from the power supply. If not, you'll need to get a Y-cable to split one connection into two. Make sure you connect the power cable correctly; if you don't you can do serious damage to your new drive. Luckily, the power connector is usually notched so that it can only go in one way.

Next, connect the data (controller) cable (the big fat one). The other end is attached to whatever card you're using to control the CD-ROM drive: SCSI card, sound card, or EIDE controller. The red-striped edge of the cable should match up with the pin marked 1 on the connector. Some thoughtful manufacturers use a triangular arrow to show you which way is "up." Be careful; on a lot of sound cards, there are multiple data connectors, keyed to specific brand CD-ROM drives, so check with the sound card's manual for help.

Plug in your CD-ROM drive.

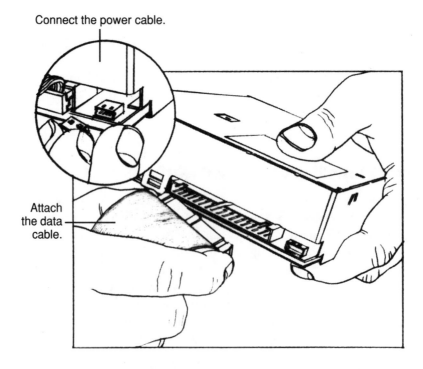

Connect the power cable.

Attach the data cable.

Finally, if your CD-ROM drive has an audio cable, plug it in. The other end goes into your sound card (you do have one, don't you?), or into the audio connector located at the upper right-hand corner of the EIDE card. Beware: the EIDE card can't function as an amplifier, so you'll have to run a patch cord from the output jack at the back of the card to your amplifier or amplified speakers. You can find a patch cord at your local Radio Shack.

Good job. The patient's alive (at least, I think so). Screw the CD-ROM drive in place and close up the PC.

Wait, You're Not Finished Yet

After you install your new drive, you should start your PC and run the setup program for your card (if you added one) and then run the setup program for your drive. The setup program for your CD-ROM drive should install two drivers in your configuration files: MSCDEX (a Microsoft driver for your CD-ROM's file system), and the specific driver that runs your CD-ROM drive. Without these two drivers, your CD-ROM won't work. If you use Windows 95, it doesn't need the MSCDEX driver, so it will automatically remove it if it finds it.

Also, if you use Windows 95 or Windows 3.1, there are some additional last-minute things you'll need to do to get Windows to acknowledge your new drive. See Part 5 for help.

Installing an External CD-ROM Drive

Adding an external CD-ROM drive is rather simple, because you don't have to get your hands dirty opening up the PC's case. Of course, you might have already had it open in order to install the controller card for your CD-ROM drive. Oh, well.

In any case, with your PC closed up, attach the cable to your CD-ROM drive. Then run the cable to the connector on the card, be it sound, IDE, or SCSI. Actually, because a SCSI cable can accommodate multiple devices, you may only have to attach your SCSI drive to any open connector on the existing SCSI chain.

Also, if your drive's a SCSI, then you'll need to set its SCSI address (device 0, 1, 2, and so on). That's done by moving a simple jumper or switch on the back of the drive. See the manual for help. Also, depending on the drive's location along the SCSI chain, you may need to remove the drive's terminating resistor. Basically, if your CD-ROM drive's not at the end of the SCSI chain, you remove its resistor. See the details on installing an internal SCSI drive for more help with this one.

If you're installing an external IDE CD-ROM drive, you'll need to make sure that you connect your hard disk to the first connector on the EIDE card, and that you disable the second connector (because you won't be using it). You'll also need to disable your existing IDE controller, which might be located on the motherboard or on a multifunction card. Also, make sure that you've set your external IDE CD-ROM drive to be a "master" because it'll be the only device running on its particular connector.

Finally, plug your drive into a surge protector and turn it on. (This is especially important if you're installing a SCSI drive, since the PC won't recognize it if you don't turn it on first.) Start your PC and run the setup programs for the card and the drive. Also, if you use Windows, you need to do some setup stuff to get Windows to acknowledge your new drive. See Part 5 for how-tos.

Connect your drive to its controller card.

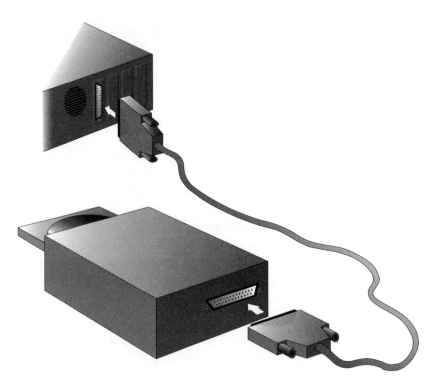

What Could Go Wrong

About a thousand things, as it turns out. Here's a list to help you narrow it down:

➤ If the drive's not working, make sure that you've connected it correctly, and that you've chosen the right IRQs and such. See Chapter 24 for help.

➤ If you're installing an IDE CD-ROM drive and you've connected it to your sound card, but it doesn't work, try connecting the CD-ROM drive to the second IDE connector on your hard disk cable. PCs have trouble dealing with two IDE controllers (in this case, the one on your sound card and the one that runs your hard disk), so putting both IDE devices (the hard disk and your CD-ROM drive) on the same controller solves the problem. Go figure.

➤ If you're having problems with an external CD-ROM drive, make sure that you've turned it on.

➤ If the drive's still not operating, make sure that you've run the setup program for the drive. When you start your PC, does it load the drivers correctly, or do you see an error? If the drivers are trying to load into high memory through the CONFIG.SYS or the AUTOEXEC.BAT, try taking out the LOADHIGH or DEVICEHIGH command so that they load into conventional memory instead. See Chapter 22 for help.

➤ If you're using an external SCSI CD-ROM drive, make sure that it's turned ON before you turn on the PC.

➤ If you're not running Windows 95, make sure that the CD-ROM setup program installed the MSCDEX driver in the CONFIG.SYS.

➤ Gotta problem running an audio CD? Make sure your CD-ROM drive supports audio. Have you installed your sound card, and did you remember to connect your CD-ROM drive to the sound card? Did you turn on the external speakers, and play with the volume knob? Are you using the software program that enables your CD-ROM to play audio CDs? Windows 95 comes with CD Player, which will do just that.

The Least You Need to Know

When shopping for a CD-ROM drive, you face an enormous amount of choices. Use this list to help you sort them out:

➤ To save money, buy a CD-ROM in a multimedia package that includes a sound card and speakers.

➤ If you buy an internal CD-ROM drive, you'll need an open 5 1/4-inch drive bay.

➤ An external drive costs more, but it's easier to install.

➤ CD-ROMs come in several speeds; most are 4x or 6x speed. To compare the speed of various drives, check out their data transfer rates, access times, and seek times.

➤ If speed is a factor, make sure that your CD-ROM drive uses a cache of at least 256 K.

➤ Make sure that your drive plays audio CDs. You might also want to check that the drive is Photo CD-compatible.

➤ If you use Windows 95, you might want a Plug and Play compatible drive.

➤ CD-ROM drives that include a caddy are more stable.

➤ A nice feature to look for in more expensive drives is a CD changer, which can store several CDs and switch between them easily.

Chapter 20

Sensational Stereophonic Sound

In This Chapter

➤ Shopping for a great sound card

➤ Tips for getting good speakers

➤ How to install the darn things

One of the most popular PC buzzwords is "multimedia." What that means varies, but most people generally include at least two elements in their definition: graphics and sound. Graphics, which require typically large, complex files, are usually stored on CD-ROM discs. So a CD-ROM drive is essential in the quest for a true multimedia system (see the preceding chapter for how to buy and install one). A sound card is also a must.

Sound cards exist at two levels: the more affordable versions provide good quality sound for casual use such as CD-ROM games and audio CDs. The more expensive sound cards appeal to the true sound artist, such as a musician, or to the multimedia maniac. In this chapter, you'll learn how to find the ultimate sound card for your needs.

Before You Buy, Here Are Some Things You Better Consider

The first consideration you will face when shopping for a sound card is really the matter of price. Cards come in 8-bit, 16-bit, 32-bit, and 64-bit styles. The higher the number of bits, the more detailed and accurate the resulting *waveform*, or sound, will be. The number of bits here does not refer to the number of bits your expansion slots can handle; in other words, you can shove most sound cards into any standard 16-bit ISA slot. (If you have an old PC that uses only 8-bit slots, you will need to search for a matching 8-bit sound card.) You can also find sound cards that fit PCMCIA slots on laptop computers. Having trouble determining what kind of slots your PC uses? See Chapter 3 for a quick refresher.

Check This Out...

So What'll This Cost Me?
An 8-bit sound card will cost you about $50 to $80, while a 16-bit card runs about $100 to $175. 32-bit sound cards cost about $200. Multimedia kits with 4x CD-ROM drives and 16-bit sound cards cost about $300 to $500.

Most sound cards support only a limited variety of CD-ROM drives. So if you plan on connecting your CD-ROM drive through your sound card, that's something to keep in mind. Also, each card only supports a particular kind of interface, either IDE or SCSI, which definitely limits your choice of a CD-ROM drive (see Chapter 19 for more info). A simple way to defeat this problem is to buy a multimedia kit (which contains a sound card, a CD-ROM drive, and speakers) for one low price. Getting these items together ensures compatibility, and can save you money.

However, if you choose to run your CD-ROM off its own adapter card (by not connecting it to the sound card), then you may or may not be able to find an audio cable to patch the CD-ROM's sound through your PC's speakers or even to your stereo amplifier. That would mean you could only listen to CDs through the headphones included with the CD-ROM drive. So in a lot of cases, the sound card and the CD-ROM drive are married to one another whether you like it or not.

Sound Card Standards

You need to make sure that your sound card is compatible with the programs you want to run it with, most notably Windows. "Sound Blaster" compatibility is a good thing to look for because most programs support some form of the Sound Blaster standard. When a sound card or a program mentions Sound Blaster compatibility, it generally means that it can accept the same sound instructions meant for an 8-bit Sound Blaster card (the oldest and least expensive of the Creative Labs product line, and thus the "least common denominator"). Also, if you use Windows 95, look for the PnP (Plug and Play) compatibility symbol.

Sound cards follow one of two standards for re-creating sound: *FM synthesis* and *wave table synthesis*. The less expensive technology, FM synthesis, creates sounds by combining pure tones of varying frequency and strength to produce a synthesized sound.

Sound cards that use wave table synthesis (sampling) contain a large table of exact digitized waveforms for various sounds. For example, a sample note is taken from an instrument, and then stored in a table as a digitized waveform. These waveforms are exact duplicates of their real-life sounds, so a wave table sound card reproduces sound more accurately than FM synthesis—but at a higher cost.

Not all wave table cards are the same; look for a minimum of 1 to 2 M of sample RAM (the area in which the samples are stored). The best-sounding (thus most expensive) sound cards support several wave tables for different octave ranges, so synthesized instruments sound more true-to-life. In other words, the best wave table sound cards contain multiple tables with several samples from each instrument, instead of just one.

> **Check This Out...**
>
> **But I Don't Know If I'll Want the Best Sound** If you're not sure if you'll really need the high-quality sound that a wave table sound card can provide, no problemo. Just shop for a sound card with a Wave Blaster-compatible expansion slot. Then if you decide to upgrade later on, you can buy a wave table daughterboard and connect it to the sound card. A daughterboard, by the way, is a small expansion board that fits into the slot next to the sound card.

> **Check This Out...**
>
> **What's a MIDI?**
>
> A MIDI device is a digital electronic instrument (such as an electric keyboard) that supports the MIDI (Musical Instrument Digital Interface) standard. MIDI enables an electronic musical instrument to communicate with your digital computer. You can use your computer to compose a musical score with multiple instruments, and your MIDI instrument set can play it.

Are You into Games?

If you want to play games and really hear the sound, make sure that your sound card is Sound Blaster- and General MIDI-compatible. (General MIDI is what most games require for the background music.) Incompatibility with General MIDI makes a lot of high-end sound cards not suitable choices for game use. You might be surprised to learn that an expensive sound card, when playing the soundtrack of a game programmed just for Sound Blaster compatibility, may sound like an elementary school band practice session compared to the simple Sound Blaster the soundtrack was based on. Another feature to look for in a good sound card for games is 3D and special effects compatibility (a kind of stereo surround sound), which adds a special dimension to game playing.

Great Composer

Most sound cards include a MIDI port, which is suitable for a joystick if you don't intend to use it as a MIDI port; however, to use a MIDI device in such a port, you'll need a separate break out box. If you're a professional musician, you might want to look for a sound card that supports either Roland GS or Yamaha XG, both of which extend the General MIDI palette.

Some Terms You'll See As You Shop

Here are some other terms you'll encounter while shopping for your sound card:

Audio line input	Special input for recording sound off of a stereo, TV, VCR, or CD-ROM. This is not the same as a microphone input, which is usually monophonic and not stereophonic.
Voice	The number of tones used in the composition of parts (instruments) on an FM synthesizer-type sound card. The more the better. A good number is 20, allowing five-part harmony from well-formed, four-voice parts. (It usually takes four voices to comprise one tone, so 20 voices allows for up to five-part harmony of four tones.)
Polyphony	The number of notes a card can play at the same time. Six-timbre polyphony can reproduce orchestral sound.
Multitimbrality	The number of different voices that a sound card can play at the same time.
DSP	Short for Digital Signal Processor, an on-board chip that takes some of the sound chores off the CPU, making the sound card faster.

A Note About Speakers

The depth of sound from speaker to speaker varies a great deal. When shopping for a set of PC speakers, look at the frequency response range. This tells the range of high to low sounds the speaker can reproduce. The best speakers can reproduce a range close to that of human hearing (from 20 Hz to 20 KHz). Some speakers add a 3D sound effect, which is a cool addition to role-playing games.

You should also make sure your new speakers contain their own amplifiers to help boost the signal coming from the sound card. Most do, so this shouldn't be a major factor. However, you should look at the total power wattage of the speakers, because the sound card produces a fairly weak signal that needs to be amplified by your speakers. Low-cost speakers offer only 4 to 7 watts, while the best offer as much as 100 watts of power output. While I'm talking about power, keep in mind that most speakers run off of two or more lowly C batteries. You might want to seriously consider investing in an AC adapter, which will prevent unnecessary trips to the store when you're in the middle of an intense dog fight. (Some speakers come with a built-in AC adapter plug.)

Sounds Nice
You don't have to spend big bucks on PC speakers if you've already spent lots of dollars on a nice home stereo system. You can easily run the output of your sound card through your stereo system. Just get the right adapter to fit the jack on the card, and the jacks on the AUX inputs in your stereo.

Total harmonic distortion is the amount of distortion (noise) level that occurs when a sound is amplified. Look for .1 percent or less.

Another feature to watch out for is the number and type of control knobs the speakers offer. Most come with a volume control, but the better ones also allow you to adjust the amount of bass, treble, and super bass (dynamic bass boost).

Keep in mind that most speakers contain magnets to create their sound. Make sure that your speakers have adequate protection around their magnetic parts—especially if you're going to put the speakers anywhere near your monitor, which is especially sensitive to magnetic fields.

One final word: if you plan on putting your speakers far away from your PC (or if you use a tower case), make sure that your speaker cables are long enough.

Installing Your Sound Card

Installing a sound card is not difficult, but getting it to work correctly often is. The main problem centers around choosing the right IRQ, DMA, and I/O addresses. The easiest way to determine which settings to use is to figure out what settings your other devices are using. Back in Chapter 4, you hopefully completed a listing of your PC's components; well, guess what—all that hard work is about to pay off.

Before you install your sound card, you should make a note of its IRQ, DMA, and I/O address settings, compare them to the settings used by other devices on your list, and change them as needed so that you end up with one big, happy computer family. You'll have to look in the manual for the location of these switches. This is a total yech, but at least you're not alone—there's more help for you in Chapter 24. Some sound cards are considerate and enable you to change their settings through software, a much more pleasant experience.

Change the sound card's settings as needed before you insert it.

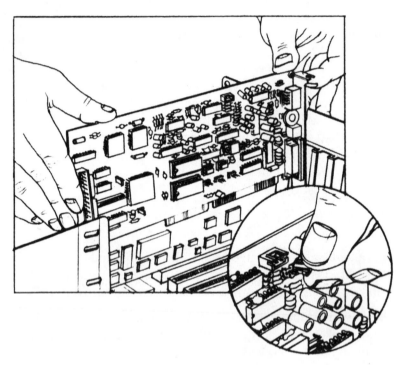

Check This Out...

That's a Shocker!

Before you remove your sound card from its static bag, clear an area on your desk. Lay down some paper to put the card on, then discharge any static you may have built up shuffling around, waiting for your sound card to arrive. Then pull the sound card from the bag and place it on the paper. Change the settings as needed.

264

Once you're ready to install your card, make sure you prepare your system by doing a backup, updating your emergency diskette, and so on. See Chapter 12 for how-tos. Then make sure you've discharged any static and open up your PC.

To install the sound card, pick out the slot you want to use and unscrew its retaining screw. This slot should be located as far away as possible from noisy components such as the hard disk and the power supply. Remove the slot's cover, but keep the thing; if you dump your sound card later, you can use it to cover up the hole. Make sure that you pick up the card at its top with both hands. Then position the edge connectors at the bottom of the card over their respective slots. Press the card into place, but don't force it—you could bend it.

Retaining screw

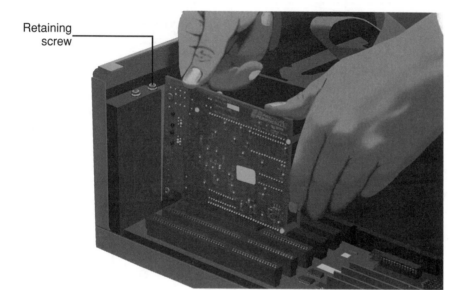

Gently press the expansion card into its slot.

Secure the card in place with its retaining screw. If you're connecting a CD-ROM drive to your sound card, plug its connector cable into the correct slot on the card. Keep in mind that many cards come with several connectors, one for each of the specific types of drives they support. These different connectors are usually well marked so you can't make much of a mistake, but check with the manual if you're not sure which one to use. You'll also want to connect the CD-ROM drive's audio cable to the sound card. See Chapter 19 if you want more help with your CD-ROM drive.

Blown Away Check This Out...
The first time you use your stereo with the sound card, turn the volume to low, to keep from accidentally blowing the speakers.

Your sound card typically comes with several outside connectors: a microphone connector, a headphone connector, an external speaker connector, and a joystick or MIDI connector. First, connect your two speakers. If your speakers come with two strands of speaker wire, then you use one strand to connect one speaker to the other speaker, and another to connect the right speaker to the sound card. If you instead have one strand of speaker wire with a connector in the middle, connect the middle part to the right speaker, one end to the other (left) speaker, and the other end to the sound card. If you want to connect your sound card to your home stereo, it's no trick, but you'll need an adapter that has a 1/8-inch mini stereo connector at one end (to fit your sound card) and regular RCA sound plugs at the other.

You can easily connect your sound card to your stereo system.

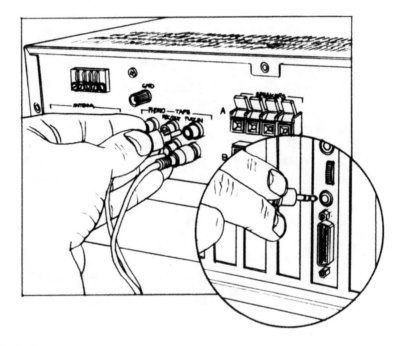

Now you can mess with the extras, such as a microphone (for recording all those wise tidbits you come up with every day) and a joystick or MIDI device. By the way, you can connect more than one MIDI device to your sound card by running the output of one device into the input of the previous one in the chain. See, MIDI devices connect to one another like SCSI devices—in a daisy-chain. So if you have a MIDI multi-timbre module, a MIDI sequencer, and a MIDI drum unit, you can connect them in a chain in any order using 5-pin DIN cable and then connect one end of the chain to the MIDI card.

Once you connect your card, close up the PC and turn it on. Next, you need to run the sound card's setup program to install the card's device driver. The device driver, you may recall, is what allows the PC to communicate with the sound card. If you use any DOS games, you'll need to select your sound card from each game's own setup program. You'll have to do some messing around in Windows too, if you use it. See Part 5 for help.

What Could Go Wrong

The main problem you'll run into when you add a sound card to your system is IRQ, DMA, and I/O address conflicts. Keeping an accurate list of the channels your other devices are using is the only real way to solve this problem. See Chapter 24 for help.

If you can't hear sound in a particular game, run its setup program and make sure that your sound card (or a compatible model that your card emulates or imitates) is selected. Also, some games only support Sound Blaster compatible cards, set at the default settings of DMA 1, IRQ 7, and I/O address 220.

Check Those Settings

Many 16-bit sound cards prefer using DMA channel 5, 6, or 7. Others prefer DMA 3. For true Sound Blaster compatibility, you may want to use DMA 1. When there's a conflict with the sound card's settings and the settings of other devices, you may get a parity error, or your PC may simply "lock up."

If you still can't hear the sound, make sure that your speakers are on, and that their batteries are working. Check the mixer program and make sure that the master volume is set high enough. In Windows 95, you can get to the master volume control by double-clicking on the speaker icon on the taskbar. You can also test the volume by running the sound card's diagnostic program and playing a test sound file. If you bought cheap speakers, they might not be amplifying the sound enough. Try connecting the sound card to your stereo to see if that solves the problem.

Another way to resolve a sound problem is to simply restart the PC and make sure that the sound card's driver loaded properly. Next, you might want to check the CONFIG.SYS settings to see if the initial volume for the driver is set too low.

One last thing to check is the cable that connects your speakers to the sound card. Make sure that you use a stereo speaker cable if your sound card is stereo. If you accidently use a mono cable, you'll either get sound of very low volume, or no sound at all.

If you get sound but it's pretty scratchy, make sure that your sound card is not too close to the hard disk or the power supply. The signal that a sound card sends to your speakers is an analog signal, which is susceptible to radio frequency distortions. These are constantly created by things like your power supply, your hard disk drive, and a hyperactive dachshund on a really tight leash. You might also want to move your speakers farther away from your monitor—unless the speakers are shielded heavily against electrical interference, your monitor may be causing a disruption.

When There's Nothing Left to Try

Sometimes your PC's BIOS may be the reason why your sound card won't work, especially if it handles its DMA channel differently than your card expects. If the BIOS' DMA timing can be changed (slowed), this usually clears up the problem. You can get to this setting through CMOS. Time to call in the nerds (and Chapter 24) for help with this one.

The Least You Need to Know

Shopping for a sound card can be a confusing experience. Here are some tips to remember:

➤ Buying a multimedia package that includes a sound card, CD-ROM drive, and speakers saves you money and ensures that you won't run into any compatibility problems. However, you won't get the best quality components.

➤ When choosing a sound card, get one that's at least 16-bit. Get a 32-bit sound card if you can afford it, because it provides a better-quality sound. A 64-bit sound card provides professional (and expensive) quality.

➤ Of course, before you buy any sound card, check the programs you want to run with it and make sure they are compatible with the sound card you choose.

➤ You should also make sure that the card you buy is Sound Blaster-compatible, because most programs support Sound Blaster sound cards. If you like to play a lot of games, look for compatibility with General MIDI too.

➤ Sound cards that use FM synthesis are less expensive, but they don't provide as nice a sound. Wave table cards are a better choice.

➤ If you want a high-quality sound card, pay particular attention to voice, polyphony, and multitimbrality. Also check to see if the sound card includes a DSP chip.

STOP FAXING!!

Chapter 21

Adding a Modem

In This Chapter

➤ Talking that modem jive

➤ What to look for in an ideal modem

➤ Installing an internal modem

➤ Installing an external modem

A modem is a device that takes digital junk coming out of your PC and changes it into analog beeps and buzzes to send over a conventional phone line. At the other end, the receiving modem unscrambles this beeping, buzzing nonsense and converts it back into digital computer data. A communications program at each end controls the whole exchange.

With a modem, you can send or receive files and electronic messages. You can even connect to an online service, bulletin board service, or your company's network. But I won't kid you—installing a modem and getting it to work is not always easy. Once you get it up and running though, a modem can be pretty useful and a lot of fun.

Talking Modem Jive

Now, when you're shopping for a modem, the salesperson is gonna use words like "error correction" and "data compression" whether you want him to or not. Here's a brief glossary you can use to decipher his modem-speak:

Online service	A pay-for-use subscription service that allows its users to send and receive files or e-mail, shop online, "chat" online with other users, and search for answers to puzzling problems. Popular online services include CompuServe, Prodigy, America Online, and Microsoft Network.
BBS	Short for *bulletin board service*. A BBS is kind of like an electronic bulletin board, but a BBS's members can leave messages and exchange information electronically. A BBS is similar to an online service, but on a smaller scale—usually locally owned and operated, sometimes in a local storefront, occasionally in someone's closet. Most BBSs are devoted to a particular topic, such as sailing, computers, gardening, and so on. You can dial up a local BBS directly by phone. Also, you can access a distant BBS through a local BBS if the local BBS supports "BBS Express," or you sometimes can reach a BBS through the Internet.
Internet	A group of interconnected networks that spans the world. The networks connected to the Internet belong to universities, businesses, libraries, and some public schools. You connect to the Internet through a service provider, which charges you a fee for the access; or from an online service, such as CompuServe or America Online. You then jump from Internet site to Internet site to find the information you need. One warning, though: no one is actually responsible for the Internet as a whole, so "surfing" the net is kind of like riding the New York City subway—you never know exactly what you're going to see.
Uploading/ Downloading	Uploading is the process of sending a file; downloading is the process of receiving a file.
BPS	Short for *bits per second*. It is a way of measuring the speed of a modem. Sometimes called *baud rate*, although that's technically incorrect.

Baud	The amount of frequency changes per second during a transmission. With early modems, this was the same as the number of bits per second, but that's not the case with today's high-speed modems.
COM port	Your PC has up to four serial ports called COM ports. A port is simply a route through which a device communicates with the CPU. Your modem uses one of these COM ports.
Protocol	A set of standards that govern how two modems communicate with each other, and how to detect errors in transmission.
Parity	The procedure for determining when an error occurs. A protocol will use either even or odd parity, where a ninth bit is added to the eight bits (which make up a character) to make the total number of 1 bits either odd, or even. If even parity is being used for example, and a modem receives the nine bits 010010111, then it'll know there's some kind of mistake because there are five 1 bits—an odd number.
Error correction	The protocol (sorry, uh, *method*) that a particular modem uses to discover whether or not an error occurs during transmission.
Data compression	The method the modem uses to shrink the data before transmitting it, so it takes less time. Popular protocols that include both error correction and data compression are V.42 and Microcom Network Protocol, or MNP, (actually, V.42 is an implementation of MNP).

More Junk on MNP and High-End Protocols

MNP can be of great help to you or, at times, no help to you at all. There are about 13 stages of MNP, having to do with greater and greater levels of error correction, data compression, and burst mode implementation (the modem version of hitting the accelerator on the straightaways). The first four levels of MNP help you no matter what modem you're talking to. But from MNP level 5 on up, you don't benefit unless the modem you're connected to supports that level or higher. Most online services support MNP 5 (which, by the way, is V.42). When choosing an Internet service provider, ask its representative how high its modems can go on the MNP scale. If they support as high as MNP 13, then by all means, go for a modem that gives you MNP 13—you really can tell the difference that high up.

Things to Consider When Shopping

Probably your top consideration when buying a modem is its speed (and the cost, of course). The speed of a modem is measured in *bits per second,* thankfully abbreviated as bps. Common speeds for modems sold today include 14,400 and 28,800 bps (these are also abbreviated, showing up on modem ads as simply 14.4 and 28.8). A 14.4 modem is cheaper, but a 28.8 modem may save you money in the long run if you use an online service (such as CompuServe) or the Internet a lot. With a faster modem, you'll use less connect time.

If You're Buying an External Modem Most external modems don't include a serial modem cable, which you need in order to connect your external modem to your PC. COM ports come in two sizes: 9- and 25-pin, so make sure you get the right cable to fit your needs. Don't accept imitations—make sure the cable says that it's appropriate for use with modems.

Modems come in both internal and external types; an external modem plugs into a spare serial port, so make sure that you have one. If you've inherited an external modem from a buddy, but you don't have an extra serial port, you can add one with something called an *I/O,* or *multifunction, card.* You can share an external modem with your coworkers, or use it with your laptop PC, if it has a spare serial port or a serial I/O PCMCIA card.

However, if you have a laptop, you might prefer a modem that fits into a PCMCIA connector. But be sure to get one with its own power supply, so it won't drain the laptop's main power.

You can buy a 14.4 bps modem for around $100. (Some cost even less!) A 28.8 bps modem costs around twice as much—around $200. A PCMCIA modem costs anywhere from $30 to $100 more than a regular modem.

Just keep in mind that you get what you pay for. Some cheap modems are so hard to install and to get working that they're just not worth the $10 or $20 you'll save by buying them. The modem you buy should be Hayes-compatible, an industry standard. Popular brands include Hayes (duh), Cardinal, USRobotics, and Zoom.

Why You Want a Fast Modem

Modems have to talk to each other at the same speed in order to communicate. but don't worry; a fast modem can always talk to a slower one, because after connecting, it automatically slows down to the speed of the other modem. But in general, the faster your modem is, the less money you will spend on connect-time to online services, and the less time it will take you to download stuff.

One feature you won't have to worry much about when choosing a modem is faxing—all modems today are capable of faxing (sending a facsimile electronically, just like a fax machine). Of course, you'll need a software program to handle the faxing details for you, but most modems include that, too. With your fax modem and the proper software, you can send a document created with your PC to either another fax modem, or to an actual fax machine. When shopping, the standard you want to look for here is called CCITT Group 3 Fax; about 98 percent of all the fax modems will support Group 3, but at least you can weed out those built on the island of Outer Gamzabia that don't.

Something you might be interested in (especially if you work in a small office or at home) is a modem that supports voice mail and caller ID. Along with the proper software, these modems enable you to set up one of those fancy voice mail systems where callers can leave messages for particular people by pressing the right button.

Cross Your Fingers, It's Time to Install

Before you install your modem, make sure that you change its COM port setting to the COM port you want to use. Usually you set the COM port by changing some DIP switches. DIP switches are kind of like light switches; they're either set on or off. By setting these switches to certain positions, you select COM1, COM2, and so on. (Of course, before you touch anything, make sure that you've discharged that darn static.)

Techno Talk

Any Port in a Storm

Before you install your modem, you'll need to decide which COM port to use. Newer PCs have four COM ports; older ones have only two. Don't get too depressed, because if you own a computer with an ISA bus, it can only use two COM ports at the same time anyway. In other words, it can only use COM1 and COM2, or COM3 and COM4, at any one time.

Trouble is, with only two COM ports to choose from, your modem is pretty likely to bump into some interference from other serial devices such as your mouse, a serial printer, or scanner. In addition, a serial port (even if it doesn't have anything attached to it) can cause a conflict unless it's disabled.

Installing an Internal Modem

Once you're ready to install your modem, go through the usual steps to prepare your system. (If you need hints, see Chapter 12 for help.) Take a moment to get rid of that nasty static cling and then open up your PC.

Unscrew the retaining screw of the slot you've picked out. Remove the slot cover and then, using both hands, pick up the modem at its top edge. Make sure that the card's edge connectors are positioned over their respective slots. Gently press the card into place. Be careful not to force the modem in—you could bend it.

Press the internal modem into its slot.

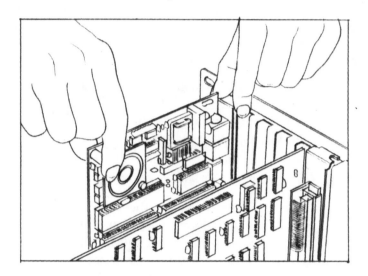

Once you have the modem in, connect the phone line. Just leave the PC open if you want; you still need to test the modem, and it's easier to correct problems if you still have access to the problem maker (uh, the modem). On the back of the modem, you'll see two connections—you need to use the one marked "To Line" or "To Wall." Connect the cord into a regular telephone jack, preferably one that's in a surge protector (many surge protectors come with a protected phone jack—use one to avoid damage to your modem from electrical surges).

If you've got only one phone jack, don't fret—you won't be able to use the modem and the phone together, but you can still get them to share. Just disconnect your phone from the wall and then connect it to the phone jack marked "To Phone." Now, when you're using one phone line for both your phone and your modem, you should get rid of extras like "call waiting," which wreak havoc on the modem's ability to send and receive data undisturbed.

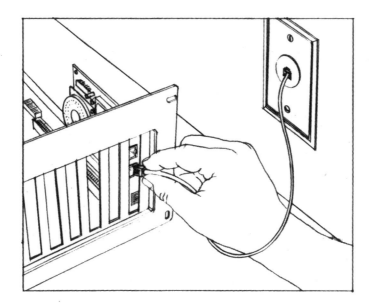

Plug in the telephone line.

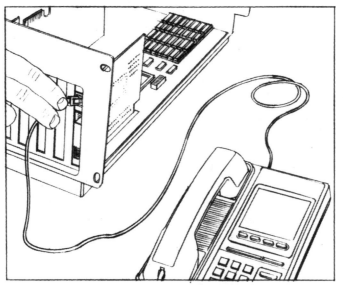

You can connect your phone to the modem if you have only one line.

Well, that's over. Leave the cover off so that you can test this thing (see "Testing Your Modem," later in this chapter).

Installing an External Modem

There's not a lot to installing an external modem, thank goodness. Just take your serial cable (you did remember to buy one didn't you?) and connect it to the back of the modem. Connect the other end to the COM port you chose.

Use a serial cable to connect your external modem.

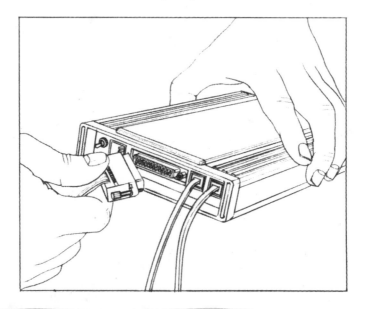

Techno Talk

You Call That a Shield?

When shopping for a serial cable to connect your external modem, you should check the level of shielding which protects your modem from nasty electrical surges. Now, just about every serial cable you'll find on a store shelf has the word "shielded" written on it someplace. As far as you know, the manufacturers may be calling that cable "shielded" because it has rubber over the wires. If the cable says "RF shielded," now that means something! This tells you that the cable is completely shielded from radio frequency interference.

Better yet, if you see the familiar "UL" label, and the cable says "RF shielded," that's the manufacturer's way of saying, "If we're lying, then we have to pay you a lot of money."

Next, plug in the power cable and connect it to a wall outlet, or preferably, a surge protector. Then connect the phone line. You'll see two telephone-type connections: use the one marked "To Line" or "To Wall." If you don't see the labels, turn the modem over. Sometimes they're on the bottom. Connect the phone cord and then plug it into a telephone (RJ11) jack, preferably in a surge protector. If you only have one phone jack, disconnect your phone from the wall and connect it to the other phone line connector on the modem—the one marked "To Phone." Of course, you won't be able to use your phone and the modem at the same time! By the way, if your modem has only one phone jack, buy an adapter, as shown below. Then plug the adapter into the wall jack and plug both your phone and your modem into the adapter.

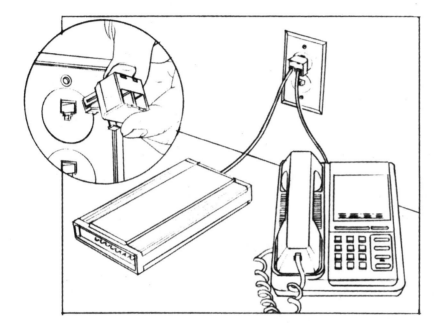

Use an adapter if your modem provides only one phone jack.

Okay. That went pretty well. Now it's time to test the darn thing.

Testing Your Modem

Power up the PC. If you have an external modem, turn it on. Now, some modems come with some software that you can use to test the thing; if you don't have any other way to test the modem, just type **ECHO ATDT>COM1** at the DOS prompt and press **Enter**.

Of course, if you connected your modem to COM2 instead, then type this: **ECHO ATDT>COM2**. You should hear a dial tone, and then the modem should reply with an "OK." If it does, then everything's fine. You can close up the PC now. If something's funky (such as a misconnected modem, or one which is connected to the same COM port as another modem) then you'll get the error message, "Write fault error writing device COM1. Abort, Retry, Ignore, Fail?". Press A for abort and check out the next section for help in determining what's wrong.

As a final step, you need to install your communications program such as ProComm Plus or CrossTalk, and select your brand of modem in the process. There are some additional things you need to do in Windows to get your modem to work, too. See Part 5 for help.

What Could Go Wrong

When testing your modem, if you get the error message: Write fault error writing device COM1 (or COM2), then either you forgot to turn the modem on, or there's something wrong with the connection. If you're using an internal modem, try taking it out and then reseating it again.

If you run into problems after you've already got your modem up and running, there could be a COM port conflict with some other device, especially if your mouse (or whatever) begins acting up, too. A conflict might also result in the modem stopping in the middle of transmission.

If your PC is old, it may not have a fast enough UART chip for your external modem to keep up. (Internal modems come with their own UARTs that override anything your PC already has.) Run MSD as described in Chapter 4 and click on **COM Ports**. Your chip should be a 16550 or higher. Older chips such as the 8250 just can't keep up. If you're getting only partial transmissions, this may be the culprit. Replace the I/O board that's connected to your external modem with something less dusty.

The Least You Need to Know

When shopping for your new communications buddy, consider these tips:

➤ Buy the fastest modem you can. It'll pay for itself in a few months, with savings on long-distance phone and online service charges.

➤ If you opt for an internal modem, make sure that you have a free slot, hopefully away from noisy devices like your hard disk or the power supply.

➤ If you buy an external modem instead, make sure you have a serial port available. Check the UART chip used by your serial port; if it's old, you'll need to buy an I/O card to update it.

➤ If you get an external modem, be sure to buy a modem cable with which to connect it.

➤ Error correction is the method by which the modem can detect errors in transmission. Data compression is the method the modem uses to compress the data prior to transmitting it.

Part 5
Getting Your PC to Figure Out What You've Done

Unfortunately, it's not enough to sweat off ten pounds in a nerve-wracking contest between you and your PC. You've installed your new device, but chances are pretty good that it's not ready to work just yet. That's because, in order to get most gadgets to work, you've got to install an interpreter called a *device driver, which is fluent in DOS-speak. The device driver then takes over the job of translating the device's requests to and from DOS, enabling them to get along quite nicely.*

And if you plan on using Windows, you're gonna have to install a different driver that talks Windows-speak. This part shows you how to add the appropriate drivers and get your new gadget going.

Chapter 22

Getting DOS to Recognize Your New Toy

In This Chapter

➤ What really goes on during startup

➤ Final steps for installing a new device

➤ The mystery behind AUTOEXEC.BAT and CONFIG.SYS

➤ How to use EDIT to edit your configuration files

➤ Using EDLIN or Notepad instead

When you start your PC, it opens its eyes, stretches a bit, and yells for somebody to tell it what day it is. After that, it reaches for its configuration files—AUTOEXEC.BAT and CONFIG.SYS—so it can get set up for the day. Among other things, these files tell your computer to load device drivers so that your computer can "talk" to the various stuff you've added, such as a sound card or a CD-ROM drive.

So, after you install your new device, you'll probably have to run some kind of setup program that makes changes to the configuration files for you. If those changes knock out your PC, or if you need to fine-tune them yourself for some reason, you'll need to know how to edit the configuration files. In this chapter, you'll learn all you need to know to get DOS to recognize your new toy.

What Really Goes On at Startup

When you start your PC, it wakes up your CPU, which gives the BIOS a good kick in the pants to get it started. BIOS then takes over the rest of the morning routine.

BIOS is your PC's basic input and output system, and it's the thing that knows how to talk to the PC's basic components, such as the floppy drives, the hard disk, and RAM. So when you add one of these items, it'll be ready to go as soon as you turn on the PC, without running any kind of setup program—as long as your BIOS isn't so old it can't recognize the technology.

BIOS then starts its POST, or Power-On Self-Test. During this part of the startup it sends a brief "hello" to all the PC's basic components such as the keyboard, RAM, and so on. CMOS keeps track of the list of components the BIOS checks during the POST. If a device that's listed in CMOS is not found, or if it's different somehow (like you've suddenly got more RAM), the BIOS will flash an error on-screen.

After POST, the BIOS looks for an operating system, such as DOS or Windows 95. BIOS starts its search at drive A, moving from there to drive C. If you've left a diskette in drive A, you'll see this message: Non system disk or disk error. Just remove the disk and press **Ctrl+Alt+Delete** to restart the PC. (If you're trying to boot from your emergency diskette in drive A, you won't see an error message, because your disk will have the files your computer needs to start itself.)

At the last part of the startup process, DOS or Windows 95 takes over, looking first for the CONFIG.SYS, and then the AUTOEXEC.BAT, carrying out any instructions it finds.

Running the Setup Program for Your New Device

Before You Run the Setup Program... Make sure you've followed the steps in Chapter 12 to update your emergency diskette. That way, if the setup program makes changes that render your PC helpless, you'll be able to undo them.

The PC's BIOS handles the job of talking to the computer's basic parts, such as the hard disk and memory. When you add other devices such as a sound card, tape backup, CD-ROM drive, printer, video card, or modem, then you have to run some kind of setup program to configure the new device and to install a program called a *device driver*. The device driver's role is to help the BIOS talk to the new device.

Your new piece of hardware usually comes with a diskette or two that includes its setup program. To run most setup programs, install your new device and turn the PC on. Then insert the setup diskette into drive A, type **A:SETUP** at the DOS prompt, and press **Enter**. (Some programs have you type **A:INSTALL** instead.)

At this point, you'll be treated to several screens that might ask you interesting questions such as "What COM port do you want to use?" or "Do you want the device driver loaded into high memory?" For the most part, just go with whatever option the program suggests. You can always rerun the setup program if you change your mind later on.

If the program asks you if you want it to make changes to the AUTOEXEC.BAT and CONFIG.SYS files, by all means answer **Yes**, because you don't really want to operate on these files all by yourself if you can help it.

Uh, I Use Windows
If you use Windows, you'll need to do some things in addition to what we've done here to get it to recognize your new toy. Luckily, that's covered in the next chapter.

Once the setup program is done, restart your PC so that the changes it made to the configuration files will take effect. The computer can't really see these changes until it has actually read them, and it doesn't read those files at any time other than at startup.

Fixing What the Setup Program Did

If you restart your PC after using the setup program only to run into a problem (like the PC won't start), use your emergency diskette. Just stick it in drive A and restart the PC again. Then edit the configuration files to either remove or change what the setup program did, so your PC and the device will work. The new changes will be easy to identify, since they'll be something you won't recognize, but you can always check the manual to be sure, or look at the unchanged files on your emergency diskette.

First, start with the manual that came with your new toy. It might suggest some changes that will help the device to work in your system. If worst comes to worst, you can always edit the files yourself to remove part or all of the changes one at a time until you find the culprit.

I'm Tired of Messing with This Junk

If you want to simply get your PC up and running quickly, then just copy old working versions of AUTOEXEC.BAT and CONFIG.SYS off of the emergency diskette. Insert the diskette into drive A and then type these two commands at the DOS prompt, pressing **Enter** after each one:

> COPY A:AUTOEXEC.BAT C:\

> COPY A:CONFIG.SYS C:\

These commands will copy the old files to the hard disk, and, after you restart the PC, you'll be right back where you were before you ran that setup program. Your new device won't work, but at least your PC will.

By the Way, What's the CONFIG.SYS?

As you may remember from Chapter 4, CONFIG.SYS is a special file that enables you to customize the original settings, or configuration, of your computer to work more efficiently with the programs and devices you use. The setup programs from the various programs and devices you install place some commands in the CONFIG.SYS, but you can add others to fit your own personal preferences.

In your CONFIG.SYS file, you'll find commands that:

➤ Change the number of files a program can open at one time.

➤ Change the number of recently opened files in memory.

➤ Enable your computer to use memory more efficiently.

➤ Run special programs called *device drivers* that tell your PC how to communicate with a particular device such as a mouse or CD-ROM drive.

Wanna Tell Me What the AUTOEXEC.BAT Is For?

When you turn on your PC, you'll normally hear only a little buzzing and a few beeps. After making the appropriate amount of racket, the PC displays a *prompt* that looks like C:\> and waits for you to tell it to do something.

If anything else happens—for example, a menu appears, or a program starts up—your computer is not possessed; it's being controlled by a file called *AUTOEXEC.BAT*.

Techno Talk

I Have Windows 95. So this AUTOEXEC Thing Doesn't Apply to Me. Right?

Wrong. Windows 95 still uses your AUTOEXEC.BAT, although it really doesn't affect how Windows 95 runs per se. When you start your PC, Windows 95 starts, but not because of any command in the AUTOEXEC.BAT. However, if you include the PATH, PROMPT, or other commands in the AUTOEXEC.BAT, they effect how DOS looks and acts when you select the **MS-DOS Prompt** command from the **Programs** menu. Also, some drivers for certain devices not recognized by Windows 95 are still loaded through the AUTOEXEC.BAT.

In addition, if you want to start a program automatically, you can place the proper command in the AUTOEXEC.BAT just like you used to do with DOS (or you can add the program to your StartUp menu, which is what most people do).

AUTOEXEC.BAT is a file that contains a series of commands that are *AUTO*matically *EXEC*uted (or carried out) when you start the computer. The AUTOEXEC.BAT can contain any command you might ordinarily type at the DOS prompt. For example, if you always use Lotus 1-2-3, you can insert a command to have the AUTOEXEC.BAT start that program for you when you turn on the PC, just by including the proper command in the AUTOEXEC.BAT. That leaves you some free time to schmooze at the coffee machine.

Sometimes, but not often, the setup program for a new device will place its device driver command in the AUTEOEXEC.BAT instead of the CONFIG.SYS. For example, your mouse driver is often loaded this way. Also, a device may place special "notes" to itself in the AUTOEXEC.BAT through something called the SET command.

But Why Does My PC Have Two Configuration Files?

It seems stupid that DOS has two files that seem to do the same thing—customize what happens when you start your computer.

Actually, DOS is not being redundant. Each file serves a specific purpose that allows it to complement, but not overlap, the other. CONFIG.SYS contains commands that change the way DOS works. The AUTOEXEC.BAT contains regular commands that can be entered at a DOS prompt, such as the command to start a program.

In your AUTOEXEC.BAT, you might find these commands:

➤ The PATH command, which helps DOS search for commands and programs in the directories you choose.

➤ The PROMPT command, which changes the default prompt from C:\> to something different.

➤ A command which displays a menu at startup.

➤ A command such as MOUSE.COM, which starts a device driver.

➤ A command such as 123, which starts a program that you use first thing every day.

Tips for Editing the Configuration Files

Before you edit your configuration files, make a copy of them. If you're editing the files to fix a problem with a setup program for a new device, then don't copy those bad files to your emergency diskette. Instead, you can just skip this step, because you already have a copy of a good version of your files on the emergency diskette.

If you're editing the configuration files for any other reason, then take the time now to copy your good versions onto the emergency diskette for safe keeping. Insert the diskette and type the following two commands, pressing **Enter** after each one.

COPY C:\AUTOEXEC.BAT A:
COPY C:\CONFIG.SYS A:

Don't Forget the PATH

If you add a command to a configuration file and you expect DOS to carry it out, you better make sure you give DOS enough information. For example, if you want to include a command that loads a device driver, you better make sure that you also include the driver's location or *path*.

A path is made up of three parts: the drive letter where the file is located, followed by a colon. This is followed by a backslash (\) and the name of the directory in which the file is kept. Finally, this nonsense is followed by another backslash and the name of the file.

So if you want to include a command to load the device driver MAXSOUND.SYS, make sure you also include its location as part of that command, like this:

DEVICE=C:\BLASTER\MAXSOUND.SYS.

Editing Your Configuration Files with EDIT

DOS version 5 and higher contains a simple editor called EDIT that you can use to edit your configuration files.

To edit your CONFIG.SYS, type **EDIT C:\CONFIG.SYS** at the prompt and press **Enter**. (To edit your AUTOEXEC.BAT instead, type: **EDIT C:\AUTOEXEC.BAT.**) You'll see something like this:

Having fun with EDIT.

```
   File  Edit  Search  Options                                    Help
                          CONFIG.SYS
 DEVICE=C:\DOS\SETVER.EXE                                              ↑
 FILES=80
 BUFFERS=10,0
 [menu]
 menuitem=std_config,Standard Configuration
 menuitem=game_config,CD Gaming Configuration
 menuitem=nonCDgame_config,Non-CD Gaming Configuration
 menuitem=nonexpmem,No expanded memory (Conventional DOS only)

 [std_config]
 DEVICE=C:\DOS\HIMEM.SYS
 DEVICE=C:\DOS\EMM386.EXE NOEMS X=A000-AFFF X=B800-C7FF WIN=B500-B7FF WIN=B200-
 DOS=UMB
 LASTDRIVE=J
 FCBS=16,0
 DEVICEHIGH /L:1,11648 =C:\ADI2C111.SYS
 SHELL=C:\DOS\COMMAND.COM C:\DOS\ /E:1024 /p
 DEVICEHIGH /L:1,2240 =C:\FSPLMSG.SYS
 DEVICEHIGH /L:1,9072 =C:\DOS\ANSI.SYS
 STACKS=9,256
 DEVICEHIGH /L:0:1,11872 /S =C:\WIN95\COMMAND\DRVSPACE.SYS /MOVE           ↓
                                                                    →
 MS-DOS Editor   <F1=Help> Press ALT to activate menus      │ N 00001:001
```

To make a change to a particular line, use the down arrow key to move to the line, or click on that line with the mouse pointer. Move over to the part of the line you want to change by pressing the left arrow key. Press **Delete** to remove any unwanted characters and then type the change.

> **Don't Forget!**
> After you edit a configuration file, you'll have to restart the computer to test your changes. The easiest way to do that is to press **Ctrl+Alt+Delete**.

To insert a line, move the cursor to the end of any line and press **Enter**. Your new line appears just under the line you chose. To type on this line, click on it.

Repeat this stuff to change what you need to. When you finish, save the file by pressing **Alt+F** and then **S**. You can also use your mouse to open the **File** menu and select **Save**.

To exit EDIT, open the **File** menu and select **Exit**, or press **Alt+F** and then **X**.

For example, suppose you need to remove a couple of lines put in the CONFIG.SYS by your new sound card, which is currently messing up your mouse. Just open the CONFIG.SYS by typing **EDIT CONFIG.SYS**. Then select the two offending lines and press **Delete** to remove them from the file. Click on the **File** menu and select **Save**, then open the **File** menu again and select **Exit**.

I've Got Windows, So I'm Using Notepad

If you have Windows 3.1 or Windows 95, you can edit your files without messing around with dumb old DOS. Just start Notepad (in Windows 3.1, it's in the Accessories group; in Windows 95, it's on the Accessories menu).

Open the **File** menu and select **Open**. In the Filename box, type either C:\AUTOEXEC.BAT or C:\CONFIG.SYS and then press **Enter**. You'll see something like the following figure appear on your screen.

Click on the line you want to edit. Press **Delete** to remove unwanted characters and then retype what you really want. You can also select text and press **Delete** to remove it.

To insert a line somewhere, just click at the end of a line and press **Enter**. A blank line is inserted after the line you chose. To type on this line, just click on it.

When you're ready to save the file, open the **File** menu and select **Save**. Then open the **File** menu and select **Exit** to get out of there.

Editing in style with Notepad.

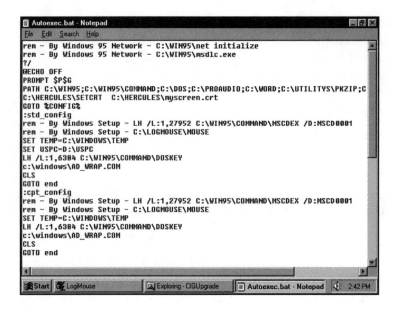

The Least You Need to Know

After you install a new device on your computer, such as a CD-ROM drive or a modem, you run the setup program that comes with the device. This program will make changes to your configuration files so that DOS can talk to the devices. If there isn't a setup program to make these changes for you, you'll have to alter your configuration files yourself so that the new devices you've added to your computer will be recognized.

➤ Thankfully, most devices provide you with a setup program to edit your configuration files for you.

➤ Before you allow the setup program to make any changes, be sure to copy the AUTOEXEC.BAT and CONFIG.SYS to your emergency diskette.

➤ If the setup program makes changes that prevent you from starting your PC, undo them by booting with your emergency diskette and copying the original configuration files back.

➤ To run the setup program, insert its diskette and type **A:SETUP** or **A:INSTALL**.

➤ Once the setup program finishes making changes, restart your PC so that the setup program's changes can take effect.

➤ If you use Windows, there are probably some other things you need to do to set up your device properly (see the next chapter).

➤ If you need to make changes to the configuration files manually, you can use EDIT (which comes with DOS version 5 or higher) or Notepad (which comes with Windows).

Chapter 23

Getting Windows to Recognize Your New Toy

Installing a driver for DOS through the CONFIG.SYS and AUTOEXEC.BAT configuration files just isn't good enough for Windows. No sir. That's because Windows has its own configuration files, WIN.INI and SYSTEM.INI. It takes a DOS device driver to make your new device officially part of the computer; but Windows needs a device driver specifically designed for Windows before it can become aware of your new toy. So, for most new devices, you'll need to install a Windows device driver as well. I know this is like learning you have to fill out your tax forms twice in the same year, but did you really expect your computer to be easy?

Most devices include a Windows driver on the diskette with the DOS driver, but if they don't, you'll find additional drivers on the Windows setup diskettes as well—you know, the diskettes you used to install Windows in the first place.

If you've got Windows 95, the newest version of Microsoft's omnipresent operating system, it's pretty easy to let it know you've added a new device. See the following section for details. If you've decided to stick with Windows 3.1 a little longer, skip ahead to the section "Telling Windows 3.1 What You've Added Instead" later in this chapter.

Telling Windows 95 About the New Hardware

After you install your new toy and restart your PC, Windows 95 may or may not recognize that something is different. That's because Plug and Play (the automatic part of Windows 95 that's supposed to figure out on its own that you've added something new) doesn't work without its other two parts: a Plug and Play BIOS, and a Plug and Play device.

In other words, if you've just added a Plug and Play CD-ROM drive, and you're using a Pentium or 486 PC with an updated BIOS chip, your PC automatically recognizes your new CD-ROM drive and begins the process to install it as soon as you turn on the PC and start Windows 95.

If you don't own a Plug and Play computer, or if you didn't buy a PnP device, no big deal—Windows 95 is pretty good at installing your new device anyway. It just needs a little shove in the right direction.

Adding Just About Anything

When Windows 95 doesn't automatically welcome your new toy, here's how to tell Windows 95 about it:

First, open the **Start** menu, select **Settings**, and then select **Control Panel**. Double-click the **Add New Hardware** icon. The Add New Hardware Wizard appears. Not much to do on this first screen, so click **Next>**.

The easiest way to handle this is to sit back, relax, and let Windows 95 do all the work. So when it asks you if you want Windows 95 to search for and detect your new hardware, by all means, click **Yes**. Then click **Next>**.

Getting Windows 95 to search for your new device is easy.

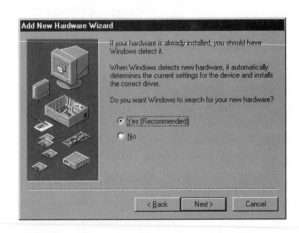

Before you continue, close all your programs. Then click **Next>**. This whole detection thing will take a few minutes, so feel free to put your feet up while you wait. Meanwhile, Windows 95 will start sniffing around, looking for something new. When Windows 95 finds your new part, it displays the name of that part (or at least what Windows believes that part to be) in a box. If the guess is right, just click **Finish**, and Windows 95 installs the proper device driver. You may be asked to provide additional information, or to perform additional steps—for example, if you're installing an external modem, Windows 95 will ask you to turn it on. Then it will ask you to enter your phone number and the COM port you're using.

If Windows doesn't find your new toy, or if it guessed wrong, you'll see a message telling you to give it another try. Click **Next>**. You'll see a list of hardware types. Select your hardware type from the list. If you don't see your hardware type listed, choose **Other devices**. Click **Next>**.

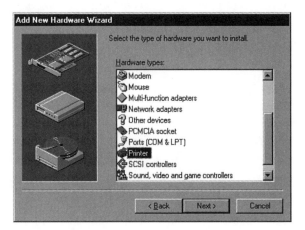

The manual method of telling Windows 95 about a new device.

You'll see a list of manufacturers for your particular device. For example, if you select **Printers**, then you'll see a list of common printers. Click the name of the manufacturer that made your printer (such as Hewlett Packard), and you'll see a list of HP printers. Pick your model from the list and click **Next>**. Windows 95 installs the driver for your new part.

If you still can't find your new part in a listing anywhere, then Windows 95 did not come with a driver for it. Click **Have Disk** and insert the setup diskette supplied by the maker of your new gadget. Select the driver file from those listed (there'll probably only be one file listed) and click **OK**. Windows 95 installs the driver.

After you've installed your new part under Windows 95, you can start using it right away. If you want to change any of your choices later on (for example, you want to change your modem's phone number) just return to the Control Panel and click the appropriate icon, such as the Modem icon.

Telling Windows 3.1 What You've Added

Once you install your new device, and DOS actually recognizes it, you'll need to perform a few extra steps to get Windows 3.1 to recognize it. Thankfully, these steps are not terribly complex, as you'll soon learn.

New Mouse, Keyboard, or Monitor? Step Right Up!

If you replace your old mouse, keyboard, or monitor with the exact same mouse, keyboard, or monitor you had before, you don't have to do a thing in Windows. You can just go ahead and start using the new device. You see, DOS and Windows need drivers in order to recognize a particular brand and model of device, but there's nothing particular about one video card that differentiates or distinguishes it from another card of the same make and model. If you replace a defective XYZ Model 12 Card with a working XYZ Model 12 Card, you don't need to run Setup for that card again.

Check This Out...

But What About My Video Card?

Suppose you have an old VGA monitor and a standard VGA card running Windows' generic VGA driver, and you buy a new video card, but not a new monitor. Chances are that you don't have to do a thing to your Windows drivers, because your old monitor is less likely to be able to take advantage of the new card's capabilities anyway. In most cases, you really need to upgrade both the video card and the monitor, because they work as a team. See Chapter 16 for help.

So again, the only time you need to change display modes with this procedure is if you upgrade *both your video card and your monitor* to a higher standard, such as upgrading from VGA to Super VGA.

However, if you upgrade to a higher quality monitor, or if you change the brand of mouse or keyboard you use, chances are you have to do something in order to tell Windows about it. Whether or not you need to do anything at all depends on whether you bought a device that operates under a different *mode*. For example, in the Windows

3.1 Setup program, under Mouse, you have only two choices: Microsoft mouse, or another brand of mouse. So you only need to change mouse modes if you switch from a Microsoft mouse to a Logitech mouse, or vice-versa.

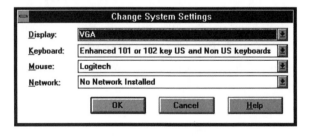

Techno Talk

Read This Before You Change Your Windows Setup

Before you attempt to change your Windows Setup, do yourself a big favor and copy the WIN.INI and SYSTEM.INI to the emergency diskette you created in Chapter 12. If you accidently change anything that makes it impossible to start Windows, you'll be able to quickly copy the original .INI files back to the Windows directory with the emergency diskette so you can get into Windows and try something else.

This is especially important to do before you change video modes, because if the current Windows selection is not compatible with your system, you won't be able to see a darn thing.

In any case, the safest thing to do is to go through this upgrade procedure, if for no other reason than to make sure that you're currently operating in the right mode. Be sure to get out any diskettes that came with your new hardware before you start; you may need them. You may also need your Windows diskettes as well, so find them and dust 'em off before you start.

Now, before you start, exit all programs, because Windows is going to restart the PC at the end of this business. Now, open up the Main window and then double-click the **Windows Setup** icon. The Windows Setup dialog pokes up its head. Open the **Options** menu and select **Change System Settings**.

Change System Settings	
D̲isplay:	VGA
K̲eyboard:	Enhanced 101 or 102 key US and Non US keyboards
M̲ouse:	Logitech
N̲etwork:	No Network Installed

| OK | Cancel | H̲elp |

Changin' Windows settings.

Click the down arrow next to the item you want to change. For example, to change your mouse, click the down arrow to open up a drop-down list of mouse options. Scroll through the list until you find your particular brand of mouse, click your mouse's brand name, and click **OK**. If your particular brand of mouse isn't listed, select the **Other** option at the bottom of the list—this means you'll need the diskette that came with your new part. Windows will read a list of (hopefully) only one mouse driver from that diskette, but you'll still need to select your one mouse brand from that one mouse list.

Feeding Windows.

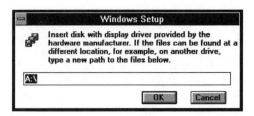

Feed Windows the appropriate diskette and then click **OK**. Windows copies the device driver to the hard disk. When asked, click **Restart Windows** so that the new driver can take effect. Your new toy is ready to play.

But Windows Didn't Ask Me for a Diskette!

If your new part is similar to the old one, Windows may already have installed the proper driver. That's because in most cases Windows installs several drivers at once in order to make it easy for you to switch modes for a device.

But if Windows allows you to install the driver that came with the new device, by all means, do so—it'll be more current than any driver that Windows might provide.

Changing Windows Setup from the DOS Prompt

If you change the display driver or whatever, and now Windows doesn't work, you can run the Windows Setup program from DOS to correct your mistake. Here's what to do:

1. First, change to the Windows directory by typing **CD\WINDOWS** and pressing **Enter**.

2. Type **SETUP** and press **Enter** to start the Windows Setup program.

3. Use the up arrow key to select the item to change and then press **Enter**.

4. Make a selection from the list that appears and press **Enter** again. If you're not sure what to select, pick something generic so you can at least get Windows running again. For example, if you select what you thought was the correct video driver for your system and then Windows blanked out on you, change to the generic VGA driver (that is, if you use VGA) and try again.

5. Finally, highlight the **Accept the configuration shown above** option. The Setup program will probably ask you for some diskettes, so oblige it. After it installs the device driver, the Setup program dumps you out at the DOS prompt.

You should now be able to start Windows. If not, try running the Windows Setup again.

Adding a Printer

To install a printer under Windows 3.1, you use a slightly different method than you use to change your monitor, keyboard, or mouse. First, open the Main window and double-click the **Control Panel** icon.

Double-click the **Printer** icon. The Printers dialog pops its head up. Click the **Add** button, and the dialog box expands, as shown.

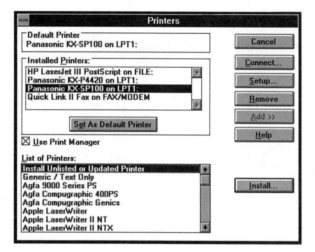

The Printer dialog box expands so that you can choose your new printer.

Select your new printer from the List of Printers list box and then click **Install**. If you don't find your printer listed, select a compatible printer instead (a printer that your printer *emulates*, or mimics).

Techno Talk

Fallback Position

Many printers have at least one "emulation mode," or fallback mode, that allows a newer brand of printer to behave, for the computer's sake, like an older, more common brand—at least until that new brand becomes more common. If you're not sure what your printer's emulation mode is, check its specifications as listed in the manual that comes with it.

Dig out the Windows diskette that Windows asks you for and click **OK**. Windows copies the printer driver to the hard disk. When you get back to the Printers dialog box, select your new printer from the **Installed Printers** list and click **Set As Default** Printer.

You can remove your old printer driver once the new one's working—it'll save you a bit of hard drive space. Just select your old printer from the **Installed Printers** list and click **Remove**.

Adding Other Junk

So far, you've learned how to install your monitor, mouse, keyboard, and printer under Windows 3.1. To install other devices, you use the generic Drivers utility.

First, open the Main window and then click the **Control Panel** icon. Double-click the **Drivers** icon. The Drivers dialog box appears on-screen. Click **Add** and you see the Add dialog box.

Select your brand.

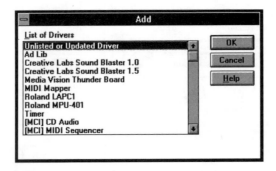

Scroll through the list until you find the brand name for your new toy. If your device's brand isn't listed, select the Unlisted option at the bottom of the list and get the diskette that came with your new part because you're going to need it.

Once you've selected your new toy from the list, click **OK**. Feed Windows the appropriate diskette and click **OK**. Windows copies the device driver to the hard disk and then asks you if it's OK to exit Windows and restart it. Click **Restart Windows**, and Windows restarts so that the new driver can take effect. Your new pal is ready to play.

Check This Out...

Use the Newest Driver Whenever possible, use the diskette that came with your new gadget to install the Windows device driver. Even if Windows already has a copy of the driver, chances are pretty good that the driver is really old.

The Least You Need to Know

After you install a new device, you have to get Windows 95 to recognize it. If you use Windows 3.1, you install the DOS device driver, and a Windows one.

➤ Windows 95 may automatically recognize and install your new device, if it's Plug and Play-compatible, and you're using a PnP computer. Otherwise, you'll need to use the Add New Hardware icon in the Control Panel to install your new device.

➤ Before you install the driver for your new gadget under Windows 95, close down your other programs, because you'll need to restart Windows for the changes to take effect.

➤ Before making any changes to your setup under Windows 3.1, update your emergency diskette.

➤ Also exit any programs before starting, because you'll have to restart Windows 3.1 for the changes to take place.

➤ You'll need either your Windows 3.1 diskettes, or the diskette that came with your new gadget, in order to install its driver.

➤ To tell Windows 3.1 about a new video card, keyboard, or mouse, use the Windows Setup icon in the Main window.

➤ To introduce Windows 3.1 to a new printer, use the Printer icon in the Control Panel instead.

➤ To let Windows 3.1 know about any other new toy, use the Drivers icon in the Main window.

➤ You can run the Windows 3.1 Setup from the DOS prompt by changing to the Windows directory and typing **SETUP**.

Chapter 24

Fiddling with Ports, IRQs, Addresses, and Such

In This Chapter

➤ Fiddling with jumpers and switches

➤ Solving annoying COM port conflicts

➤ Dealing with IRQs

➤ The mystery behind DMA

➤ Messing around with the CMOS

When you install some new gadgets in your PC, they bring wine, flowers, and candy, eager to be loved by all the other parts. Other parts bully their way in, steal Dad's favorite chair, and refuse to behave.

I'm guessing that you just installed one of these brutes, or you wouldn't be boring yourself with this chapter. Here, you'll learn to tame your beast and get everyone working happily together again.

Before You Mess Inside
Before you take the cover off your PC in order to mess with jumpers, switches, and other junk, take out some insurance in the form of an emergency diskette. See Chapter 12 for details.

Fiddling with Jumpers and Switches and Such

Back in the days of cave men and stegosauruses, PCs got most of their configuration information from tiny pins called *jumpers*, or small switches called *DIPs*. But even with all their fancy-schmancy hardware, some computer parts still prefer this primitive method of communication.

A jumper is made up of two or more parallel pins, which are part of a circuit. If the pins are sticking up in the air, then obviously the circuit is open, which is the same as having a switch turned off. To turn on an electric circuit, you need to close, or complete, it; with a jumper, you close the circuit with a little rectangular doodad called a *shunt*, which you slip onto a pair of pins, as shown. The pins are labeled; check the device's manual to find out which pins the jumper is supposed to be put on.

Place the jumper over the correct pins to change the setting of the device.

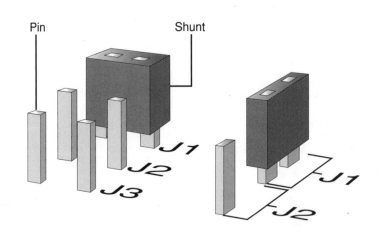

If you need to remove a shunt, let it hang over one pin, like this

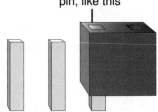

For example, if you're installing a modem and the manual tells you to set the jumper to J5 in order to set the modem to COM2, then remove the shunt from its current resting spot and place it over the two J5 pins. As if this junk isn't hard enough, some jumpers are set in a row and not in pairs. Here you place the shunt over two numbered pins, such as pins 4 and 5. The number points to the pair of pins that together form the jumper; and you have to be careful here, because one pin can be part of two jumper pairs. For instance, you might find three pins (not four) in one row, with markings for J1 and J2. The J1 pair will most likely be the top pair (the first and second pin from the top), and J2 will probably be the bottom pair (the second and third pin).

To remove the shunt from the jumper, just pull up. If the shunt's stuck, you may find tweezers or threats helpful. Be careful not to let the metal tweezers touch anything it might short out.

Check This Out...

Don't Remove Under Penalty of Law

Don't remove a shunt entirely from a card even if the manual tells you to; you're likely to lose the little guy. Instead, leave the shunt hanging over one of the two pins, as shown in the figure. (A jumper is formed by joining two pins with a shunt in order to work, so putting it over one pin will have no effect.) That way, it'll be easier to find the next time you need to change the gadget's settings.

DIP switches (sometimes called rocker switches) are like tiny light switches: they can only be set to on or off. By setting the correct switches to either on or off, you can reconfigure a device. Oh, in case you care, DIP is short for *dual in-line package*. Yes, it's the same DIP as in "DIP chip"; the term refers to the way the item is mounted to the circuit board. You'll notice two (thus the "dual") rows of prongs (thus the "in-line") sticking out of opposite sides of both a DIP chip and a DIP switch set. They could've called it "two row package" but then the acronym would have been "TRP chip," and you'd have to pronounce it

Check This Out...

Before You Rock You may want to write down the device's switch settings before you start messing with them, so you can at least go back to the original settings if things go wrong. It might not be what you want, but hey, at least it works.

I'm Feeling a Bit Left Out Don't be bummed out if your PC doesn't use old-style jumpers and DIP switches. A lot of modems let you set the jumpers for the COM port selection using the software program included with the modem.

"trip" or "twerp." Although "twerp chip" sounds fitting, it doesn't have that whole double entendre thing going for it.

To change a DIP switch, use a ballpoint pen—your fingernails will thank you. Flip the switch to the side marked on (sometimes marked with just an arrow symbol) if you want to activate it, or to the other side to turn it off.

These aren't Grandma's rockers.

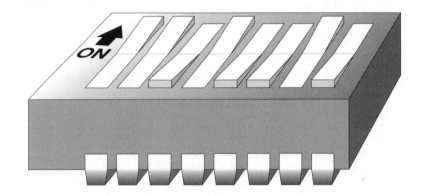

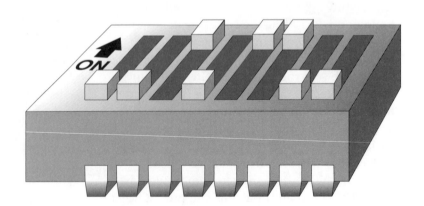

What to Do When Your COM Ports Start a Fight

Various serial devices such as a modem, mouse, scanner, and serial printer use COM ports to communicate with your PC. All's well and good, as long as you only use two of these critters, and you set them to use different COM ports.

But if you install a new serial device and it grabs somebody else's COM port as its own, you're gonna have what's commonly called a mess. Sorry—I mean a COM port conflict.

Another Fine Mess

The easiest way to avoid this problem is to write down the settings your gadgets use. Then, before you install anything new, just choose some settings that aren't being used. You can use this method to avoid not just COM port conflicts, but also IRQ and DMA conflicts as well.

Most PCs can support up to four COM ports, but you can use only two of them at any one time. That's because COM1 and COM3 both use the same *interrupt* to talk to the CPU. (More on interrupts in a minute.) Same goes with COM2 and COM4. So you need to limit yourself to two serial devices and use only COM1 and COM2.

I Don't Think I Have a COM3 or COM4

Some devices don't want to use the higher COM ports, so you can't set them to COM3 or COM4 even if you want to. Likewise, some PCs, such as old XTs or those that use a DOS version earlier than DOS 3.3, don't support COM3 or COM4.

Now, most PCs come with two serial ports on the back, marked COM1 and COM2. It's important to remember that these two ports are active, *even if you have nothing connected to them*. So if you insert a serial device such as a modem, it'll conflict with one of these two. To deactivate a COM port, you usually remove some jumper. Check your PC manual for help.

Check This Out...

It's Still Not Working! If you set up one device to COM1 and the other to COM2, and they're still not working, switch them. (Some devices just don't like being number two.)

To change the COM port an external device uses, plug it into a different serial port. To change an internal device, you usually have to flip some silly DIP switches or move a stupid jumper. (If you're lucky, you get to use software for this nonsense instead of setting the COM port through switches.)

After changing COM settings, reset the device by turning it off and then back on, so that the new settings take effect. If the gadget's an internal one, restart the PC to reset it.

Fixing What IRQs You

When a child wants to get someone's attention, he usually yells. When a boss wants an employee's attention, she usually yells. (Notice the trend...) When a computer part wants to get the CPU's attention, it uses an *interrupt*, or *IRQ*.

You see, your computer's CPU is busy all the time. If some device needs immediate attention, it sends an S.O.S. along its private interrupt. For example, if you start pressing keys on the keyboard, the keyboard controller sends an interrupt signal to the CPU so that it knows that someone's pressing keys. If two devices are accidently assigned the same interrupt, the CPU doesn't know what device actually needs its attention, so either of two catastrophic things can happen:

➤ Either the CPU just ignores any messages it gets,

or

➤ the CPU processes one device's message as though it came from the other device.

So imagine what can happen when the CPU thinks that someone's typing "DELETE *.*" on your printer.

So what you need to do is assign a unique interrupt to each device. Sounds simple, but it's not, since most of the interrupts are already taken by the PC's inner few. Here's a list of the various IRQs and who normally occupies them:

Interrupt	Who Owns It	Problems
IRQ 0	System timer	
IRQ 1	Keyboard controller	

Interrupt	Who Owns It	Problems
IRQ 2	Controller for IRQ 8 to 15	If you have an old XT, then this one's available. (IRQs 8 through 15 don't exist in older PCs.) If you own a newer PC, you can set a gadget to IRQ 2 (but it actually ends up using IRQ 9).
IRQ 3	COM2 and COM4	This is why you can't use COM2 and COM4 at the same time.
IRQ 4	COM1 and COM3	This is why you can't use COM1 and COM3 at the same time.
IRQ 5	LPT2	This is usually unused by anything.
IRQ 6	Floppy disk drive controller	
IRQ 7	LPT1	This is usually taken by your printer.
IRQ 8	Clock	
IRQ 9	Unused	Since IRQ2 is used as a controller for IRQ8 to 15, the computer automatically switches any device set to IRQ 2 to IRQ9. A network card often grabs it.
IRQ 10	Unused	Some gadgets don't support an IRQ this high.
IRQ 11	Unused	Some gadgets don't support an IRQ this high.
IRQ 12	Motherboard mouse port	
IRQ 13	Math coprocessor	Even if your PC doesn't have a coprocessor, you can't use this because it's not wired to the expansion slots.
IRQ 14	Hard disk controller	
IRQ 15	Unused	Some gadgets don't support an IRQ this high.

As you can see, the only way you're going to get out of this mess is to know what IRQs your other devices are using. See Chapter 4 for help in figuring out what's what.

To assign an interrupt to a particular device, you usually need to move a jumper or two, or a series of switches. If you need help with these monsters, see the first section in this chapter. By the way, some civilized devices actually enable you to assign the IRQ through software, which makes guessing a bit easier.

Messing with DMA Address Junk

First, the good news: Not every device needs a DMA channel. Now, the bad news: There aren't that many of them. Good news again: Although there aren't that many DMA addresses, hardly any of them are taken; this means they're up for grabs by the first device that claims them.

DMA is short for *direct memory access*, and it's a method that some devices use to shove big chunks of data at the CPU. Data-intense devices such as your hard disk, floppy diskette drive, CD-ROM drive, and so on use DMA addresses.

Again, the best way to figure out this nonsense is to make a list of the DMA addresses that your gadgets are using and then select an unused one for your new toy.

DMA Address	Who Owns It
DMA 0	Unused
DMA 1	Unused
DMA 2	Floppy disk controller
DMA 3	Unused
DMA 4	DMA controller
DMA 5	Unused
DMA 6	Unused
DMA 7	Unused

To change a device's DMA address, again, you resort to flipping switches or pulling jumper shunts. Some nice toys enable you to set this nonsense with software, but if you're stuck with switches and jumpers, see the first section in this chapter for help.

What's My Address?

Many devices use an I/O address, which is their home place in memory. Devices shuffle input and output through this tiny space in memory. The I/O addresses for devices can come into conflict just like those other addresses, DMAs. Video cards, disk drive controllers, sound cards, SCSI adapters, network cards, and the COM and LPT ports all use I/O addresses.

Dealing with CMOS

As you learned in Chapter 4, CMOS is kind of like your PC's reminder pad, keeping track of important stuff like how much memory the computer has, how large the hard disk is, how many floppy drives there are, and so on.

When you upgrade certain basic PC parts, you need to upgrade the information in CMOS too, or your computer's gonna be mighty confused. You see, each time you start your system, the BIOS checks the information in CMOS and uses that to test each basic component to see if it's awake and functioning. If something in the CMOS doesn't jive with reality, then the BIOS gets real mad and flashes some kind of nasty message on-screen.

CMOS Protection Since the information in CMOS is irreplaceable, you should make a copy of it. Follow the steps here to start CMOS and then print the information out by turning on the printer and pressing the **Print Screen** key on your keyboard.

By the way, if you own an old XT or earlier type PC, then it doesn't use CMOS. Instead, it uses a more primitive system of jumpers and DIP switches. Jump back to the section "Fiddling with Jumpers and Switches and Such" for help in how to deal with them.

To change the CMOS, exit Windows or any other program. Then try one of these tricks to start CMOS:

➤ Reboot your computer and watch the screen for a message telling you what key to press for Setup. Then press it. Most likely, it'll tell you to press **F1**, **F2**, or **Delete**.

➤ If that doesn't work, try rebooting your computer and pressing **Ctrl+Alt+Escape** or **Ctrl+Alt+S**. You can also try **Ctrl+Alt+Enter** or **Ctrl+Alt+Insert**.

➤ If you own a 286 PC, restart your computer with its setup diskette in drive A.

Once you have CMOS up and running, change whatever information you need. If you've just changed the battery, whatever was in CMOS is gonno; use your printout to restore the settings.

To move from item to item, you usually press the Tab key or the down arrow key. You typically use the left or right arrow key to change a setting. Just follow the tips provided at the bottom of the screen.

When you're done making changes, be sure to save them. Usually you just press **Esc** and select **Yes** to save the changes. You'll end up at the DOS prompt. Restart the computer so your changes take effect.

The Least You Need to Know

Some devices refuse to play well with others. Here's how to deal with them:

➤ To move a shunt from a jumper, pull it off the two pins it currently occupies and slide it back on top of two other pins.

➤ Flipping a DIP switch is similar to flipping a light switch: the switch itself is either on or off.

➤ You can't set two devices to the same COM port. Also, COM1 and COM3 conflict, and so do COM2 and COM4. So you can't set devices to conflicting ports.

➤ COM ports (serial ports) are active, even when nothing is connected to them.

➤ An IRQ (interrupt) is a way for a device to get the CPU's attention.

➤ A DMA channel is a high-speed channel for data transfer to the CPU.

➤ CMOS keeps track of important info like the number and type of floppy diskette drives, the size of hard disks, and the amount of memory.

Index

Symbols

8 bits
    expansion slots, 31
    sound cards, 260
16 bits (expansion
    slots), 32

A

accelerator cards
    graphics accelerator
        cards, 13
    video cards, 214
accessing
    CMOS
        (Complementary
        Metal-Oxide
        Semiconductor),
        52
accidents, 106
    sticky keys, 106
adapters, 108
    CGA (Color
        Graphics Adapter),
        209
    EGA (Enhanced
        Graphics Adapter),
        209

Hercules graphics
    adapter, 209
MDA (Monochrome
    Display Adapter),
    209
Add dialog box, 296
adding
    CD-ROM drives, 57,
        250-251
        controller cards,
            251-252
    hard disks, 56
    memory, 56,
        195-197
        laser printers, 135
    modems, 58
    printers, 56
    sound cards, 57
    tape backups, 56
    video cards,
        216-218
    Windows 95
        hardware,
        290-292
addresses (DMA),
    305-306
Advanced Technology
    PC, 9

anti-virus utilities, 95
arrays
    CGA (Color
        Graphics Array),
        12
    EGA (Enhanced
        Graphics Array),
        12
    SVGA (Super Video
        Graphics Array),
        13, 210
    VGA (Video
        Graphics Array),
        12, 209
    XGA (eXtended
        Graphics Array),
        209
assigning (IRQs),
    304-305
AT-style (keyboard
    types), 109
AUTOEXEC.BAT file,
    48-49
    defined, 285
    Windows 95, 284

M

N-O

323

disks, defragging, 88-89
drivers, 217
Explorer, 67
hard disks, compressing, 82-83
hardware
  adding, 290-292
  installing, 290
Inbox, 68
MemMaker, 81
Microsoft Network, 68
My Briefcase, 68
My Computer, 67
Network Neighborhood, 68
Plug & Play, 70, 248
Recycle Bin, 68
ScanDisk, 91
software, upgrading, 70
speed, 72
Start button, 67
Startup groups, 76
swap files, 73
system
  requirements, 68-70
    prices, 69
taskbars, 67
upgrading PCs, 5
utilities, 71
Windows Setup dialog box, 293
Windows Setup program, changing, 294
wires (CPUs), 166
write-protected disks, 223

X-Y-Z

XGA (eXtended Graphics Array), 209
XT (eXtended Technology) PC, 9
XT-style (keyboard types), 109

ZIF (zero insertion force), 165
ZIP (Zigzag In-Line Packages), 25

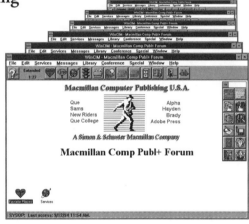

PLUG YOURSELF INTO...

THE MACMILLAN INFORMATION SUPERLIBRARY™

Free information and vast computer resources from the world's leading computer book publisher—online!

FIND THE BOOKS THAT ARE RIGHT FOR YOU!

A complete online catalog, plus sample chapters and tables of contents give you an in-depth look at *all* of our books, including hard-to-find titles. It's the best way to find the books you need!

- STAY INFORMED with the latest computer industry news through our online newsletter, press releases, and customized Information SuperLibrary Reports.

- GET FAST ANSWERS to your questions about MCP books and software.

- VISIT our online bookstore for the latest information and editions!

- COMMUNICATE with our expert authors through e-mail and conferences.

- DOWNLOAD SOFTWARE from the immense MCP library:
  - Source code and files from MCP books
  - The best shareware, freeware, and demos

- DISCOVER HOT SPOTS on other parts of the Internet.

- WIN BOOKS in ongoing contests and giveaways!

TO PLUG INTO MCP: → WORLD WIDE WEB: **http://www.mcp.com**

GOPHER: gopher.mcp.com

FTP: ftp.mcp.com

What's on the Disk

The disk is loaded with programs you can use to find out more about your computer, which will make upgrading and troubleshooting a breeze.

The System Analyst for Windows (SAW)

SAW is a diagnostic utility that can help you identify your system's CPU, memory, BIOS, hard disks, floppy drives, mouse, joystick, sound card, DMA addresses, IRQs, and so on. SAW also monitors Windows resources/events/errors in the background. *Windows: needs 1.53M free hard disk space.*

System Checkout (SYSCHK)

Like SAW, SYSCHK is a diagnostic program that provides valuable information about devices installed in your PC. Use both programs for the most comprehensive picture of your system. *Windows/DOS: needs 134K free hard disk space.*

PC-Doctor

PC-Doctor/Pro is a diagnostic tool similar to SAW and SYSCHK. However, the registered version provides several diagnostic tests that detect failures in system components from the CPU to SCSI devices, CD-ROM drives, and PCMCIA cards—so you'll want to check this one out. *DOS: needs 750K free hard disk space.*

CTS Serial Port Utilities

The CTS Serial Port Utilities are a collection of utilities designed to help you with serial port problems such as failed UART chips, more than one port at the same address, PCs that can't use Com4, conflicting IRQ assignments, Com ports that can't generate IRQs, and non-standard BIOS port assignments. When you register your copy of CTS Utilities, be sure to ask for Install-It for Modems, a simple-to-use interface that makes it easier to use the various CTS Utilities. For the latest versions of these and other CTS products, see the Computer Telecommunications Systems home page at http://comminfo.com. *Windows/DOS: needs 727K free hard disk space.*

IRQ Info

Part of the CTS suite of utilities, IRQ Info detects IRQ use, and is a great supplement to the PortInfo program in the CTS Serial Port Utility set. *Windows/DOS: needs 199K free hard disk space.*

SwapIRQ Utility

Also part of the CTS utilities, SwapIRQ lets DOS software use any IRQ by redirecting the interrupts (IRQs) from your modem, sound card, or any other device. SwapIRQ can be used with some game software that requires a specific IRQ for the sound card, or with communications software that does not support non-standard IRQs. *Windows/DOS: needs 153K free hard disk space.*

How to Use the Programs on the Disk

1. Copy all directories from the disk to your hard drive.

    Windows 3.1: Select the directories in File Manager, and then drag them to the C: drive window.

    Windows 95: Select the directories in Windows Explorer. Select **Copy** from the **Edit** menu. Make the C: drive current and then select **Paste** from the **Edit** menu.

    If you are using DOS rather than Windows, you can optionally go into each directory on the floppy disk and copy the .EXE files directly to your hard drive. Setting up a directory structure similar to the one on the disk will make it easier to see which files go with which program, but it is not necessary.

2. Go to the directory that contains the program you want to extract (all programs on the disk except for SYSCHK must be extracted before you can run them). In Windows, double-click the file name; in DOS, type the file name (omitting the .EXE part) at the DOS prompt.

IRQ Info program	IRQINFOD.EXE
PC-Doctor	PCDR15-D.EXE
System Analyst (SAW)	SAW103-D.EXE (after the files are extracted, double-click the INSTALL.EXE file to install the program)
SwapIRQ Utility	SWAPIRQD.EXE
CTS Serial Port Utilities	CTSSPU-D.EXE

3. Most of these utilities (except SAW, which you can run by double-clicking SAW.EXE in File Manager or Windows 95 Explorer) will give you more accurate information if you run them at the DOS prompt. If you are using Windows 3.1, choose **Exit** from the Program Manager's **File** menu. If you are using Windows 95, close all open programs and then select **Shut Down** from the **Start** menu. In the dialog box that appears, click the **Restart the Computer in MS-DOS Mode?** option.

4. Change to the directory that contains the program you want to run (for example, type **CD \SYSCHK** to go to the SYSCHK directory).

5. Type the name of the program you want to run:

IRQ Info program	IRQINFO
PC-Doctor	PCDR
SwapIRQ Utility	SWAPIRQ
SYSCHK System Checkout/Info	SYSCHK
CTS Serial Port Utilities	BIOS_FIX, BUFFER, COM_BPS, COM_FMT, DOS_COM, DOS_SWAP, DTR, HANGUP, IRQ, PORTINFO, RESETCOM, RESETMOD, or RTS

Legal Stuff

This software is sold *as is* without warranty of any kind, either expressed or implied, including but not limited to the implied warranties of merchantability and fitness for a particular purpose. Neither the publisher nor its dealers or distributors assumes any liability for any alleged or actual damages arising from the use of these programs. (Some states do not allow for the exclusion of implied warranties, so the exclusion may not apply to you.)

Most of the programs included on the disk are *shareware*. Shareware programs give users a chance to try software before buying—but it is not free. If you try one of the shareware programs on the disk and continue using it, you are required to register it. You'll find details for doing so in a text file included with each program. By registering your shareware, you'll often get a lot of helpful extras, such as a printed manual, free updates, or a version of the software that includes additional features.